32 President's Square

ACROPOLIS BOOKS LTD.
Washington, D.C. 20009

32 President's Square

Part I of a Two-Part Narrative of The Riggs Bank and its Founders

Roland T. Carr
Foreword by Richard Walsh, Ph.D.
Professor of History, Georgetown University

Illustrations by Frederic Schuler Briggs

The Acropolis International Business History Series

© Copyright 1980 by Roland T. Carr

All rights reserved. Except for the inclusion of brief quotations in a review, no part of this book may be reproduced or utilized in any form or by any means, electronic or mechanical, including photocopying, recording or by any information storage and retrieval system, without permission in writing from the publisher.

ACROPOLIS BOOKS LTD.
Colortone Building, 2400 17th St., N.W.
Washington, D.C. 20009

Printed in the United States of America by
COLORTONE PRESS, Creative Graphics Inc.
Washington, D.C. 20009

Library of Congress Catalog Number 80-11260
ISBN 87491-079-X

Also by Roland T. Carr
To Sea In Haste

The story of a small World War II warship that was engaged in anti-submarine and Convoy activities in the Eastern Sea Frontier of the United States — a frontier that extended roughly from Halifax to Florida and Cuba. (Acropolis Books Ltd. ©1975)

Library of Congress Cataloging in Publication Data

Carr, Roland T.
   32 President's Square.

  Bibliography: p.
  Includes index.
  1. Riggs National Bank of Washington, D.C.—History. 2. Riggs, George Washington, 1813-1881. 3. Corcoran, William Wilson, 1798-1888. 4. Bankers—United States—Biography. I. Title.
HG2613.W34R5124   332'.092'2 [B]   80-11474
ISBN 0-87491-079-X

32 President's Square

To Frank G. Burrough, Assistant Vice President and Personnel Officer of Riggs National Bank, and to Avon M. Nevius, a Vice President of the bank, who argued vehemently in 1926 over my application as a bank runner (Mr. Nevius in favor and Mr. Burrough undecided and not about to be pushed), but finally offered me a 90-day trial, which lasted 47 years.

And to my father, Paul C. L. Carr, Chief Clerk of the Money Department of the old Adams Express Company, at 2nd and Eye streets, Northwest, adjacent to the Union Station, who wanted one of his sons to work at Riggs Bank. . . and to my mother, Eidth May (Taylor) Carr, who encouraged me to enroll in night classes at George Washington University and sometimes forgave the payment of my board money at tuition time.

Thankfully and affectionately,
RTC

ACKNOWLEDGEMENTS

Special acknowledgment is due Mrs. Isabel Mangum for her editorial skill, advice and assistance in the launching of this book and for her wise counsel in solving difficult problems that arose later. Mr. Robert Lyle, Curator of the Peabody Room of Georgetown Public Library, was of great assistance in establishing for the first time the ownership of a number of real estate properties mentioned in this volume. Mr. Robert Truax, of the Columbia Historical Society, was another most helpful consultant in checking obscure historical facts as well as in the obtaining of copies of old photographs, plats and directory and newspaper references. The late Mathilde Williams, beloved longtime former curator of the Peabody Room was also most helpful through her wide recollections from a lifetime of historical research.

Through the courteous assistance of Mrs. Jane Sween, of the Montgomery County Historical Society of Rockville, Maryland, I obtained an introduction to Mr. Samuel Riggs, IV, of Olney, who proved to be not only a lively direct descendant of Samuel and Amelia Dorsey Riggs of Pleasant Hill at Brookeville, but a pleasant, knowledgeable, influential and enormously helpful associate in this endeavor. With his guidance I soon climbed the long hill running up to the ruins of Pleasant Hill and the adjacent old Riggs burying ground, and stood, almost miraculously, at the very place of origin of the Riggs family of our story.

Special thanks are due, too, to Mr. John M. Christie, Chairman Emeritus of the Board of Directors of Riggs National Bank, who persuaded me to undertake this narrative in the first place, and to his lovely wife, Dottie, for her gracious encouragement.

Strong support came also from the pressurized domain of the current Chairman of the Board of Directors and Chief Executive Officer, Mr. Vincent C. Burke, Jr., who indicated repeatedly the keen interest of himself and his charming wife, Teeney, in the coming chronicle of their predecessors.

I cannot close without mentioning the loyal assistance throughout this project of my former secretary and associate, Mrs. Maria B. Ruhe.

FOREWORD

Author Roland T. Carr explains in the following work, *32 President's Square: The Story of the Riggs Bank and its Founders,* that there are essentially two types of Washingtonians. The first are the politicos who since the early days of John C. Calhoun, Daniel Webster, and Henry Clay to Abraham Lincoln took up residence that everyone knew was seasonal and impermanent. Their interests in the Washington area were at best transient. The other residents and their families held deep roots in the city and its environs and gave the place natural permanence. Carr's book tells of both type of Washingtonians through one of its most steady families — the Riggs of Maryland and Washington.

At the same time, Carr relates to us another important topic in history — the story of a business — one of the more renowned and most stable in the country — that of the Riggs Bank of Washington. This business history is intrinsically combined with family history. Carr tells of the steady growth of the bank and banking in the early Republic. Riggs was unique because its customers were the famous men of American history and the bank became identified intimately with national events and figures. The bank held the accounts of the Presidents from John Tyler to Andrew Johnson. In its business, the bank helped to finance many of the most important national projects of the early Republic including loans to the federal government for the Mexican War. Carr's narrative also describes the almost forgotten tragedy of the ill-fated Collins Steamship Line, in which one of the senior members of the Riggs family was an important investor. This bold enterprise helped give primacy in world shipping to the United States for a brief period in the early part of the 19th century.

Interspered with business and national history, one finds anecdotal tales such as Madison's retreat to the Riggs farm at Brookville, Maryland, after the disaster of the battle of Bladensburg and the burning of Washington in the War of 1812. Carr relates how the Riggs managed to save the shrine at Mount Vernon especially during the trying days of the Civil War when the head of the bank and the heroines of Mount Vernon Ladies Association doggedly preserved the national homestead. Personal stories of William W. Corcoran and his interests and philanthropies, and of George Peabody, add to local history and lend insights into the nature of the men of wealth and affairs of that day.

Roland Carr's gentle exploitation of the Riggs Bank Papers — the accounts, drafts, and personal letters contained in its vaults — is the heart of the book. These materials make for excellent social history. Witness the draft by "A. Lincoln, Pay to Mr. Johns (a sick man) bearer, Three Dollars."

> Richard Walsh, Ph.D.
> Professor of History
> Georgetown University

Chapter 1

In 1834, the leading bankers and businessmen of Washington — faced with the almost certain passing of the Second Bank of the United States, which furnished a substantial portion of the city's credit and currency — petitioned Congress to establish a new Bank of the District of Columbia, with branches in the towns of Washington, Georgetown and Alexandria. The plan failed to materialize, however, and two years later, under the onslaught of President Andrew Jackson, its implacable foe, the charter of the government bank expired with no substitute in sight.

The Washington office of the Second Bank of the United States was located at the corner of 15th Street and President's Square — President's Square then being that portion of Pennsylvania Avenue between 15th and 17th streets, Northwest. In its employ was a native son of Georgetown, William W. Corcoran, who for the previous eight years had managed its real estate and suspended debt departments. Corcoran must have been aware of the plans to establish the new bank, and when these plans bogged down so woefully, he decided, somewhat brashly, to enter the banking business himself in the young national capital.

At the time Corcoran was nearing his 38th birthday, and with two notable exceptions, had lived an uneventful and mostly private life. This would soon prove to be in startling contrast with the flamboyant, amazingly successful, rich and powerful public career he would enjoy for the balance of his long life, which extended over another half century.

What we know of William W. Corcoran prior to 1836 is largely what he has told us in the foreword of his autobiography, which chiefly takes the form of a collection of his personal letters. Entitled *A Grandfather's Legacy*, it was published in 1879 when he was 81 years old. He died on Feb. 24, 1888, in his 90th year, leaving many intangible legacies to be found in Washington landmarks, private philanthropies, and intriguing legends.

He begins his "sketch" of his life by telling us that his father, Thomas Corcoran, was born in Limerick, Ireland, in 1754. Thomas' father, it is stated, was from London, and his mother was Elizabeth Wilson, the sister of William Wilson, who had emigrated to Baltimore in 1769 and become one of the principal shipping merchants of that city and the owner of several large vessels.

The success of his uncle evidently lured young Thomas Corcoran to join him in Baltimore in 1783, and he made three voyages on Wilson's vessels, two to Cork and one to Amsterdam. In 1788 he married Hannah Lemmon, the niece of Mrs. William Wilson, and moved with her to the small Potomac River port of Georgetown. There he commenced the shoe and leather business on Congress (now 31st) Street, below Bridge (M) Street in a house rented from Mr. Robert Peter, in which he and his family lived until he built the three story brick house at 122 Bridge Street. This was later 3119 M Street, between 31st and Wisconsin, now part of the site of Woolworth's. He also purchased for the account of his uncle, William Wilson, large quantities of tobacco and flaxseed for shipment — Georgetown, Bladensburg and Baltimore being the three rival tobacco markets of the State of Maryland.

Thomas Corcoran was well regarded in the community and was appointed by President Jefferson a magistrate and member of the Levy Court of the District and was reappointed by all successive presidents until his death in 1830. In 1815, he

CHAPTER 1

was appointed by President Madison postmaster of Georgetown, which office he held during his lifetime, and was succeeded by his son, James, who continued in it until his death. On two occasions, from 1805-1806, and from 1808-1811, he had served as Mayor of Georgetown.

Thomas and Hannah Corcoran had twelve children, six boys and six girls, of whom three boys and three girls lived to maturity, as follows:

James Corcoran	born	1789
Eliza Corcoran	born	1791
Thomas Corcoran	born	1794
Sarah Corcoran	born	1797
William Wilson Corcoran	born	1798
Martha Ellen Corcoran	born	1807

William Wilson, born on the 27th of December, 1798, commenced his schooling in 1803 with a widow Nicholson who kept a school for young children in Beall (O) Street. Thereafter he was placed with a series of highly qualified private tutors until he entered Georgetown College as a day-scholar in 1811.

In 1815, contrary to his father's wishes that he continue his classical education, he went into the dry goods business of his brothers, James and Thomas Corcoran. In 1817 they established him, at the age of nineteen, in a separate store in a small building owned by his father on the northwest corner of High (Wisconsin) and First (N) streets, under the firm of W. W. Corcoran & Co. This modest structure, still standing today, and with appropriate modernization, is the Citizens Branch of Interstate Federal Savings and Loan Association.

The business of young Corcoran and his brothers continued to be extensive and prosperous, until the disastrous spring of 1823, when like so many others — perhaps a third or more of Washington's merchants and those in Baltimore — they were obliged to close up their business. Eventually they were able to pay off in full all of the confidential debts, consisting of endorsements, commission accounts and borrowed money, but they were forced to compromise with their remaining creditors at fifty "percentum", and received from them a discharge in full.

After the failure and compromise, W. W. Corcoran devoted himself to the interests and businesses of his aging father —

13

collecting rents and superintending property. His mother died on June 2, 1823, at the age of fifty-eight years.

In 1823 he entered the employ of the Second Bank of the United States and eventually was managing the real estate and suspended debts departments. He performed a similar function for the Bank of Columbia of Georgetown which had failed in 1826.

After serving in several units of volunteers, Corcoran was appointed a lieutenant-colonel of artillery in 1830 by President Andrew Jackson and in 1832 a colonel

One historian has noted that "the uniform consisted of blue coat, white pantaloons, white vest, black hat, and black stock or cravat." The colonel "must have cut a rather handsome figure as a popular man about town, maintaining his own carriage and in demand for squiring the ladies" she adds.[1]

Among those he was "squiring" in 1831, and for some months thereafter, was Susan Decatur, the widow of the naval hero, who was then living in Georgetown. The first several letters in the *"Grandfather's Legacy"* are from her, and they give us our first brief glimpse into the personal and private life of W. W. Corcoran during that period.

The widow Decatur was apparently quite actively seeking his company and he was responding, sending his carriage for her when asked, corresponding when she was out of town, and escorting her to church and to social functions in the fashion of the day.

A typical letter from her reads:

My Dear Mr. Corcoran,

If you should find yourself destitute of amusement this evening, while the belles are at church, I beg of you to come and listen to some of my lamentations.

Yours, Sincerely,
S. Decatur

Another brief Sunday morning message states:

My Dear Mr. Corcoran,

I am happy to say that I can take you under my wing today on the way to heaven, and I pray you to call for me at ten o'clock.

Yours, Sincerely,
S. Decatur

CHAPTER 1

Some time after these meetings with Susan Decatur, Corcoran met and fell madly in love with the girl he was to marry. Ironically enough, Mrs. Decatur may have unwittingly played a part in their introduction through her friendship with the young lady's father. Commodore Charles Morris was a naval officer and close friend of her late husband, and was then living with his family in Georgetown's Cox's Row, at the corner of First (N) and Frederick (34th) streets.

These old "service friends" might have encountered Mrs. Decatur and her escort at church with their family, or strolling down High street, or even in the lobby of the Union Hotel on Bridge Street, then the most fashionable hostelry in the area where Susan Decatur was residing for a time.

In any case, the resulting marriage led to W.W. Corcoran's second emergence into the public eye. He covers it quite simply in the "sketch" with one sentence, or rather, the first part of a sentence: "On the twenty-third of December, 1835, W. W. Corcoran married Louise Amory Morris, daughter of Commodore Charles Morris..."

But this was no ordinary marriage, and Commodore Morris, no ordinary father-in-law. At fifty-one, he was one of the senior officers of the Navy and one of its greatest heroes. He had served under the gallant Decatur in 1804, in entering the harbor of Tripoli on the occasion of the recapture and destruction of the frigate *Philadelphia*. Midshipman Morris, who had volunteered for the mission, was the first on the deck of the *Philadelphia* and his heroic conduct was rewarded by a citation and immediate promotion. In the War of 1812, he was executive officer of the frigate *Constitution*, Captain Hull commanding, when that ship fell in with the British frigate *Guerriere*. The two vessels came for a moment into close quarters and, "on their sides touching, Lieutenant Morris lashed them together". They soon parted but in the fierce fight of musketry and short swords that ensued he was wounded when a musket ball passed through his body but missed vital organs. The bloody conflict was crowned with victory and Lieutenant Morris in September 1813, was again promoted for special services.

This victory, one of the earliest in our naval conflict with Great Britain, caught the imagination of the American people and immeasurably raised the stature of the U.S. Navy, its ships and officers, in the public mind.[2]

Mr. Corcoran's marriage, as can be imagined, caused a great deal of public excitement and comment. In fact, it has ever been the subject of much controversy, gossip and speculation, by reason of the prominence of the father-in-law, the age of his daughter, and the subsequent fame and fortune of W. W. Corcoran. The age of the bride has variously been reported in the press from thirteen to seventeen.[3] But the records of Oak Hill Cemetery are accurate and available, and they reveal for any one genuinely interested in the truth, that she was indeed born on December 19, 1818 and was, therefore, on December 19, 1835, seventeen years of age. Corcoran was born on December 27, 1798 and would have been thirty-seven on December 27, 1835. Thus, she was four days past her seventeenth birthday, he four days before his thirty-seventh, on their marriage day, December 23, 1835.

There are several versions of the marriage, but since Corcoran makes no mention of any details in his "sketch", or elsewhere, as far as is known, the exact order of events remains uncertain.

The version of John Clagett Proctor, who for many years was a weekly columnist for THE SUNDAY STAR on local historical subjects, reads as follows:

> Commodore Morris was a hardy martinet and would not believe it possible that his daughter could care for any one outside 'the service.' All appeals to his reason were vain against the walls of his prejudice and the way of true love was rough indeed. But Louise Morris had a pretty fair share of her father's courage, and she consented to an elopement. However, when the night came for the runaway, and the fair Louise was about ready to flee from the window into the arms of her lover, the Commodore — being accustomed to night watches — snatched her back into his house.
>
> The Commodore was outwardly stern, as all his men knew, but when he realized that his daughter was seriously in earnest, and that "love laughs at locksmiths," he sent the would-be bridegroom for the previously engaged minister and, calling together

> *the rest of the household, had the marriage ceremony performed then and there at midnight.*

Other versions state that Corcoran's sister-in-law, Harriet Reynolds Corcoran, widow of his brother, James, who had died in 1834, had forewarned the Commodore and persuaded him to relent in his opposition to the marriage. In any case, Harriet was the recipient of much devotion and affection from her brother-in-law throughout their long lives.

This marriage took place, of course, before Corcoran had actually launched his extraordinary career as a banker. The first directory of Georgetown, published in 1830 lists him simply as "clerk, U. S. Bank, r. Bridge St.".

Strangely enough the first composite directory of Washington and Georgetown for 1834, an error-prone, sometimes unalphabetical affair, lists him as: "Corcoran, William, hatter, West St., south side". West was P Street east of Wisconsin.

Could this possibly mean that, being uncertain of his future, he was taking a final fling at "dry goods" on the side? At this juncture one is tempted to draw some parallels between the careers of Harry Truman and Corcoran. Truman failed in the haberdashery business in Kansas City circa 1922, and acceded to the Presidency twenty-three years later. Corcoran, who failed almost a century earlier in 1823, had become twenty-three years later, in 1846, one of the richest and most influential men in the Capital City, known and respected throughout the financial world.

The marriage was apparently a love match, but it was also filled with sorrow. The complete sentence covering Corcoran's marriage in the "sketch" reads as follows:

> *On the twenty-third of December, 1835, W. W. Corcoran married Louise Amory Morris, daughter of Commodore Charles Morris; the issue of which marriage was: Harriet Louise, born September 22, 1836, died September 5, 1837; Louise Morris, born March 20, 1838, died December 4, 1867; Charles Morris, born July 16, 1840, died August 11, 1841.*

What the sentence did not include, perhaps because it was already quite long and burdoned with bitter reminiscences, was the sad fact that Corcoran's lovely bride, Louise Amory

Morris, predeceased her third child, the little son (who lived only a little over one year) and died of consumption on November 28, 1840, at the age of twenty-one.

CHAPTER 1

Chapter Notes

[1] This description of W. W. Corcoran in his military uniform is from *William Wilson Corcoran*, a private memorandum by the late Miss Mathilde D. Williams, the longtime helpful and brilliant curator of the Peabody Room, Georgetown Branch, D.C. Public Library.

[2] During this engagement with the *Guerriere* the *Constitution* won her famous nickname. When her crew saw enemy shot bouncing off her thick oaken sides, they dubbed her "Old Ironsides." Still preserved and afloat, she is moored as a national shrine in Boston harbor.

[3] As late as January 23, 1976, Mr. Paul Richards, in an article in the *Washington Post*, wrote: *"No one was more delighted with the society of intelligent and agreeable women than Mr. Corcoran.*

It seems he liked them young. Louise Amory Morris was but 13 when Corcoran, then 20 years her senior, first began to court her. They eloped two years later."

Chapter 2

The exact date of Corcoran's entrance into business is unknown, although it was long thought to have been in 1836, the year of the closing of the Second Bank of the United States.

Following World War II, a rare copy of *A Grandfather's Legacy* came into possession of the Riggs National Bank and an examination of the gilt-edged pages disclosed that Corcoran, himself, had partially set the record straight in the biographical preface by stating: *In 1837 he [W. W. Corcoran] commenced the brokerage business in Washington in a small store, ten by sixteen feet, on Pennsylvania Avenue, near Fifteenth street.*

And so we knew at least that the founding year was 1837, not 1836. The location given was on the north side of the avenue on a site now covered by the Washington Hotel.

Whatever the exact date of his entrance into business, Corcoran's venture appears to have been an immediate success, and he set about moving his family to Washington from Georgetown. His home appears in early directories as located on the north side of H street, northwest, between Vermont Avenue and 15th Street, near the center of the block.

His progress was such that in 1839, he was able to move his office further up 15th Street to occupy the larger quarters vacated by the old Bank of the Metropolis on the northeast corner of 15th and F streets. This building, a portion of which still stands today and houses a newsstand and a souvenir shop, was once occupied by the tavern of a Mrs. Suter, the daughter-in-law of the proprietor of the earlier and more famous Suter's Tavern of Georgetown. It was in this tavern at 15th and F streets, during the War of 1812, that British Admiral, Sir George Cockburn, and his aides supped while they watched the burning of the White House.

Although no notice of Corcoran's entrance into business in 1837 has been discovered, his move in 1839 was accompanied by a circular which survives in the archives of the Corcoran Gallery of Art and reads as follows:

> *Washington, D.C.,*
> *May 1, 1839,*
> *I beg leave to inform you that I have established myself in this city for the prosecution of a general stock and exchange business.*
>
> *I will attend to the purchase and sale of all kinds of Government, bank and other stocks, as well as domestic and foreign exchange.*
>
> *Claims against the Government will be collected and promptly remitted.*
>
> *I annex a list of references with an offer of my services and remain.*
>
> *Very respectfully yours,*
> *W. W. Corcoran.*

Having worked for the previous eight years only two blocks up the street on the northwest corner of Fifteenth Street and President's Square, at the Second Bank of the United States, then the financial hub of the city, Corcoran undoubtedly had made a number of important friends among the clientele of the Government bank.

He had also become something of an authority on the value of real estate, of bank notes and currency, and of state and municipal securities. Many surviving examples of the correspondence of that era of prominent businessmen in Georgetown, Baltimore, Philadelphia, New York, and elsewhere, contain statements such as "I took Corcoran's value for the stock," or "Corcoran states there is no market for the bonds at present," etc.[1] He was also demonstrating the popular concept that exists even in today's banking world, that "the best way to learn about good loans is to be a collector of bad ones".

But above all, Corcoran was possessed of an abiding faith in the future of the capital city and its neighboring Potomac River port of Georgetown, as well as in the vigorous and expanding young nation itself. He was a genuine disciple of the inevitable greatness of the United States and he arrived on the scene at a most fateful moment.

It had long been Corcoran's dream to open a bank of deposit, but he lacked capital for such an undertaking. As his business continued to grow, he was forced to consider accepting a partner and he was soon in communication with Elisha Riggs, an old Georgetown friend and neighbor of his family who had become a leading banker in New York City.

And at this point we must switch somewhat from the history of the Corcorans to that of the Riggs', to bring these two great families into juxtaposition and perspective.

Elisha Riggs and his brothers, George Washington and Romulus, had come down from their father's plantation in the hills of Montgomery County, Maryland, around 1800 and settled in Georgetown. They were lured by the great promise, excitement and opportunity of the new federal city, which, despite the vigorous and vociferous competition of more affluent and influential areas of the country, was being carved out of their home county.

Georgetown, formerly part of Montgomery County, but now included in the new District of Columbia, was the largest and most flourishing town on the north side of the Potomac. Its population still exceeded that of the newly laid-out city of Washington and was considerably larger than that of the eastern branch port of Bladensburg. Alexandria, eight miles down the river in the Virginia portion of the new District, was still a large rival, but Georgetowners considered their proximity across Rock Creek to the new capital a great and growing advantage.

The exact date of the arrival of the brothers in Georgetown is unknown, but there is some evidence that George Washington, the oldest of the three, born August 4, 1777 (and named for General Washington), may have come first. Or, he may have come with his next younger brother, Elisha, born June 13, 1779. Romulus, born December 22, 1782, came last, but he was to stay in Georgetown longer than any of them.

The Riggs brothers came from a family of twelve children, five girls and seven boys, all of whom lived to maturity except one brother who died at age nineteen.

Their father, Samuel Riggs, also came from a family of twelve children and was the ninth child of John and Mary (Davis) Riggs, born October 6, 1740, at their plantation "Riggs Hills" and "Rich Neck," in Huntington Hundred, Queen Caroline Parish, Anne Arundel County, Maryland.

John Riggs was "the first known ancestor of the Riggs family in Maryland, and was born, according to record, in 1687. Whether he was born in England or the Province still remains unknown". The "record" was an entry in an old family book similar to a bible, stating that when he died in 1762, "he was in the 75th year of his age".

His marriage to Mary, daughter of Thomas Davis, "took place on January 16, 1721, in St. Ann's Parish, Middle Neck Hundred, Anne Arundel County. Her family was of Virginia origin, identified with the very earliest years of the Jamestown settlement".

This we are told by the accomplished geneologist, historian and author, John Beverly Riggs, in his massive and magnificent work entitled, *The Riggs Family of Maryland*, published in 1939.

John Riggs' plantation, "Riggs Hills" and "Rich Neck", was located near the present town of Laurel. Nothing remains of the buildings and much of the site itself was apparently destroyed in the building of the Washington-Baltimore Boulevard.

Upon the death of his father in 1762, Samuel Riggs inherited 200 acres of the tract "Bordley's Choice", in Newfoundland Hundred of the lower District of Frederick (now Montgomery) County. After his marriage to Amelia Dorsey, youngest of the five daughters of Captain Philemon and Catharine (Ridgely) Dorsey, "he removed to Bordley's Choice where he established

CHAPTER 2

himself as a planter, and in 1768-69 built 'Pleasant Hill' on a part of his plantation, which eventually consisted of about 500 acres."

Pleasant Hill was located on a beautiful hilltop overlooking the present town of Brookeville, a verdant region of swift streams and bubbling springs. Behind the plantation flowed the steep banked Hawlings River where the people in the neighborhood had blasted out the stone for their houses and fireplaces and found cool, limpid swimming holes and some lively fishing in summer.

The settlers of this area came up the Patuxent River (of which the Hawlings was a tributary) from Anne Arundel County and bought their land from the original patentees and speculators or their heirs. "They had been neighbors and kin and they continued to be neighbors and to intermarry. They bores names like Dorsey and Gaither, Riggs and Davis, Griffith and Waters. They were largely English descended and they belonged to the Church of England".[2]

This was the fringe of Tidewater, and while the people lived a plantation way of life, there was one great difference — tobacco was not their sole corp — their lands had been given over to the raising of a more diverse crop of corn, wheat and other grains, and to the raising of livestock — and they did not own many slaves.

Such was the bountiful area where the three Riggs brothers were born and had passed their young lives, until they entered the beckoning and burgeoning world at the waterside of commerce and industry and banking.

Chapter Notes

[1] From miscellaneous ancient correspondence from the files of the old Farmers and Mechanics Bank of Georgetown, merged with Riggs National Bank in 1928.

[2] From the outstanding publication of the Brookeville Bicentennial Committee, 1976.

Chapter 3

The old real estate records of the District of Columbia reveal that George Washington Riggs made his initial purchase of property in Georgetown on October 4, 1800. On that date, according to the description in the deed, he bought "a three story building on Bridge Street, of the estate of William H. Dorsey, with the use of an alley". This building still stands in a row of old dwellings converted to commercial usage on the north side of M Street, east of the Old Stone House, one of the major landmarks in the area. Numbered 3019, it is now occupied by the "In Town Gallery."[1]

This is the earliest recorded date of George Riggs' presence in Georgetown, but he may have been there much earlier. He had passed his twenty-third birthday in August of that year, and many young men were coming down from their farms or emigrating to the bustling port in their late teens. He had unquestionably seen the town on visits with his brothers and uncles in bringing their plantation produce to market. And there is the possibility he may have seen and become fascinated by the workshop of a silversmith somewhere in the teeming waterfront area.

27

For George Riggs became a silversmith. How, and to whom apprenticed, is unknown. But he became a good craftsman and his work is regarded as having finer artistic qualities than that of many of the silversmiths of the period. He used several marks, of which five are known.

He probably engaged in other commercial pursuits and the records disclose he bought and sold numerous parcels of real estate. But, nonetheless, he produced a lot of fine silver which is still sought after by collectors today. The Baltimore Museum of Art has an excellent representation of his work, including a porringer and a punch ladle thought to be from his Georgetown period.

His Georgetown period did not last long. He bought a second house on M Street on May 1, 1802, and brought his Montgomery County bride, Eliza Robertson, there to establish their home upon their marriage on January 8, 1803. This house was also on the north side of M Street in the same block as his first house, but closer to the Old Stone House — only three doors east. Now numbered 3033-35 M Street, it at present houses an art shop called "Spectro."[2]

George Riggs apparently moved his family to Baltimore in 1810, as shown by his signature on a deed of sale for the second property, which reads "George W. Riggs of Baltimore."[3] He later appears in Baltimore directories as a member of a prominent mercantile firm, and subsequently engaged in the exporting of tobacco from which he accumulated an ample fortune. He continued to make silver during his residence in Baltimore, but in view of his absorption in general business affairs, the craft probably became an avocation or hobby. He never sold his first house on M street, perhaps because it had been his original silversmith factory, but left it at his death to a stepson by his second marriage.

Elisha Riggs also appears as a purchaser of real estate in Georgetown in 1801 and 1802, but, as in the case of George Washington Riggs, he must have been in town for some time prior to those transactions.

This fact becomes startingly evident by reason of a large and sophisticated advertisement he placed in the *Federalist* newspaper for September 3, 1802. In order to have been knowledgeable in the wide variety of dry goods items listed for sale, this twenty-three year old former farm boy obviously had been tutored and trained by older and more experienced hands in the business. The advertisement also reveals that he knew his way around the waterfront and had already established valuable contacts with some of the ship captains sailing directly into port from the far ends of the earth, or via coastal packet boats from Baltimore, Philadelphia and New York.

The full text of the ad, printed in the old English style: reads!

> "The Federalist, Georgetown, D.C., September 3, 1802
>
> ### SEASONABLE GOODS
> ### ELISHA RIGGS
>
> At his store, Bridge Street, has a general supply of SPRING GOODS which being selected of the best terms, will be sold very low for cash, Viz: Chintzes, Calicoes, Dimities, Muslinets & Jenets; Irish Linens; Brownholland, Bretagnias, & bro. Irish Linens, Cambrick muslins — White Black, bro. plain and glazed India mulinul, Book and Camrick Muslins; Damask and plain Silk & Cambrick Muslin Shawls & Tippets; Lace shades, Thread Laces, and Lace, Paris Net and Gauze Veils; Italian Crepes, Pealongs; Sarcenet, white Sattin and fashionable Ribbons; Indian Persians, Black modes, Lutestrings, Silk Velvets and Velvet Ribbons; Summer Cloths, Cashmers, Hairbines, Bombozets, and Silk Nankeens Mersailles Quilting; Printed Jeans, Fustians, & fine white Jeans, Spangled Kid Shoes, Morroco leather and stuff do, and men's leather do.; Fine linen Pocket Handerkerchiefs, Long, Lawn, Cambricks, Diaper, and Table Cloths; Womens and Mens Silk, Cotton, and Thread Hosiery and Gloves; Fine Bed Ticking, Drillings, Dowlas, and white Rolls: Ladies and Gentlemens Umbrellas; with Cane and hooks; Gentlemens Fine Hats, Mans, Boys and Children Coarse do; Fine white Russia Sheeting, Brown do, and fine Cress; Ticklinburg, Oznabrigs, Stripes, Checks, and Striped Holland; Gurrahs, Bastas, Mamoodis, and fine Shirting Muslins; ALSO; A large quantity of very cheap Hollow Glass; Paper Hangings of the newest figures, & fresh hyson, Young Hyson, Hysonskin & Souchong TEAS; Sugars and Coffee. And many other Articles not mentioned.
>
> May 29, 1802

Elisha was obviously an early believer in the effectiveness of advertising, and the date at the bottom of this ad, May 20, 1802, shows that it was written for the spring market and had been running intermittently in the same format for over three months.

As an interesting sidelight, the same edition of the Friday, September 3, 1802 *Federalist* carries at the top of the page over Elisha's large ad an announcement of the Annapolis and Georgetown Mail Stage, giving a revealing glimpse of the transportation of the day. A two-column illustration shows a four-horse stage coach and has the footnote, "To run twice a week after the first of September, next". It was then the 3rd. The announcement reads as follows:

ANNAPOLIS and GEORGETOWN
MAIL STAGE

The public are respectfully informed that the Mail Stage will leave Mr. Caton's Inn, Annapolis, every Tuesday and Thursday, (after the above date) at five o'clock A.M. and arrive at Georgetown at six P.M. RETURNING will leave Mr. M'Laughlin's Tavern, Georgetown, every Wednesday and Saturday, at 5 o'clock A.M. and arrive at Annapolis at six P.M. FARE, three dollars for each passenger, with an allowance of Twenty weight of baggage. One hundred and fifty weight of extra baggage to pay fare as a Passenger. All Baggage to be at risk of the owners.

HENRY COOK
THOMAS COCKENDERFER

August 18, 1802

In 1806 Elisha purchased a large brick residence on Bridge Street, still standing today as 3107-09 M Street.[4] This house was only three doors east of the home Thomas Corcoran had built in 1791 which was later 3119-21 M Street. The Union Bank was next door to Elisha and he and Thomas Corcoran both became directors of the bank. His father, Samuel, was a stockholder.

The two men were also original pew holders at Saint John's Church in Georgetown. There were forty-eight boxes "which had doors with good strong hinges and button fastenings" Elisha held pew No. 6 and Corcoran No. 28.

These mutual interests would seem to indicate a close and cordial relationship between Elisha Riggs and Thomas Corcoran and their families. And they were soon joined by Romulus Riggs, who entered the exchange and brokerage business, as would Mr. Corcoran's youngest son thirty years later. Romulus married on May 29, 1810, at Christ Church in Alexandria, Mercy Ann Lawrason, born there October 24, 1789, the daughter of James and Alice (Levering) Lawrason.

How Romulus met Mercy Ann Lawrason is unknown, but it is a good guess that his brother, Elisha, met her younger sister, Alice, at the wedding, and another romance immediately developed. Elisha and Alice Lawrason were also married at Christ Church on September 17, 1812 and came to Georgetown to live in Elisha's house on Bridge Street. He was thirty-three and his pretty bride twenty. An evocation of her done some years later shows a pert, buxom young lady with a firm chin, a thin-lipped smile and two little curls dangling coquettishly at her temples.

James Lawrason, the father of these two sisters, was a prominent merchant and one of the leading citizens of Alexandria, and would certainly be considered a most satisfactory father-in-law for these two ambitious, business-minded young men. Both of them, we can assume, learned a few tough business axioms from James Lawrason. He had been very successful in the tanning and leather business and had reputedly made a fortune outfitting settlers going west in coonskin caps, leather jackets and boots. His first home was on the waterfront at what is now the southwest corner of Prince and Union streets. Beside it was his tannery, which has been replaced in recent years with another house. He later built, in 1819, a fine residence uptown, still standing today on the southwest corner of St. Asaph and Duke streets.

It is interesting to note here that at the time of Lafayette's last visit to the United States in 1824, the Lawrason mansion was selected as "the most elegant in the city," and was put at the disposal of the Marquis. When he concluded his visit, he is said to have referred to his reception in Alexandria as "the most pleasing hours of his life." Sadly enough, both the Lawrason parents had died just prior to the General's visit.

The first child of Romulus and Mercy Ann Riggs, a son, was born on August 14, 1811, and named for both their fathers,

Samuel James Riggs. Shortly thereafter, Romulus, having prospered in business and feeling his family needed larger quarters, purchased the handsome brick house at what is now 3038 N Street.

Then on July 4, 1813, very much in the middle of the War of 1812, Elisha's bride, Alice, presented him with a son who was named George Washington Riggs, Junior, obviously for his uncle who had been named for General Washington, but also, apparently because of the patriotic date.

The recollection of the naming of the first son after George Washington in 1777, probably recalled for the family with great pride the fact that Samuel Riggs had joined the cause of the patriots during the American Revolution and was commissioned a second lieutenant in the Montgomery County Militia (originally Frederick County) on May 14, 1776. He served in the company of Captain Nathaniel Pigman, and since it is known that Pigman's company fought at the Battle of Germantown, October 4, 1777, it is possible Samuel Riggs saw action there.

Now in the War of 1812, over in Baltimore the General's namesake, George Washington Riggs, was serving as a private in Captain Samuel Moale's Company of the Columbia Artillery.

Elisha, himself, "was commissioned an ensign in the company of Captain Thomas Owings of the 32nd Regiment of Militia of Anne Arundel County, Maryland.[5]

On August 24, 1814, Elisha was serving as an aide to General William Winder at Bladensburg when his forces were soundly defeated by the British after a brief battle.

In those dire circumstances Elisha was said to have been dispatched to the Executive Mansion "to warn the President and Mrs. Madison to depart at once." Since Dolley Madison had left the White House in midafternoon carrying the Gilbert Stuart portrait of Washington, along with other valuables, and since the President was elsewhere with his escorts, no record exist as to what Elisha may have accomplished or what action he took after reaching the White House.

But a letter in the possession of the Riggs family appears to throw some light on the subject. Written on April 12, 1891, by George Smith Riggs, son of George Washington Riggs, and his second wife, and addressed to E. Francis Riggs of Washington, D.C., grandson of Elisha, the letter reads as follows:

George W. Riggs, Jr.
(c. 1866)
Courtesy University Club

Right, Samuel Riggs. *Below,* Pleasant Hill, built circa 1769, home of Samuel Riggs.

Photograph of the first George Washington Riggs, the first brother to come to Georgetown, and the uncle of George Washington Riggs, Jr. Also his second wife, Rebecca (Smith) Norris.

Elisha Riggs and his first wife, Alice Lawrason.

The Union Hotel

The Thomas Sim Lee complex at 30th and M streets, approximately as it looks today. The store next to corner with two display windows was owned by Elisha Riggs.

3337 N Street, northwest, home of Mrs. Cecilia Shedden and her Seminary.

George W. Riggs and his wife Janet M. C. Shedden.

The Cruttenden House a 3114 O Street, a 1972 photograph. Home of Sophia Theresa Cruttenden, first wife of Lawrason Riggs.

A quaint view of the former Second Bank of the United States Building on the northwest corner of 15th Street and President's Square, as it was depicted on the checks of Riggs & Co. in the 1860's.

Left, silhouette of Elisha Riggs. *Below,* the New Corcoran Building, 15th & F Streets, N.W., built in 1878, demolished in 1916, Present site of Washington Hotel. *Courtesy, W. Lloyd Wright Collection of Washingtoniana, The George Washington University Permanent Collection.*

Drawing of the first Treasury Building on the southwest corner of Fifteenth Street President's Square, facing east on Fifteenth Street. Built in 1800, it was burned by the British in 1814, but rebuilt.

Left, in 1861 the same small building on the corner is now flanked by the east front of the new Treasury Building. *Below*, old Treasury Building now seems part of the State Department in this 1865 view.

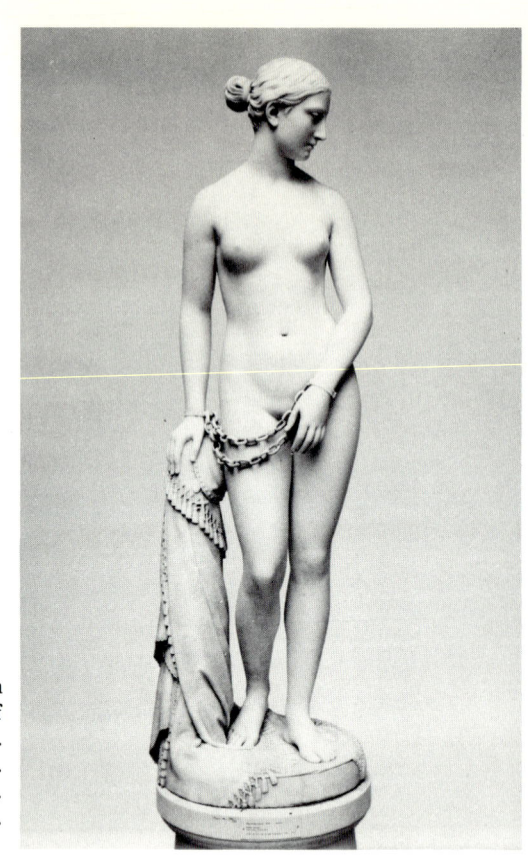

Right, Hiram Powers, *The Greek Slave*, in the collection of the Corcoran Gallery of Art, Gift of William W. Corcoran. *Below*, an engraved portrait of W. W. Corcoran, circa 1847-1850. *Bottom right*, Elisha Riggs, Jr.

CHAPTER 3

> *I have heard that your grandfather, Elisha Riggs, used to laughingly tell that he was . . . the first to see the British, the first to inform the President, the first on the field and the first off it, and that he did not stop until he reached his father's home near Brookeville.*[6]

There must have been as much panic in Georgetown as in Washington, and doubtless Elisha's wife and little son and Romulus and his wife and children had set off in their carriages for the eighteen-mile drive to Pleasant Hill. They may even have invited neighboring families, including the Corcorans, to join them, since there were a half dozen or more Riggs-related planations where they would be welcome.

Elisha probably galloped out the George Town-Frederick Town Road until he came to the major fork in Tenleytown, now known as Tenley Circle. Here he veered to the right on old Belt Road, which traversed in a northerly direction the land granted to Colonel Joseph Belt by Lord Baltimore for his services in the French & Indian Wars, and which he named "Chievy Chase", after a chase or hunting ground in the Cheviot Hills of his native Northumberland. This road corssed the District Line at the site of the present Chevy Chase Circle, where it became Brookeville Road.

Brookeville, a small town founded in 1794 by Richard Thomas who named it for his wife, Deborah Brooke, had at least fourteen houses in 1814 built along the two main streets. There were "two mills, a tan yard, two stores, a blacksmith, a post office, a school — and a town constable to watch over all".[7] And for one brief moment on August 24, 1814, this tiny community took its place in history.

One Montgomery County historian states that "the tide of misfortune that night washed up on its doorstep, not only dozens of refugees from the burning of Washington, but the President of the United States as well." Madison and his party went to the house of Caleb Bentley, who ran the general store and had been appointed postmaster by Jefferson. His escort of soldiers camped behind the house in the meadow beside Reddy Branch. Across a ford and up the slope was Pleasant Hill, where the Riggs family was most certainly holding an extraordinary reunion.

Regretably, old Samuel was not present, having died in his seventy-fourth year the preceding May 25, and been laid away in the nearby grove of pine and cedar of the Riggs burying ground beside his wife, Amelia Dorsey, who had died in 1807.

One wonders if Elisha actually encountered the President on his mission and if he might have suggested Brookeville as a safe destination.

For many years, it is said, there hung on the wall of the Bentley house the following letter written by Madison to Dolley:

> *My dearest —*
> *Finding that our army had left Montgomery Court House, we pushed on to this place, with a view to joining it, or proceed to the city as further information might prescribe. I have just received a line from Colonel Monroe saying the enemy were out of Washington and on the return to their ships, and advising our immediate return to Washington. We shall accordingly set out thither immediately. You will all of course take the same resolution.*
>
> *Truly yours,*
> *James Madison.*

Chapter Notes

[1] Deed, F-228; Made, Oct. 4, 1800; Recorded, February 24, 1801
[2] Deed, H-384; Made, May 1, 1802, Recorded, August 20, 1802.
[3] Bond of Conveyance, Liber X-495; Made, April 26, 1810, Recorded, Aug. 1810.
[4] Deed P-367; Made, March 25, 1806; Recorded, July 17, 1806.
[5] All these details of service are duly recorded in *The Riggs Family of Maryland* as follows: Samuel p 155; George W. p. 297; Elisha, p. 321.
[6] *The Riggs Family of Maryland*, 1939 p. 321.
[7] Sylvia Nash. Brookeville Bicentennial Committee.

Chapter 4

Romulus Riggs did not serve in the armed forces during the War of 1812, but he did play a part in rendering a valuable service to the Federal government.

He was one of the ten founding directors of the Farmers & Mechanics Bank of Georgetown, organized on February 14, 1814, barely six months before the invasion of Washington. Among his fellow directors was George C. Washington, a great nephew of the First President who had served as a member of Congress from Maryland and was president of the Chesapeake and Ohio Canal Company.

The young banking house was called upon for assistance when the Government's credit had sunk to its lowest ebb. The valiant response was the approval of a series of advances totaling over $200,000 in the first year of its existence. This was accomplished through the solid financial standing and patriotic support of its directors.

One loan in particular was of special significance. It involved making $50,000 available to support the tough, frontiersman army Andrew Jackson had mustered to meet the threat of the British at New Orleans. The credit was approved in October of 1814, and Jackson's victory came on January 8, 1815. No matter that, unkown to the combatants, a peace treaty had already been signed in Paris. This victory had great political and psychological importance in allowing the dispirited country to congratulate itself and finish the war in a blaze of glory. And it also made a national hero and future President of Jackson.

A letter regarding this loan signed by James Monroe, Secretary of State under Madison and Acting Secretary of War (he was the "Colonel Monroe" of Madison's letter to Dolley from Brookeville) reads as follows:[1]

*War Department,
October 12, 1814*

Sir:
It is important for the Department as well as for the drawers, Messrs. Ward and Taylor, who are contractors for supplying rations to the expedition down the Mississippi that their bills should be paid. I have therefore to request that you will receive their drafts to the amount of fifty thousand dollars when presented if they have been previously accepted.

As soon as the Secretary of the Treasury arrives, which will be in a few days, arrangements shall be made to repay this amount.

*I have the honor to be
With great respect,
Your obdt. servt.
James Monroe.*

C. Smith, Esq, Cashier,
Farmers & Mechanics Bank, Geo. Town.

Elisha soon returned to his business, the war having moved away from the charred and blackened capital. He had had a series of partners in his mercantile endeavors, all of whom were announced in the press with great promise, but all apparently were temporary. For example, back in the June 2, 1810, *Independent American*, it was advertised that "W.D. Ridgeley & Elisha Riggs beg leave to inform their friends and the public, that they have formed a co-partnership in business

CHAPTER 4

under the firm of Ridgeley & Riggs," and further that, "they have just returned from Philadelphia and New York and are now opening for sale at their store next door to the Union Bank [Elisha's house] with a well selected assortment". W. D. Ridgeley may have been a cousin, inasmuch as Elisha's grandmother, the wife of Captain Philomen Dorsey and the mother of Amelia Dorsey, was a Ridgeley.

But regardless of whether or not Ridgeley was a relative, three years later in the April 9, 1813, *Federal Republican*, appeared the announcement that "Clagett & Riggs have this day received the best assortment that has been in Georgetown, and to enable them to make quick sales, they will be offered at very reduced prices, at their wholesale and retail store two doors above the Union Tavern."

Several things catch our attention here in addition to the naming of a new partner and the inclusion of the word "wholesale" in describing their business. Clagett became the fourth partner, since Elisha had previously had a partner named Baker and another named Beeding before Ridgeley. The new location itself is of special interest, being in the block east of Elisha's house and "two doors above the Union Tavern" instead of "next door to the Union Bank." This location, if described in today's parlance, might be said to have been the "hottest business section" in Georgetown, and is worth a pause to explore the circumstances surrounding that fact.

The new and commodious Union Tavern (also at times called the Union Hotel) on the northeast corner of Washington (30th) and Bridge (M) streets, was the favorite rendezvous of the citizens of Georgetown and the transient home of many members of Congress and government officials. The huge (for its day) five story structure which occupied half a block on Bridge Street and extended back the full block on Washington to Olive street, was built in 1796 by popular subscription. Many notables enjoyed its hospitality including George Washington himself. Washington's diary for August 7, 1797, states he was in Georgetown on that date and "attended an annual meeting of the Potomac Company at the Union Tavern." On February 8, the following year, his diary states he "visited the Public Buildings in the morning . . . and met the Company [Potomac — forerunner of the C. & O. Canal Co.] at the Union Tavern and dined there."

Finally, on August 5, 1799, Washington writes, "Went up to Geo. Town to a general meeting of Potomac Company and dined at the Union Tavern." This was his last visit to the Tavern. He died December 14, 1799.

During the previous February, at the time of Washington's last birthday, his sixty-seventh, the newspapers printed a notice that "the birthnight ball in honor of George Washington would be held at Union Tavern." If George Washington Riggs and Elisha were both in Georgetown at that time, it is likely they attended the ball, although there is no evidence the General appeared.

From 1796 until 1800, the tavern had been leased, but the original terms of the public subscription had stipulated that in 1800 the building be sold at public auction to the highest bidder. Thus, it went to Mr. McLaughlin who ran it successfully until 1806, the year in which he died.

During his proprietorship, "accommodations were made in the rear of the hotel for horses and for the stages that connected with Alexandria, Annapolis and Frederick Town." So, the reference in the *Federalist* for September 3, 1802, that the Annapolis and George Town Mail Stage, "RETURNING, will leave Mr. McLaughlin's Tavern, George Town, every Wednesday and Saturday, at 5 o'clock A.M. —." At least the "passengers" could sleep comfortably in Mr. McLaughlin's City Tavern (Union Hotel) until stage time.

There was a second reason why the intersection of Washington (30th) and Bridge (M) was so attractive to Elisha and his partner, Darius Clagett. On the northwest corner, opposite Union Tavern, stood another interesting and important structure. There, *circa* 1794, the distinguished Thomas Sim Lee had built an imposing residence, one of the largest and finest in Georgetown (Georgetown then being in Montgomery County, Maryland). Lee was the second governor of Maryland in 1779-1782, and the seventh governor from 1792 to 1794. It was after his last term that he "retired to Georgetown to live as a Federalist and friend of George Washington whom he had known for almost thirty years."[2]

Lee's dwelling became a hospitable center for Federalists living in the Federal city, although with advancing years he spent an increasing amount of time at his large estate in Frederick County. In 1803, he sold his residence and very soon

CHAPTER 4

the handsome building, with six windows on the Bridge Street side across both the second and third floors and two magnificent dormers above, was divided into two houses. Subsequent owners built two more houses of similar size and appearance next door on Bridge Street, and the entire complex, a property measuring 120 by 120 feet square, was and still is known as the Thomas Sim Lee corner.

It was in the second half of Lee's former residence, now numbered 3003 M Street, next to the corner property that Clagett & Riggs were announcing their "wholesale and retail store two doors above the Union Tavern." With the splendid hotel, having the stage terminal at its rear as a center of public attraction, the adjacent area was without question a prime business location. Elisha was so certain of its value that in July of 1816, he bought the building they were occupying and held it throughout his lifetime.[3]

Meanwhile, his young wife, Alice, had born him a second son on November 22, 1814, who was named for her family, simply Lawrason Riggs. Things seemed to be going very well indeed.

But suddenly the scourge of so many "young marrieds" of that day intervened, and on April 16, 1817, a sudden and untimely death took Elisha's young wife of twenty-five, and little George, three years and nine months and Lawrason, two years and four months lost their mother.

Alice Lawrason Riggs was buried beneath a marble slab supported by four classical columns in the Lawrason plot in the annex of Christ Church cemetery, located at the south edge of Alexandria beside the old post road of legendary fame that ran into the south.

Her two little boys would soon be living with their aunt Mercy Ann and their uncle Romulus and their children.

Elisha, desolate, but already a rich man at thirty-eight, threw himself with greater urgency and vigor than ever into the expansion and advancement of his business ventures, enroute to being the first native of Montgomery County to become a millionaire.

Shortly before he lost his wife Elisha had hired a young man as office boy who would eventually prove to be a valuable associate. George Peabody, sixteen years junior to Elisha, was born February 18, 1795, and had had four years of schooling and four years of apprenticeship in a general store in Danvers, Massachusetts. In 1811, after his father died and a fire had destroyed his brother's establishment in Newburyport, Massachusetts, young Peabody emigrated to Georgetown and was employed temporarily in the store of his Uncle John. But at seventeen, this impatient young man struck out on his own, as per an advertisement in the *Federal Republican and Commercial Gazette* of Georgetown of December 28, 1812:

> *Just received and for sale by George Peabody, Bridge Street, . . . 30 pair Rose Blankets . . . 20 dozen Gentlemen's leather gloves . . . 1000 pair Ladies Morocco shoes . . . 200 pieces India cotton . . . 1 case Nuns Thread . . . 20 cases Men's fine Hats . . .*

Elisha soon took this "wise beyond his years" young man into the firm as a junior partner and changed its name to Riggs, Peabody & Co.

Back up in the Maryland countryside, Elisha's family and neighbors had proliferated spectacularly and the hills were full of his cousins and kin and prospective customers. George Peabody traveled tirelessly and extensively for the firm, journeying on horseback with loaded backpack and bulging saddlebags through the hills of Maryland, and eventually into western Virginia and Pennsylvania. Through his wide-ranging soliciting, the name and reputation of the firm grew rapidly.

The partners soon opened a branch in Baltimore, it being evident that shipping traffic and population there were moving ahead of those of Georgetown.[4]

Leaving his two sons with Romulus and his family in Georgetown where they were attending school, Elisha moved to Baltimore around 1820. He remarried there on July 16, 1822, Mary Ann Karrick and the next year she bore him the first of eight children, of whom four, three sons and a daughter, lived to maturity.[5]

The association of Riggs and Peabody had proved to be a catalyst that accelerated the sensational careers of both men, and their business grew beyond all expectations. As might be expected, they had emerged unscathed from the disastrous panic of 1823 that had forced the Corcorans into bankruptcy.

The firm opened additional offices in Philadelphia and New York, and in 1825, Elisha moved his family to Philadelphia, where on November 28, 1826, his first son by his second marriage was born and named for him, Elisha, Jr.

After a brief residence in Philadelphia, the family moved on to New York and, in 1829, the firm of Riggs, Peabody & Company was dissolved and Elisha withdrew. On March 1, 1834, he purchased a large residence at No. 6 Bowling Green which remained his home until his death.

He established himself as a banker on Pearl Street in 1837 and subsequently at Hanover Place and Exchange Place.[6] He was elected to the Board of Directors of the Farmers Loan & Trust Company of New York on June 5, 1837.[7] Elisha had followed an unswerving course from his father's plantation in Brookeville to the financial center of the United States.

George Peabody had gone even farther, for in the same year, 1837, at forty-two, he had established himself in London, then the money capital of the world, under the firm name George Peabody and Company, Merchants and Money Brokers, in Warnford Court.

The great distance between the countries did not change the friendship and high regard Elisha Riggs and George Peabody had for each other, and through the years their business contracts remained cordial and profitable for both of them.

Chapter Notes

[1] The original letter of James Monroe reposed in the files of the Farmers & Mechanics Bank for over a century until transferred to the archives of The Riggs National Bank upon the merge of the two institutions in 1928.

[2] In his youth Mr. Lee had visited Mount Vernon and was active during the Revolution in both the Maryland militia and politics. The quote about Gov. Lee appears in article by Mary Mitchell entitled *The Thomas Sim Lee Corner in Georgetown,* Mary Mitchell, Columbia Historical Society, Vol, 1969-70, page 510.

[3] Deed of trust, Robert Anderson of John to Elisha Riggs; Liber AO—14, dated May 13, 1816; recorded July 15, 1816.

[4] The Baltimore office was originally at 113 Baltimore Street; later 208 West Baltimore Street.

[5] Elisha's home in Baltimore was on the west side of Hanover Street, south of Conway, until 1825-26. *The Riggs Family of Maryland,* p. 322.

[6] The Riggs National Bank possesses in its archives a letter dated George Town, July 19, 1837, addressed to E. Riggs, Esqr., Pearl Street, New York. *The Riggs Family of Maryland* states he was subsequently at Hanover Place and Exchange Place.

[7] This bank was later merged into the United States Trust Company at 45 Wall Street.

Chapter 5

After Elisha moved to Baltimore, remarried and moved again briefly to Philadelphia and finally to New York, his two sons, George Washington, Jr., and Lawrason, continued to live with the Romulus Riggs family in Georgetown and went to school there.

We know this by reason of a letter that has come down to us from the family of Anthony Hyde, W. W. Corcoran's longtime secretary and accountant. This letter was written to him on June 14, 1848 by his brother, George A. Hyde, who had gone West and settled in St. Louis, where he became a judge. The Hydes were a Georgetown family and both the brothers went to school there.

After apologizing for not having answered Anthony Hyde's letter because of "an attack of inflamatory rheumatism which disabled me for a time from even signing my name," George A. Hyde touched upon the "lights and shades of human nature" that came before his court, and added, "but enough of my Court."

He then reports the following:

A brother of your Mr. Riggs lives here in St. Louis [this was Lawrason]. I know him well and a most

> excellent man he is. Don't you remember that we all
> used to go to Searles & Smiths school together when
> we were boys? The Riggs boys then lived in a large
> brick house opposite Dick's Garden.
>
> Henry, afterwards, Dr. Reintzel, & his cousin, &
> Uriah Hyde & Bill Gosler & his brother, Henry, were
> all at the school. They were "big boys" and we were
> the small fry. They used to make my back ache
> sometimes playing "crack and crack again".

The "large brick house" we recognized immediately as Romulus's red-brick house at what is now 3038 N Street. But "opposite Dick's Garden" puzzled us temporarily. It sounded somewhat like the name of an outdoor tavern. But the friendly and helpful experts on Georgetown lore in the Peabody Room of the Georgetown Public Library had the answer.

Dick's Garden, they said, referred to Beall House at 3033 N Street, almost across the street from the home of Romulus. It was built, according to them, by George Beall on land inherited from his father, Col. Ninian Beall, in 1717 and was one of the oldest in Georgetown.

Mrs. Grace Dunlop Ecker, they pointed out, in her *A Portrait of Old Georgetown,* says of it, "Adjoining the house on the east was the garden, and the little summer house and the fruit trees were still there many years afterward". The "Dick" was not an abbreviation for Richard, but was a surname.[1]

Mrs. Robert Peter, widow of the mayor of Georgetown, lived there for many years with her daughter, Margaret, who later became the wife of Thomas Dick. He tended the large garden faithfully — hence "Dick's Garden".

Wherever Searles and Smith's school was located, it was down N Street toward 31st or beyond, since the inference is that the Hyde boys, who lived on 30th Street, walked past the Riggs and Dick houses on their way to school.

We may never know the exact location of the school because the time when the Hyde and Riggs boys were in attendance there was in that murky period before the publication of the first Georgetown Directory in 1830.

"Why did they need a directory", scoffed one of the Peabody Room apologists," it was a small town and everybody felt they knew everybody and every place." And probably they did. But the Hydes never mentioned the location of the school and no direct record of its location exists at the Peabody Room.

By 1831, when the 1830 *Directory* made its appearance, George Washington Riggs, Jr. was seventeen and in his second year at Yale College, and Lawrason, one year younger, was following in his footsteps at Round Hill School in Northampton, Massachusetts.

The 1830 *Directory* does list two school teachers named Searle and Smith, *viz;* Searle, Ann, Teacher, Bank of Columbia [this bank had closed in 1826], and Smith, Mrs. Isabella, Teacher, Seminary Second Street (O Street west of Wisconsin). Although this sheds no light on where their joint establishment was located, we can be sure after reading an advertisement Miss Searle had placed for her school in the December 19, 1823 *National Intelligencer,* that the boys received a fine education from these two schoolmarms.

The ad reads as follows:

> *Courses of studies comprise:—*
> *Reading, writing, arithmetic, the English language,*
> *Geography, with the use of Globes, History,*
> *Rhetoric, Philosophy, Chemistry, Logic, Animated*
> *Nature, the Principles and Evidences of the Christian*
> *Religion, with such other studies as time and*
> *proficiency may allow.*
>
> *Drawing and painting will be taught in superior*
> *style by Mr. Gibson, and the Piano Forte by a*
> *lady well qualified to instruct. Needle work, if*
> *desired, will receive its due share of attention.*
>
> *Terms: First class $10.00, Second class $6.00,*
> *Third class, $5.00 per quarter. The first class*
> *will include all but music, which will be at an*
> *additional charge of $12.00 Young ladies can be*
> *admitted at the usual hours for drawing only, for*
> *$6.00 per quarter. The winter session will commence*
> *the 29th Inst.*

There was another interesting school on N Street in the general area where the Searles and Smith school must have been located. That was the seminary for young ladies run by the future mother-in-law of George Washington Riggs, Jr., Mrs. Cecelia Shedden.

The initial facts of what we know about Mrs. Shedden come to us from another Riggs great grandson, Franz von Recum, of

Hampton Bays, Long Island, an avid and lifelong student of his forebears.

Mrs. Shedden, he tells us, was born Matilda Cecelia Dowdall, in April of 1781, in County Meath, Ireland, and was in New York around the turn of the century. She married Thomas William Shedden, a native of Glasgow, Scotland. They had three daughters, Jane Agnes, born in 1807 in New York, Catharine Ann Teresa, born July 12, 1809 in Newark, and Janet Madeleine Cecelia, born August 20, 1815 in Newark.

Thomas Shedden died in 1817-18 in Newark, leaving his wife and three little girls largely unprovided for. His family in Glasgow offered to help raise the children but on the condition it would be in the Presbyterian faith, which Mrs. Shedden, a staunch Roman Catholic, refused. Shortly thereafter, attracted by the prospects and opportunities of the new Federal city, she moved to Georgetown and bravely opened a school for young ladies which was called, "Mrs. Shedden's Seminary."

The school was located in Cox's Row, which consisted of five houses on the north side of N Street, the last of which was at the corner of 34th street. The house she rented, says Franz von Recum, was the second from the corner and is now numbered 3337 N Street. "I have seen it on every trip to Washington," he adds.

Col. John Cox, a prominent citizen, completed the building of these houses in 1818 and he lived for a time on the one on the corner. Since it was in that year or the previous one that Mrs. Shedden lost her husband, the time of her arrival appears to be fairly well established.

In 1818 her little girls were aged eleven, nine and three years. George W. Riggs, Jr., who was living with the Romulus Riggs family only four blocks down N Street, was five and Lawrason four. The girls in the Riggs family were five, four and three; therefore, all of these children were quite close in age to Mrs. Shedden's (the youngest born in 1815), and probably grew up in this small community as childhood friends.

Her move to Georgetown was again in that shadowy period before the publication of a directory, but von Recum's dates and other information dovetail well enough to make it all seem plausible. But if we had only his facts, we might still be somewhat skeptical.

CHAPTER 5

Fortunately, Mrs. Shedden soon emerges from another source as a definite person and a lady of some distinction. Lafayette and his celebrated visit in 1824 again plays a part in the picture at this point.

Colonel Cox, having been elected mayor in 1823, inherited the honor and duty of acting as host for the city to the Marquis de Lafayette during his visit. Meanwhile, he and his second wife, Jane Threlkeld, had moved from the corner house to a large residence they had built called "The Cedars," which stood on the present site of Western High School.

A new arrival was imminent in the Cox family, which made it inadvisable to have a party at their home. Consequently, Cox used one of the houses which was then vacant, number 3337, second from the corner. He had it handsomely furnished throughout and his eldest daughter, Sally, was nominated to act as hostess in her mother's place for the distinguished occasion. And all went well.

But where were Mrs. Shedden and her daughters and the school at the time of the General's party? We finally discovered that she had moved to the City of Washington. She appears in the directory there for 1827, a separate one, not including Georgetown. This was the second directory for the city, the first one being for 1822. Her listing is as follows: *Mrs. Shedden, widow, seminary for young ladies, south side of Penn. Ave., btw 10th and 11th.*

Mrs. Shedden had made the same decision Elisha's former partner, Darius Clagett was soon to make. In a paper presented before the Columbia Historical Society, entitled, "Three Generations of Clagetts," the following appears:

> *As the city of Washington grew, Darius must have decided that it presented greater business opportunities than the more static, and still quite separate Georgetown. By 1834 (and probably 1827, since he had moved his residence to Washington by then) he was operating the firm of Darius Clagett & Co., dry goods, at the northeast corner of 11th and Pennsylvania Avenue.*

Not only did Mrs. Shedden move first, but she moved to within half a block of the location selected by one of the more astute merchants in the area.

This plucky little widow, thirty-seven when she arrived in Georgetown, deserves our admiration and applause for her successful entry into the crowded academic field to maintain herself and her daughters. The extent of her achievements is revealed in another paper read before the Columbia Historical Society back in 1909.

That paper, entitled "Richard Forrest and His Time (1795-1834)" contains the following paragraph:

> The fashionable school for young ladies about that period was conducted by Mrs. Cecelia Shedden, an accomplished Irish lady who came here with her four [sic] young daughters, one of whom, Janet, married George W. Riggs. Mrs. Shedden was not only a thorough teacher in the English branches, but a proficient French scholar, which her French spelling book will amply testify. This book was recommended by the President of Georgetown College and was in use there. I doubt if any succeeding work of the kind was so successful. I still have my mother's thumb-worn copy.

The author, Mrs. Kate Kearney Henry, then goes on to disclose that her father, a fleet surgeon in the Navy, lived in the family property located on the site of the old Willard Hotel. Her mother, who was a Forrest, lived in their family home on the southeast corner of F at Fourteenth street, later covered by the Ebbitt House, thus illustrating that the neighborhood had been a fine residential section.

But what is there here about the romance of George W. Riggs, Jr., and Janet Madeleine Cecelia Shedden? Well, perhaps quite a bit — reasonable proximity, an age differential of only two years, a swarm of brothers and sisters and cousins and perhaps even some classmates in Mrs. Shedden's prestigious school for young ladies. Romance often develops among a certain generation or age group in a certain location, and it could have happened here.

The fact that George W. Riggs, Jr., lived with the Romulus Riggs family and grew up in Georgetown has only been known since our recent investigation and the discovery of the George A. Hyde letter. It had always been assumed he had lived with his father and stepmother in Baltimore and Philadelphia and New York.

CHAPTER 5

At the very least, our brief excursion down these minor historic trails has provided a much more reasonable assumption as to how George, Jr., and Janet met and later fell in love.

Concerning Romulus's "large brick house" which now has a one story addition erected later, and many other expansions and improvements, it may also be noted that the house received considerable latter-day publicity as the residence of Averell Harriman which was loaned to Mrs. Jacqueline Kennedy and her children after the assassination of President Kennedy.

After a brief residence there Mrs. Kennedy bought the house across the street at 3017 N Street, built by Thomas Beall, son of George, which had originally adjoined the old garden to the east. However, the resulting crush of tourist traffic, including not only pedestrians and individual cars, but tourist busses as well, caused her to move to New York in the fall of 1964 and the house was later sold.

Chapter Notes

[1] A Portrait of Old Georgetown, by Mrs. Grace Dunlop Ecker, p. 142, Dietz Press, Inc., Richmond, Va., 1951.

Chapter 6

In the latter part of 1826, Romulus moved his family from Georgetown to Philadelphia. Six years before, he had sold the drygoods portion of his business to a nephew, George R. Gaither, son of his older sister, Henrietta, and Gaither subsequently had moved the business to Baltimore.

Romulus had continued in the banking and brokerage field and to provide additional capital had sold the acreage in Montgomery County which old Samuel had willed him in 1814. An advertisement in the January 20, 1816, *National Intelligencer* provides an interesting insight into his activities:

> *I will give the highest premium on drafts and bank notes of the following kinds, viz; Georgia, South Carolina, North Carolina, Virginia, Boston, New York and Philadelphia. I also wish to purchase treasury notes, specie, United States' stock and bills of exchange. Notes and drafts collected and remitted in any kind of funds. Persons remitting or traveling to any part of the United States may be supplied; all kinds of western bank notes bought and sold*

Also, Romulus had developed a prosperous land business in Illinois by buying up land warrants given as bonuses to soldiers after the War of 1812. He was so enamored of this lucrative phase of his business that on January 15, 1826, just before leaving Georgetown, he named his ninth and last child, a daughter, Illinois Riggs.

In Philadelphia, Romulus and Elisha were in partnership briefly under the firm of R & E Riggs and Co. at No. 96 High (now Market) Street. Presumably, at that time, George, Jr., and Lawrason, on their summer vacations and excursions from school, had rejoined their father and his young wife, Mary Ann Karrick [she was nineteen years younger than Elisha]. The family soon moved on to New York because "She wanted the 'bright lights'" said a granddaughter many years later.

George W. Riggs, Jr., appears to have been the first member of his family to go to college. He entered Yale in 1829 when he was sixteen, but, strangely enough, left there after two and a half years. By a rare coincidence, the bank possesses the original memorandum of the president of Yale College dismissing him on February 16, 1832, "at his father's request." This yellowing document was brought into the bank in the late 1950's by a genial Irish gentleman, Mr. J. B. McMullen, whose sister, Miss Mary McMullen, had inherited the contents of the old Riggs mansion at 1617 Eye Street, N.W., from the last surviving daughter, Miss Jane Riggs. The message reads simply:

> George W. Riggs, a member of the Junior Class in this college, of fair character, is hereby dismissed at his father's request.
>
> Jeremiah Day,
> President.

Yale College, Feb. 16, 1832.

The word "fair" has been downgraded in our lifetimes, partly because it was used years ago in grading school papers as "fair, good or excellent." But the second definition in Webster's New World Dictionary still gives the usage popular in President Day's time, which was "Unblemished; clean; as a 'fair reputation' ".

To seek as much information as possible, and to follow through on our good fortune in obtaining the letter in the first

CHAPTER 6

place, we dispatched an inquiry through friends at Yale and eventually received the following reply:

> Riggs was present at Yale for his freshman, sophomore, and part of his junior year. He did not graduate. He is listed in the yearly catalogues for his first three years, but there is no mention of him in the catalogue for 1833, which would have been his senior year.
>
> The Class Book of 1833 [in its 3rd decennial edition — 1863] provides a biography of Riggs in the non-graduates section. This biography includes the following 'was a member of the Calliopean Society and the North Division; roomed with Colt sophomore year, and was also a roommate of W. P. Johnston; left College in the course of the junior year. After visiting Europe, he became a merchant in New York City...'

This letter was signed by Professor G. W. Pierson of the Department of History, Yale University, who added that a further investigation would be made and another report sent to us. Six weeks later we received the second report signed by his secretary, Mrs. Glynn Marini. The pertinent sections are as follows:

> At Professor Pierson's request I resumed my search for information about George Washington Riggs, Jr....
>
> I must now report that I have been unable to find any information or piece of evidence which positively identifies the reason for Riggs's departure from Yale in 1832. The letter which, one supposes, must have been written by Riggs's father to President Jeremiah Day is not to be found in the Day papers at Yale.
>
> Enclosed you will find a photocopy of a page from the Book of Averages. You will note that Riggs received grades of 3.3, 3.23 and 2.73. To give you some idea of what these figures mean I will say that a 2.00 was the equivalent of a passing mark of 60, a grade of 2.75 would be the equivalent of a 75, and a mark over 3.00 would have been considered an honors grade by the standards of that time. It would appear, even on the basis of incomplete records of Riggs's grades, that he most probably did not leave Yale for academic reasons.

55

> In my opinion, you may be reasonably certain that Riggs did not leave Yale College for disciplinary reasons. Had he been guilty of any infractions of College rules or had his behavior warranted dismissal, there is little doubt that I would have much more information to report to you. The very fact that there is so little information about Riggs's departure from Yale indicates to me and to those more experienced than I, that he left of his own volition or, at worst, at the request of his father.

Thus, we were left with little more information than we already possessed, except the comforting assurance that George Riggs, Jr., did not leave Yale for disciplinary reasons, and he was, moreover, a good student. The information in the reprinted Class Book of 1833 that, "After visiting Europe, he became a merchant in New York," is consistent with the statements covering that period in *The Riggs Family of Maryland*, as follows: "In 1833, he [G.W.R.] went abroad. He later returned, and was employed in the banking business with his father, in the firm of Riggs, Taylor and Company."

But we still had a small mystery here. Who was Taylor? Nothing in the Index and not even a footnote amplifies or explains his presence in the firm. Obviously the author did not know who he was, or he would have set forth the facts in his customary meticulous fashion.

The answer to his identity came later from a totally unexpected source and added another interesting dimension to our story.

In early 1965, a charming lady of middle age was ushered into the author's office from the Information Desk in the main lobby of Riggs National Bank. She very quickly explained that she was seeking information on her great grandfather, Samuel Taylor, who had been in partnership in New York with Elisha Riggs and his two sons, George Washington, Jr., and Lawrason.

When I looked at her a little incredulously, she asked, "Did you know about him?"

"We knew there was a partnership," I told her, "but we didn't even know his first name."

"Then you don't have any of his letters," she said dejectedly, and I told her we didn't.

CHAPTER 6

It turned out that this attractive history buff was Mrs. George Heitz of 2 Lancaster Lane, Lincolnshire, P.O. Deerfield, Illinois. Our rapport as two amateur historians at opposite poles of a mutual quest was instantaneous.

When she learned my middle name was Taylor, inherited from a grandfather, Charles Franklin Taylor, of Burke Station on the Southern Railroad in Fairfax County, Virginia, she was delighted and I was promptly dubbed "cousin Taylor." We have since met on three or four occasions, and our correspondence has become voluminous. Our files now contain more information about Samuel Taylor than about many of the members of the Riggs family.

To begin with, she had seen copies of thirty or forty letters owned by an aged cousin, that were written by Samuel Taylor to Elisha Riggs in 1833-34 while he was accompanying George Washington, Jr., and Lawrason on a buying trip to England, Ireland and Scotland. A number of the letters were written from Manchester, Samuel Taylor's home town, which was apparently headquarters for the buying expedition.

He had come to America in 1823, she said, and first served an apprenticeship in a firm of which George Peabody was a partner. She speculated this was where he had met Elisha Riggs. I speculated she was absolutely correct.

She had also jotted down some details about a contract signed by the four on 1 November, 1833, to run for two years, in which the capital contributions were, Elisha $20,000, Samuel Taylor $10,000, George, Jr., $5,000 and Lawrason $5,000. Her notes indicated Elisha was then 54, Samuel Taylor, 31, George, Jr., 20 and Lawrason a year younger.

She also said all her family records indicated the partners were wiped out, lost their store and stock, in the "great fire of 1835" in New York.

After that, she said, there was a second contract signed in 1836, between the three younger men only — S.T., G.W.R., Jr. and L.R. It was to have run for one year from June 1, 1836, but she didn't know what happened after that. She believed the fire had hurt business badly, and some time later, Samuel Taylor had gone West with a surveying party and finally settled in Wisconsin Territory.

We had talked longer than we realized and Mrs. Heitz had to rush off for an appointment. Before she left, we promised to correspond, filling out as many gaps as possible in our separate statistics.

Subsequently, I learned that the great fire in New York in 1835 had been truly devastating — a conflagration originating at Hanover Place and Pearl street, which had destroyed six hundred buildings and caused a loss of $15,000,000 in the heart of what was then New York's business district. Unquestionably business had suffered severely for months thereafter. Fortunately, Elisha's home on Bowling Green and his banking office, which had been moved from its original location, emerged unscathed.

Lawrason left New York in 1838 for Peoria, Illinois, where he handled some land business for his father. Later he moved on to St. Louis, the frontier city on the bluff overlooking "the father of waters," with its bustling and opulent steamboat traffic. He was much taken with the business opportunities there and he opened a mercantile business with his father known as E. Riggs & Son.

George, Jr. had returned to England in 1838, to further his knowledge of dry goods and trade generally "at the patronage of Mr. George Peabody".[1] He must have considered entering this fabulously successful firm, but, for whatever reasons, returned home in time to learn of the proposed partnership in Washington. He wrote Mr. Corcoran in December, 1839, that he and his father were considering "the prospects for business."

Franz von Recum states that he had always heard from the members of the Riggs family that George, Jr. fell in love with Janet Shedden around 1831, the year he left Yale. Some family gossips even maintained that Elisha had yanked him out of Yale to show his displeasure with her Roman Catholic background. But we now know, or think we know, that George, Jr., was anxious to go into business like the rest of his family and to get on with becoming settled sufficiently to marry. The opportunity in Washington may have attracted him for that reason.

If George, Jr. had had a childhood sweetheart in Georgetown, it followed that Lawrason might have had one too, which, it soon developed, he did. In his case, the young lady was Sophia Theresa Cruttenden, the daughter of Joel Cruttenden, a prominent merchant on Water (now K) Street

CHAPTER 6

and a member of the Board of Common Council of the town. He and his wife, Mary, had come to Georgetown at an early date and owned a house on O Street, which they bought in 1815, shortly after the birth of their daughter. The tidy residence still stands today at 3114 O Street, N.W.

Since Sophia Theresa was the same age as Janet, they might have been classmates. Mrs. Shedden certainly taught her own little girls and she may have taught other young children; or the girls might have met through the Riggs brothers, or vice versa.

In any case, Lawrason, having settled in St. Louis and gone into business, returned to Georgetown and married Sophia Cruttenden in Christ Church on February 4, 1840. Her family was then living in Cox's Row, where the wedding reception probably was held.

Afterwards, the young couple returned to St. Louis to establish their home in that exciting "gateway to the west".

The partnership agreement between W. W. Corcoran and George W. Riggs, Jr. was signed a little over two months later on April 15, 1840, and the firm commenced business at once at their 15th Street location as a bank of deposit. George, Jr. must have taken a very early vacation, since he married Janet Shedden on June 23, 1840, in Madison, New Jersey — at that time the residence of Mrs. Shedden. The couple soon returned to Washington and made their home "on the south side of New York Avenue, between 13th and 14th, nearer 14th."[2]

The year had begun happily but the tide turned when Corcoran's striken young wife died on November 21, 1840.

Tragedy struck again almost before the New Year's bells had stopped peeling, when Lawrason's bride, Sophia, died in child-birth on January 4, 1841 and was buried in Bellefontaine Cemetery in St. Louis. Her distraught parents who had moved to St. Louis to be near their daughter and her first born, lived out their lives in that city and were buried in the same cemetery.

This recurrent tragedy of young lives in those precarious times is recounted in a letter to General Washington from his only sister, Betty, dated May 18, 1790. In it she apologizes for not having written sooner, and then explains in the harsh, fatalistic jargon of her day:

"I was on a Visit to my Son Lawrence in Essex at the time I Expect'd his wife to lyin, Pore thing it Proved fatal to her, she was taken with Fitts and died in twelve Ours without being Deliver'd."[3]

Chapter Notes

[1]*The Riggs Family of Maryland*, p. 328.
[2]Letter of Franz von Recum, November 18, 1950.
[3]Mount Vernon Ladies Association, *Annual Report*, 1976.

Chapter 7

In April of 1841, on the eve of the celebration of the first anniversary of the young banking house of Corcoran & Riggs, a national crisis of formidable proportions loomed when William Henry Harrison, who had been sworn in as the nation's ninth President on March 4, 1841, died on April 4, 1841. His tenure — thirty days — was the shortest in our history.

Harrison was the first member of the Whig party to be elected President and the first President to die in office. He had succeeded Van Buren and was himself succeeded by Virginian, John Tyler, his Vice-Presidential running mate under the slogan, "Tippecanoe and Tyler too."

So stunned was the country by this unprecedented situation that some members of Congress were "actually demanding a clarification of the Presidential powers that had evolved upon Tyler".[1] But the constitution and the resourceful Tyler were equal to the challenge and the course of the nation proceeded resolutely onward.

Harrison had named one of the original organizers of the Whig party from Pittsburgh to be the first Comptroller of the

Currency in the reorganized Treasury. The latter, who bore the promising name, Walter Forward, was an august seventy-five-year-old lawyer and politician who had served one term in Congress back in the 1820's.

Upon Harrison's death and Tyler's accession to the Presidency, Forward was named Secretary of the Treasury in the new cabinet. While he set out optimistically enough upon his duties, he was scarcely equipped to handle the nation's finances. As a matter of fact, few, if any, of the executive and legislative leaders of the period had any training in fiscal affairs.

To make matters worse, the new government was badly in need of funds. Secretary Forward made several vain attempts to raise money at home. After being summarily rebuffed by the New York financial community, he booked passage to London to seek a loan. This must have been a difficult trip for the elderly secretary, and, following his failure to accomplish his object, he returned a weary and discouraged cabinet officer. To the President he reported that the conduct of the repudiating states was still fresh in the minds of the overseas capitalists and was an insurmountable obstacle in his negotiations.

At this juncture, Daniel Webster, who had somehow become a close friend of Mr. Corcoran, and who had been named Secretary of State in the new cabinet, interceded and requested Corcoran & Riggs to help the beleaguered government to place a loan. This required that Corcoran hurry to New York to discuss the proposal with Elisha Riggs, the firm's backer and silent partner, and to seek his personal guarantee, without which the new firm was powerless to be of any significant assistance.

From that mission W. W. Corcoran first began to emerge as a banker statesman. Apparently his eloquence persuaded Elisha to consent to give his guarantee, and the firm bid and received an award of a $5,000,000 government loan at 101.[2] This bold and courageous transaction not only caused an immense sigh of relief across 15th Street at the Treasury Department, but brought the fledgling firm into the national spotlight.

The venture was crowned with success when the entire loan was disposed of at a handsome profit. There followed some bitter and belated jealousy in banking circles but the words "sagacious" and "skillfull" also began to be applied to the Washington firm.

Secretary Forward had less trouble floating subsequent loans, but he gratefully remembered his rescuers by keeping them and their associates represented in future financing.

In a letter in the archives of Riggs National Bank, dated "Washington City, Feb. 25th, 1843," W. W. Corcoran, in writing to George Newbold, Esq. of New York City, states:

> Under the circumstances I think we are fairly entitled to the amount we proposed to subscribe for, [but] strange things are going on here in relation to the loan.
>
> Mr. Forward throws up the reins on Monday. He sent over for me this morning with a view to arrange our old difficulty. He says he wishes to do what is right in the matter. You will see his manifesto in a few days.
>
> We have various names mentioned as likely to succeed him in the Treas. Dept. — We will write you when we have direct information on the subject.

A second letter dated two days later, February 27, 1843, contains the following:

> The President in a representation of the case to him wrote a letter to the Secretary of the Treasury to withhold $300,000 of the stock until we heard from you.
>
> Nothing has transpired to induce me to doubt the correctness of what I wrote you yesterday. An effort will be made, or rather has been made, to induce Mr. Forward to hold on until after the adjournment of Congress, that it may not be necessary to send nominations to the Senate. It will not succeed.

Secretary Forward actually resigned his postion the next day, February 28th, 1843, "to return to the practice of law." Thus, he not only vindicated Corcoran's judgment, but terminated his service in government just short of his second anniversary. The distinguished barrister, then seventy-seven, richly deserved to return to private pursuits, where, it may happily be reported, he passed another nine years, reflecting, perhaps, ruefully or philosophically, on the perils of public financing.

Corcoran & Riggs appear to have had only minor dealings at the Treasury Department with his successor. But when the Democrats returned to power in March of 1845, the firm would begin another and even closer affiliation with the government which would raise it to a new pinnacle of fame and fortune.

In the interim W. W. Corcoran and George W. Riggs, Jr., both used their newly acquired profits to make investments in real estate.

Corcoran appears to have been fascinated with the possibilities of the block bounded by 14th Street on the east, 15th Street on the west, Pennsylvania Avenue on the south and F Street on the north — the very block where he had started in business on the north side of Pennsylvania Avenue, near 15th Street.

This block, designated in the city's real estate records as square 225, today contains the landmark old Willard Hotel, scheduled for renovation, on the east, and the more modern Washington Hotel, on the west. Corcoran's initial investments were all made in the site now covered by the Washington Hotel. Ultimately, this astute financier would own the entire site on which, in 1878, he would erect a massive six-story office building, the largest and finest of its kind in the city, and the predecessor of the present hotel.

George W. Riggs, Jr., on the other hand, followed in the footsteps of his forebears and purchased a beautiful 200-acre farm in what was then known as Washington County, being the portion of the District of Columbia west and north of Bladensburg, north of the Boundary (now Florida Avenue) in Washington and north of 8th (now R) Street in Georgetown. The property was located some seven miles out 7th Street Turnpike, and near St. Paul's Church in Rock Creek Parish.

Young Riggs was influenced by the fact he had a family of two little daughters, with a third child expected, when he made the purchase in 1843. Recalling his own childhood visits to Pleasant Hill and the other plantations near Brookeville, he obviously wanted his children to grow up in a farm-oriented atmosphere. In addition, he felt that the land, being very advantageously located on high ground overlooking the some-

CHAPTER 7

times fever-plagued, low-lying sections of the District, was a sound investment. Two very different backgrounds and personalities were possessed by these founding fathers of what would eventually become The Riggs National Bank — Washington's largest.

Riggs seems to have assembled his tract by purchases from several owners, including the glebe of Rock Creek Parish. There was apparently an older building on the property which was restored and remodeled. John Clagett Proctor, already mentioned as the local historian whose columns appeared some years ago in the *Sunday Star*, has given us detailed information on the building of George Riggs's house, including even the names of the craftsmen who worked on it — there being no general contractors in that era.

The supervisor was William H. Degges, whose occupation is given in the city directory at that period as a house carpenter. The specifications called for "venetian blinds to all windows except those in gable end of garret," and that the veranda on south side be "according to plan given by John Skirving." Skirving appears in the directory of 1843 as a bricklayer.

At completion, the handsome balconies and veranda on the south side of the house provided an inspiring view of the capital city in the distance. Riggs named the place "Corn Rigs," a reference to the Scotch word "rig," meaning a ridge or furrow. It was an allusion to the farm with its "corn fields" stretching between areas of beautiful woodlands.

An old plat of the farm shows a well beside the main house and a second well between the managers cottage and the barn. There was also a stable and a pond, and downhill in the lower quarter, a tenant house and well and another barn. And all this rusticity was only eight miles from Riggs' office.

The original ledger of Corcoran & Riggs for the years 1842-43, an elongated, dusty tome weighing twenty pounds, (the first one for 1840-41 is unaccountably missing) discloses that President Tyler favored the partners by opening his Presidential account with them. He also established a "furniture account," into which were credited substantial sums appropriated by Congress for the refurbishing of the White House. Tyler was a borrower, too, as shown in his letter of February 4, 1843, which reads:

> Gentlemen:
> Above you have an order for my month's salary due this day. Will you do me the favor to redeem the note at bank, notice of which is enclosed — amount $1,195.48.
>
> Yrs. Truly,
> J. Tyler
> Feb. 4, 1843

Secretary of State Daniel Webster and Postmaster General Charles A. Wickliffe were both depositors, and Wickliffe was apparently so taken with George Riggs's new status as a country gentleman, that in a letter from his Kentucky plantation he wrote, "I have caused to be sent to Mr. Riggs one barrel of blue grass seed — one half of which is for the President of the United States."

One can picture the scene that resulted when the barrel of blue grass seed arrived at the office of Corcoran & Riggs opposite the Treasury and George Riggs hastily summoned his coachman to deliver half of it to President Tyler at the White House, and to reload the balance for the trip to Corn Rigs.

And the President, by the way, was about to establish another Presidential first — a marriage while in office. Five months prior to his letter requesting the bank to retire his note, he had lost his invalid wife, Letitia Christian Tyler. Shortly thereafter, at a White House reception he met and became enamored of the beautiful New York socialite, Julia Gardner, who had left a trail of broken romances on the Continent and in New York and Washington. She eventually accepted his proposal and on June 26, 1844, the urbane fifty-four-year-old widower and the twenty-four-year-old Julia were married.

Notwithstanding the gossip this romance had provoked, the union proved a happy one that lasted for 18 years. Julia bore Tyler seven children (he had eight by his first wife), making him the most prolific President.

At this time a formidable array of bank correspondents was represented on the firm's books, including the American Exchange Bank, the Chemical Bank, Phenix Bank, Leather Manufacturers Bank and the Bank of America, New York; the Chesapeake Bank, the Franklin Bank, Western Bank and the Bank of Baltimore, Baltimore; the Bank of Potomac, Alexandria; the Hagerstown Bank; the Farmers Bank of Virginia, Fredericksburg; the Exchange Bank of Petersburg and the same of Norfolk; the Bank of the Valley of Virginia, Leesburg and Winchester; the Bank of Missouri and the Merchants Insurance and Trust Company, Nashville.

George Peabody of London was carrying substantial balances as was August Belmont, New York representative of the Rothschilds, always looking for new and influential contacts.

There was even an account in the name of W. H. Degges who, presumably, was the William H. Degges named by Proctor as the builder of George Riggs's house. And thus was the modest beginning of the tradition of "Riggs Bank" being the favorite depository of many of the leading builders in the capital city.

Everything considered, the firm's first years had exceeded all expectations.

We have from the year 1843 an extraordinary likeness of the firm's silent partner, or godfather, Elisha Riggs, who guaranteed their first $5,000,000 purchase of U. S. Treasury notes.

He was evidently relaxing at his favorite spa, Saratoga Springs, New York, when, on August 3, 1843, the eminent French artist, August Edouart (1788-1861) cut his silhouette. This fact is attested in Elisha's own handwriting on the back of the glass-framed portrait.

Silhouettes were all the rage at the time. There were no cameras, few daguerreotypes, and the almost instant black and white cut-outs, done rapidly by talented artists, were the "Polaroids" of the day. Edouart cut nearly 4,000 silhouettes during the decade 1839-49, traveling back and forth between Saratoga Springs, Boston, New York and Washington.

He always used a double fold of paper and bound the duplicates for himself into more than 50 albums. All but sixteen were lost at sea when Edouart's homebound ship sank in a winter storm near Guernsey in the Channel Islands.

We obtained our silhouette from our good friend Franz von Recum who was the first to recount to us the story of Edouart's disastrous voyage home. According to his version, the artist gave the surviving albums to his valiant rescuers, and the silhouettes eventually found their way to London, and finally to New York where they were sold at auction.

Ours was purchased by von Recum's cousin, Karrick Riggs (1853-1935), Elisha's grandson, and Franz received it after the death of Karrick's only daughter, Pauline Riggs Noyes, in 1942. We learned recently that the National Portrait Gallery has a collection of 348 of Edouart's silhouettes, evidently originating from the same auction. A press release issued by the Gallery confirms the story of the shipwreck and hails the silhouettes as "an invaluable snapshot of our world of 120 years ago."[3]

We took another careful look at our full-length portrait of Elisha, attired in an elegant tailcoat, with high collar, watch fob and slippers. It was done from his right side while he was standing at ease, arms folded, left foot slightly forward of the right. It reveals a fine head of hair even at age sixty-four and a prominent but well-formed nose and chin — the confident and relaxed bearing of a successful and self-assured businessman and banker, luxuriating, perhaps in the latest highly profitable guarantee for his son's firm.

Franz von Recum said of the splendid shape of the head in the silhouette, that "it was a fine head, and was inherited by George W. Riggs, Jr., and his grandson, Col. E. Francis Riggs."

We now view this isolated remnant of a cruel shipwreck as a portentous addition to our collection of Elisha Riggs memorabilia. Ships and shipping were destined to play a profound part in the last decade of his life.

Chapter Notes

[1] Robert John Walker, *A Politician From Jackson to Lincoln* p. 30.
[2] Corcoran Gallery of Art Scrapbook, 1886-1888, pp. 19-20.
[3] "Profiles in Cutouts; The Famous and Obscure", by Jeannette Smyth, The Washington Post, December 28, 1977.

Chapter 8

In the year 1845, the firm of Corcoran & Riggs employed a portion of its mounting profits to purchase the former Washington Office of the Second Bank of the United States at the intersection of 15th Street and President's Square. The transaction included a considerable amount of the assets of the defunct institution (of which Corcoran was a qualified judge) as well as the vaults and furnishings. Thus, did the new firm put on the very vestments of the old government bank where Corcoran had worked nine years before.

This was no average building. It had been designed by the brilliant English architect, George Hadfield, who supervised its construction in 1824. He had been commissioned, as a very young man in 1795, one of the architects of the U.S. Capitol Building. We know now from recent additions to history that he obtained that exhalted position via our minister to Paris, Thomas Jefferson, who had succeeded the venerable Benjamin Franklin there in 1785.

Jefferson, forty-three and a recent widower, had fallen in love with Hadfield's twenty-seven-year-old sister, Maria Cosway, whose husband was a year older than Jefferson and a noted miniature painter. The romance of Jefferson and Maria was touching and brief (she took herself out of his life when convinced he was probably in line to be President of the United States), but the two remained friends and correspondents for the balance of their lives.[1]

In any case, under Jefferson's lofty sponsorship, Hadfield obtained many important commissions, including the first Treasury Building constructed in 1800 at the southwest corner of 15th Street and President's Square, facing east, on Fifteenth. This was directly south across the Square from the location of the Second Bank of the United States, and the two buildings bore a marked similarity. The Treasury Building had been burned by the British in 1814, and reconstructed under Hadfield's supervision in 1817. It later became part of the old State Department which stood on President's Square north of the Treasury and east of the White House during the Civil War.

Hadfield's greatest work, however, was City Hall, built in 1821, the third oldest government building still standing today and now part of our Court House complex. But his government bank building was hailed as one of the finest of its day and its occupancy by Corcoran & Riggs was regarded as another mark of distinction for the rising young firm.

The administration of President Polk, who took office on March 4, 1845, was one of the true golden ages of our history. Three new states, Texas, Iowa and Wisconsin were admitted to the Union during his presidency. The War with Mexico was fought to a triumphant end and the acquisition thereby of the vast territories of New Mexico and California carried our national borders to the Pacific. The long-smoldering Oregon boundary dispute was settled by a treaty with Great Britain. Polk was the only president other than Washington to carry out every item of his political platform.

His administration was also a golden age for Corcoran & Riggs. Around the corner on 15th Street, Robert John Walker, the new Secretary of the Treasury, was an aggressive, controversial little politician who had emerged as one of the leaders of the Democratic party. At college, Walker had somehow met and married Mary Bache, the granddaughter of Benjamin Franklin, and thus became a member of the influential Bache

CHAPTER 8

and Dallas families. Mary's maternal grandfather, Alexander J. Dallas, had been Secretary of the Treasury in the cabinet of James Madison, and her uncle, George Miflin Dallas, would soon become Vice-President under Polk.

This fiery little Secretary, five-feet-two inches in height and weighing scarcely one hundred pounds, was described by one contemporary as "a mere whiffet of a man." Though small in stature, Walker possessed an inordinate pride and an explosive temper, which caused him to challenge to a duel "no less than Henry Clay, Thomas Hart Benton, and Jeremiah Black, all of whom declined, probably assuming that Walker would be honor bound to shoot to kill."[2]

Walker played an important role in the Baltimore convention of the Democratic party in 1844, in securing the nomination of Polk for president and "Uncle George" Dallas for Vice-President. He aspired to be Secretary of State, but after that post fell to fellow Pennsylvanian, James Buchanan, accepted appointment as Secretary of the Treasury.

Walker was sitting in the Senate at the time of Secretary Forward's difficulties in raising money for the government, and he obviously knew of the brilliant services Corcoran & Riggs had rendered at that time to the Treasury Department.

Now, in his own term as Secretary of the Treasury, Walker faced an unprecedented demand for funds to finance the conflict with Mexico. He immediately enlisted the aid of W. W. Corcoran as an emissary between the government and the private banks. There is ample evidence of the close cooperation between the two men. To charges of favoritism, the Secretary blandly countered that he had made the government more money as a result of Corcoran's higher bids.

The Treasury Report of 1847, states one authority, discloses that "of the $15,469,800 in Treasury notes accounted for, $11,713,850 had either been taken directly by Corcoran & Riggs or by Elisha Riggs as an individual. Another $1,987,500 went to firms . . . closely associated with C & R . . . they thus bagged over 80 percent of the loan."[3]

Throughout the crucial year of 1847, there appeared increasingly favorable comments across the country on Walker's handling of the Treasury's affairs. This reflected favorably on the Secretary and on the firm of Corcoran &

Riggs and on Corcoran himself. There is some evidence Walker resented his reliance on the latter, but he knew of no alternative. Corcoran delighted in the experience, and the accompanying rich profits that accrued to the firm and to himself.

Meanwhile, President Polk had opened his personal account with the firm and also a second account entitled, "The President's House, J.K.P., President," presumably for White House expenses. The bank was thus favored with its second consecutive Presidential client, a circumstance that added enormously to its prestige.

Corcoran's own prestige as a banker statesman had continued to grow, as indicated by a letter he had received in March of 1847 from Robert C. Winthrop of Massachusetts, Speaker of the House of Representatives. In this remarkable document Winthrop asks Corcoran if he could obtain "some assurance from headquarters [meaning, apparently, from the President]" to help him decide whether to undertake a short trip to Europe. Put quite simply, Winthrop wanted to know if there might be in contemplation a call for a special session of Congress . . . hence the curious letter which follows:

Boston, March 24, 1847

My Dear Sir:

In view of a short visit to Europe which, you know, I am preparing to make, I am extremely anxious to know whether the late news from the Rio Grande is likely to involve an extra session of Congress. I do not see what Congress can do to help matters . . Still I would like some assurance from headquarters as to what may be in the contemplation of the Executive. I have actually taken passage on the Hibernia, which sails next week. But if I thought that Congress could be wanted before August, at the earliest, I would abandon all idea of going. You have a golden key for unlocking the mysteries of Walker-dom if not of Polk-dom. Will you do me the favor to give me a line at your earliest convenience, communicating, as confidentially as you please, such intimations or assurances as you are able to obtain?

I am, very truly and
respectfully yours,
Rob. V. Winthrop

CHAPTER 8

Mr. Corcoran:
It would greatly oblige me if I might hear from you by return mail.

Corcoran had already added to his personal image in another and most admirable manner when he used a part of his newly acquired wealth to pay off the debts he and his brothers had compromised with creditors back in 1823. He not only paid the portion which had legally been forgiven by the settlement, but he made the unheard of gesture of paying interest due from 1823 to 1847, which more than doubled the debt from $23,000 to $47,000.

Locating the holders of the individual items of indebtedness and/or their heirs, must have been in itself, a laborious, time-consuming and expensive process. The letters he received from payees are eloquent testimony to the unusual nature of this high-minded and generous act. Three examples will probably suffice to portray the gratitude and astonishment of the beneficiaries, as follows:

New York, 23 May, 1847

Dear Sir:
I received yesterday, through Mr. McCall, your check for three hundred and fifteen dollars, being, he informed me, the balance of a debt due my father, under the late firm of Smith, McCall & Co., which, however, had been honorably compromised and settled many years ago; and, had not your high sense of rectitude and equity revived this moral debt, I, at least would always have remained ignorant of its existence...

I cannot allow this opportunity to pass without contributing my mite... in encircling your name with the enviable motto "just man"....

I know that acts of this nature bear with them their own appropriate fruits, and the pleasure they engender is in no way dependent on the opinion of the world; still, if these few lines of grateful acknowledgment should serve to heighten that pleasure, my purpose will then be attained.

77

I fervently trust, sir, that prosperity (which you much deserve) and happiness may always be your attendants.

>Very respectfully, yours,
>Gam. G Smith
>(in behalf of the heirs of
>the late Gamaliel Smith).

W. W. Corcoran, Esq.

>Philadelphia,
>May 27, 1847

Dear Sir:

Mr. William Whitney has handed me upwards of nineteen hundred dollars, the amount received from you on account of the balance of a debt contracted with my lamented husband, the late R. M. Whitney, many years since, and which was legally and honorably arranged by you at the time.

This act of voluntarily discharging the balance, after the lapse of so many years, seems to me so noble and so creditable, and has given to me and my friends to whom I have mentioned the matter so high an estimate of Your character and honorable views, that I cannot refrain from this simple expression of feeling, and of assuring you of the gratitude I feel, and of the glad heart which it has made of an almost dependent widow.

Permit me to congratulate you on your success in business and to offer you my best wishes for your future prosperity and happiness and that of each member of your family.

>Your obliged friend,
>Julia Whitney.

W. W. Corcoran, Esq.
Washington

CHAPTER 8

> Philadelphia,
> July 12, 1847
>
> W. W. Corcoran, Esq.
> Dear Sir:
> I have this day received from you fourteen hundred and fifteen dollars and fifty cents, being principal and interest on the balance of the claim compromised at fifty per cent, twenty years ago. This extraordinary act has been done by you without solicitation on my part, and I will take this occasion to say that, having been engaged in mercantile pursuits for thirty years, and, during that period having sold upwards of twenty-three million of dollars to the various persons in different states of the Union, and having compromised claims for a very large amount, yours is the only instance in which a man ever came forward after recovering his fortune, in the honorable manner you have done, and paid me in full. Be assured it will not be forgotten by me, and whenever occasion may occur by which I can, directly or indirectly, serve you, it will be remembered then also.
> With my best wishes for your health and prosperity,
>
> Believe me, yours truly,
> T. C. Rockhill

This generous settlement of old debts by Corcoran reveals him to have been a person of unusual integrity and character. Very few bankers and businessmen will witness in their lifetime any financial transation to match it. For "tax benefits," yes, but not simply in the name of family pride and honor.

Not surprisingly, he also remembered his boyhood home in the little colonial river port of Georgetown, awarding to that community the sum of $10,000 "as a fund for the aid and comfort... of the dependent population."

At about this time he was also distributing to friends and relatives a handsome engraving of himself in which he is portrayed as a sort of middle-aged Lord Byron. He had achieved an immense fortune in an unbelievably short time and he possessed the accompanying amounts of pride and vanity.

But gratitude and charity were to be henceforth the leading characteristics of this remarkable man.

W. W. Corcoran was already beginning to deserve his legend.

CHAPTER 8

Chapter Notes

[1]"Jefferson in Paris," Joseph Barry, *Saturday Review*, January 10, 1976.
[2]*Robert John Walker, A Politician from Jackson to Lincoln*, James P. Shenton, p. 2.
[3]Ibid. p. 97.

Chapter 9

The year 1848 was a notable one for the country in many respects. First, gold was discovered in California at Sutter's Mill on the American River on January 24 — a date of enormous significance and excitement. And exactly nine days later, on February 2, a treaty of peace was signed in the little village of Guadalupe Hidalgo, near Mexico City, bringing to a close the war which had been waged for nearly twenty-one months.

President Polk's stature had never been higher, but he was a cold, reserved and colorless individual who lacked the personality and appeal to be a genuine national hero. However, he was acknowledged to be firm and hard working and his honesty and integrity had never been questioned.

He had demonstrated his stern code of ethics on one occasion when Corcoran & Riggs, with the best of intentions, had invested for him in U.S. Treasury bonds (then called "public stock") $3,000 he held in trust for a ward (the Polks were childless), and he wrote to Corcoran:

> *I do not doubt my lawful right to make such an investment, but in view of my official position, I deem*

> *it proper to relinquish the stock ... and invest the funds in some other mode ....*

The year was an extraordinary one for the young banking firm also. In response to a Treasury Department advertisement of April 17, 1848, for bids on another $16,000,000 in United States stock, Corcoran & Riggs, for themselves, Baring Brothers & Company, London, and others, bid for the entire amount. The "script" was the same. They were awarded $14,065,550, or eighty-seven percent. Of that amount, $1,250,000 was for Baring Brothers, $250,000 for a correspondent in San Francisco, and $1,400,000 for other foreign accounts. It might be noted that Elisha's name does not appear and it is possible, in the light of later developments, he did not join in this bid.

For some time, George Riggs, Jr. had been in disagreement with Mr. Corcoran over the extent of the firm's participation in the government loans. George Riggs was obviously the "in house" member of the firm, handling day to day transactions and not always sure where his senior partner was engaged with his "higher connections."

Letters of that period in the bank's files give a sampling of the daily items with which George Riggs was occupied. There was, for example, a letter from Mansfield, Ohio, enclosing a draft for $216 to purchase two land warrants at $100 each, and stating, "I shall be happy to deal with you, as I am acquainted with no other house in Washington City, and with you only by reputation. I wish you to see that the warrants are genuine and assigned by the Soldier, not by Power of Attorney."

Another, from New York, enclosed a land office receipt from Springfield, Missouri, for 1,924 and 24/100's acres of land and added, "Your Mr. Riggs' father told me that you would get the patents for me which I will thank you to do as soon as practicable & forward them to me & I will cheerfully pay the expense to Mr. Riggs here."

A third, from Betsey C. Mason of Alexandria, enclosed a check for $500 to apply to her note for $1,500 and asked for a renewal of the balance, "to get a portion of our crop to market." Such were some of the ordinary but necessary services of the growing firm.

CHAPTER 9

Riggs was unquestionably, also, a family man, much devoted to his wife and five daughters and his comfortable and flourishing country estate.

He was happy with his share of the enormous profits from the government financing. Our information on this subject is limited and conjectural at times, but it is believed that on those loans guaranteed by Elisha, he received fifty percent of the profits. Of the remaining fifty percent, Corcoran and George Riggs may have shared it at a ratio of three-fifths and two-fifths (a best guess, considering the fact Corcoran was senior partner and originated the loans). In any event, this was a handsome return on loans ranging from $5,000,000 to upwards of $13,000,000.

The fees they actually received will never be known; there was no income tax in those days and no tell-tale personal income tax statements. The fees might have ranged from 1 percent to 3 percent or higher. One percent on $1,000,000 was $10,000, three percent, $30,000. So, on the very first loan of $5,000,000 made to assist Treasury Secretary Forward, which was said to have been disposed of "at a handsome profit," assuming the profit to be three points (and it might have been more) the firm's total profit was five times $30,000, or $150,000. Elisha would have received $75,000 and Corcoran and George Riggs, $45,000 and $30,000 respectively. And this at a time of practically no taxes when money was worth an estimated twenty times what it is worth today.

On the $11,717,000 of the 1847 loan "said to have been taken directly by Corcoran & Riggs or by Elisha Riggs as an individual," the firm would have received, at three percent, nearly twelve times $30,000 or close to $360,000. Again, Elisha's share (assuming he guaranteed the whole amount) would have been $180,000 and Corcoran and George Riggs would have received $108,000 and $72,000 respectively.

These figures are entirely separate from the partners' commissions on loans taken by "firms closely associated with them", and smaller loans under the firm's sponsorship sold from time to time without any formal bidding or advertising. The whole operation was an almost unbelievable bonanza for the still young organization.

It was such a bonanza that it unsettled George Riggs who wanted very much to be a conservative banker. He was swept along in the tides of history and the profits involved, but he knew that in operations of such large and unprecedented magnitude, serious risks were inherent. And he also knew, that as a partner, he would be responsible for his portion of the risks.

W. W. Corcoran was the optimist, the expansionist, like Secretary Walker, a believer in "Manifest Destiny." He proposed to see the government through its needed financing come the proverbial "hell or high water."

Both men were right. Before many years had elapsed, legislation was enacted separating banking entirely from its more optimistic and speculative and profitable cousin — the stock brokerage business. But on July 1, 1848, George Riggs felt, with much reluctance, that it was necessary for him to withdraw from the firm and was succeeded by his younger half-brother, Elisha Riggs, Jr., who had graduated with high honors the year before from the University of Heidelberg. The firm then continued under the same name. The parting of George Riggs and Corcoran was not personal and they always remained friends.

Corcoran continued to thrive in his role as the banker-statesman, as shown by a succinct note from Daniel Webster, as follows:

My Dear Sir:
I wish you would come to my house about 8 this evening and tell me, in five words, what are the best reasons to be given to friends of the administration for not passing the sub-treasury bill at present.

Yours,
D. Webster.

But the misgivings that had haunted George Riggs almost caught up with W. W. Corcoran.

There was suddenly something approaching a moratorium on the purchase of the 1848 government issue — a cautionary wait-and-see attitude, a conviction the price would be lower if all waited, perhaps out of offended pride or resentment in certain financial sections, even though there was tacit admission Corcoran & Riggs had done a superb job of attempting to supply the government's and Secretary Walker's enormous wartime needs. As a result the market declined, and prospective purchasers still stood by awaiting a more favorable price which they felt their actions might secure. (A perfect test case for conspiracy and restraint of trade in another century.) And suddenly the hard-pressed Treasury made a demand for an advance of $2,000,000 from the expected proceeds of sale.

This might have panicked a less formidable financier, but not W. W. Corcoran. He tells the balance of the story in his own words in a section of his autobiography, *A Grandfather's Legacy*, as follows:

> In August, 1848, having about $12,000,000 of the six percent loan of 1848, and the demand for it falling off in this country, and the stock being one percent lower than the price at which Corcoran & Riggs took it, Mr. Corcoran determined to try the European market; and after one day's reflection, embarked for London, where, on arrival, he was told by Mr. Bates of the house of Baring Bros. & Co., and Mr. George Peabody, that no sale could be made of the stock and no money could be raised by hypothecation thereof, and they regretted that he had not written to them to inquire before coming over. He replied that he was perfectly satisfied that such would be their views, and therfore came, confident that he would convince them of the expediency of taking an interest in the securities; and that the very fact that London bankers had taken them would make it successful.
>
> Ten days after his first interview with them, Mr. Thomas Baring returned from the continent, and with him he was more successful; and a sale of five million at about cost (one hundred and one) was made to six of the most eminent and wealthy houses in London, viz: Baring Bros. & Co., George Peabody, Overend, Gurney & Co., Dennison & Co., Samuel Jones Lloyd, and James Morrison.
>
> ...On his return to New York, he was greeted by every one with marked expressions of satisfaction; his success being a great relief to the money market by securing that amount of exchange in favor of the United States.
>
> On his success being announced the stock gradually advanced until it reached one hundred

and nineteen and one-half, thus securing by his prompt and successful action a handsome profit which would otherwise have resulted in a serious loss.

And it might be added, that Corcoran thus established the credit of the United States abroad, where it has never wavered except for a brief period in the Civil War. One imagines that he thoroughly enjoyed writing the foregoing account of his trip.

Dramatic events seemed to hover around Mr. Corcoran. While he was away he almost suffered the loss of his only daughter, ten-year old Louise, who was seeking to escape the August heat of Washington with her Aunt Harriett at the fashionable New England resort of Stonington, Connecticut. She was caught in an undertow and rescued at the last moment by a young man, a native, who happened to be nearby.

Upon his return, Corcoran rewarded him in characteristic fashion with a gift of one thousand dollars, for which he received the eloquent letter which follows:

> Stonington, Oct. 30, 1848
> Dear Sir:
>
> I received your letter enclosing a draft for a thousand dollars this morning, having been absent from home since Wednesday.
>
> With the deepest gratitude and the most sincere thanks, I accept your munificent present, your generous thanks, and kind wishes for my welfare. Dear Sir, I am surprised at your bounty. I considered myself repaid a hundredfold by the approbation of my own heart, for my trifling exertions in behalf of your child.
>
> ...I was more than satisfied with no other compensation. So little did I desire any, that I made no inquiry, and was absolutely ignorant of her being your child, until your interview with Mr. Williams. I am, therefore.. to the last moment of my life your debtor for what, to me, is a fortune.
>
> Your humble friend,
> Gurdon B. Smith.

CHAPTER 9

Undeterred, or perhaps even emboldened by his success in rescuing the market for the 1848 loan, Corcoran plunged again into the government market.

The treaty of Guadalupe Hidalgo called for the payment to Mexico of $15,000,000 for the annexed territories in the gold and silver coin of that country. Although August Belmont and others had bid for this business, the former, in behalf of the Rothschilds, Corcoran & Riggs, Baring Brothers, and other associated with them, were once more the successful bidders. An agent for the banks, E. J. Forestall, collected the required gold and silver coins under the protection of the U. S. and Mexican governments. The payments extended over four years — the final installment being paid by Corcoran & Riggs, agents, on June 18, 1852 — the cancelled drafts now being on file in the National Archives.

On November 15, 1848, nearing the close of an eventful year, Corcoran received a letter from the distinguished educator, historian and statesman, George Bancroft, then our minister to London, which contained the following:

> We are very much distressed to hear of the terrible danger to which your daughter was exposed. Thank God! there was someone at hand to rescue her.
>
> I was sorry for your long passage home. The Brittannia was more than eqully long in her return.
>
> ...The stock is here in great and increassng demand; all the purchasers are delighted.
>
> Yours sincerely,
> George Bancroft.

Shortly after what must have been a very jubilant New Year's celebration, Mr. Corcoran was in receipt of a letter from Baring Brothers, as follows:

> London,
> 12th January, 1849
>
> Dear Sir:
> We beg to thank you very much for your private lines of December 23rd, and we do not doubt that our connection with you in the contract for the payment of the Mexican indemnity money will be as

satisfactory as the operation in the Federal stock. Whatever, however, may be the result, we feel much indebted to you for the attention and ability you have devoted to this matter.

. . .All goes on smoothly here, and the demand for United States stock runs away with all we have or wish to sell.

*Yours very truly,
Baring Brothers.*

And so, eight years after the formation of the firm of Corcoran & Riggs, Mr. Corcoran was the confidant of statesmen, ministers and international financiers.

No small accomplishment for the "hatter, West st., south side" of the *Washington and Georgetown Directory of 1834!*

Chapter 10

For information on the affairs of Corcoran & Riggs after George W. Riggs, Jr. was succeeded by his young half-brother, we are partially dependent on a series of letters between Elisha, Jr. and his father in New York.

This correspondence was part of the senior Elisha's personal files which turned up miraculously many years later in the possession of a Syracuse (N.Y.) physician whose hobby was philately. He wrote the bank in the 1930's, saying he had some letters which might interest them or the Riggs family and indicated he was getting on in years and wished to dispose of them. His letter was found in the bank's files fifteen years later, after World War II, and a hasty and apprehensive telephone call was rewarded by the voice of the good doctor himself, declaring "Yes, I still have them." Whereupon we entrained the next day for Syracuse.

This proved to be a valuable collection, containing not only much family correspondence, but letters from many notables, including Daniel Webster, August Belmont, George Peabody, Charles Wickliffe (the "blue grass letter" previously referred to), plus an early telegram sent on the original telegraph line between Washington and Baltimore. We purchased the lot.

By a fortunate coincidence the collection included a series of letters from Elisha, Jr. to his father, written in 1848 shortly after he joined the firm. They give us a rare insight into his introduction to the banking business and some of the frustrations and problems he encountered. Old-timers in the industry find much that is familiar and nostalgic in his complaints. Since all of the letters started with the salutation "Dear Father", they are known in the bank's collection as the "Dear Father" letters.

Elisha, Jr.'s first letter was dated "Washington, 7 July, 1848," five days after he joined the firm, and opens simply,

> *Dear Father:*
> *I duly rec'd yours of the 5th Inst. this morning and note contents. I shall endeavor to break myself of smoking by degrees, but find it impossible to stop all at once. Your advice with respect to dining at 3 o'clock it is impossible to carry into effect. I have not been able to leave the office for the last week till after 6 o'clock P.M. Our business is excessively onerous, and we feel much the want of a competent man to superintend the keeping of our accounts. Such a one would be a great relief to me, as our accounts are already getting confused . . . . . .*
>
> *George and family are well as also Lawry [Lawrason]. Lawry and myself are going to Balt. tomorrow afternoon to pass Sunday.*
>
> > *In haste,*
> > *Yours truly,*
> > *E. Riggs, Jr.*

It is past 6 o'clock and office closing.

The second letter was penned four days later and repeats the young neophyte's call for assistance:

> *Dear Father:*
> *In yours of the 8th Inst. you make inquiry how we are situated with regard to a bookkeeper. The young man we now have from Georgetown is industrious and quick, but by no means such a man as we*

require. Our business is so extensive that we still want extra force, and could we procure a man thoroughly acquainted with accounts, who would be able to order entries, see that everything was attended to and carry on a part of the correspondence, it would be relieving me of a great deal of anxiety. At present the work of the office if conducted correctly is more than I can attend to. At every instant I am called off from what I am about, to sign a check or attend to a customer. Mr. Corcoran is all the time occupied with the outdoor business and has in reality no time to attend to the correspondence.

What we want is a thorough Accountant, active, correct man; with such an addition we might easily manage our business in such a manner that nobody would be overworked, which is not the case at present. Mr. Corcoran will be in N.Y. in a few days and will consult you on this point. In the meantime do not cease to inform yourself if any person is to be found of the character we require. Our office expenses are already heavy and we should not feel disposed to give a higher salary than $1200 or $1500.

I have taken rooms in the neighborhood of the office . . . If you could send me a box of claret or sherry it would be most acceptable. Am obliged at present to drink cold water, which after a hard day's work is rather tasteless.

Yours truly.

Elisha, Jr. was the third son of his illustrious father, and the first by his second marriage to Mary Ann (Karrick) Riggs. Born in Philadelphia on November 28, 1826, he was three months shy of his 22nd birthday when he joined the firm. Careful examination and reexamination of his letters and his photograph brings one to the reluctant conclusion that he was a somewhat severe young man, lacking at least in this early period, any sense of humor or humility and undoubtedly affected by the sytlized, prestigious atmosphere of the University of Heidelberg where he had matriculated. Franz von Recum, great grandson of George W. Riggs, Jr. and our family informant, states that the difference between George Jr. and

Lawrason and their three half-brothers, Elisha, Jr., Joe and Willie, was "like day and night." "The latter were far from kind or nice and sometimes mean", he added. "We always called it the 'Karrick blood'."

At any rate, in this third letter, Elisha's "pressure" had eased not the slightest, and the fact that the family sent him a horse seems not to have left him overjoyed:

> I received the other day from the country the horse sent me by Elisha Riggs of Montgomery County [son of his father's older brother, Thomas]. It is a beautiful mare 7 years old, and Elisha warrants her perfectly sound... The price with all accoutrements is $135- that of the horse $100. I have not had time as yet to get a good trial, having been at the office every day till after 5 o'clock.

Letter number four is dated 13, September, 1848, and continues his complaints:

> Your letter (without date) came duly to hand... I have been exceptionally busy during the last few days, as I am obliged to be much of my time out of the office at the Treasury Dept., and also am much interrupted by persons coming into the office on business, who I am obliged to dispatch. My duties here are no sinecure... I get at present but little opportunity for exercise as by half past six it begins to get dark, and I am seldom through with my dinner before this hour. I hope the Messrs, Ward will conclude to come to Washington and pass a few days, although the attractions here are few...
> Very truly yours,

We can be more sympathetic with this young aristocrat's evident dislike of the capital city to which he came in 1848 and its probable impact on his disposition. In speaking of the region known as the Mall, one contemporary described it as, "a magnificent Sahara of solitude and waste — appropriated as a cow pasture, frog pond and decorated with a stone-cutter's yard, a slaughter-house and pig-pen." Pennsylvania Avenue, the only macadamized roadway, had become so badly worn that one lady who crossed the Avenue near the old National

CHAPTER 10

Hotel at 6th street "incautiously stepped in a puddle and plunged into three feet of mire."

Shortly before Elisha's arrival the "Great National Broadway of the Metropolis" was cobbled and street gas lights were erected between the White House and the Capitol. They were lighted, however, only on moonless nights and extinguished at midnight. The rest of the city was in darkness and its 40,000 inhabitants traveled at great risk in certain localities. . . . A lawyer broke his leg when he plunged off one of the unprotected crossings into Goose Creek and sued the City Fathers for "parsimony."

Young Elisha proved to be in no happier a frame of mind when he wrote his next letter on October 9, 1848:

> *I am scarcely able to attend to business today and nothing but absolute necessity would compel me. Yesterday about three o'clock P.M. I was attacked by a severe cramp colic, and for upwards of three hours suffered the most intense agony. By copious doses of Laudinum, applications of mustard poultices, etc., I was somewhat relieved, but am still exceedingly weak, and on leaving the office I shall retire immediately to bed. I mention this in order that you may account to our correspondents for my short letters, as I have been totally unable to exert myself much, and should not be at all surprised if I were obliged to remain at home for two or three days.*

Still harassed on October 31, he wrote:

> *We have received no northern mail this morning. The Messrs. Ward arrived safely, but I have not had much time as yet to see them, in consequence of my business engagements. Have not had time to read your letter as yet — will answer tomorrow.*
>
> *Mr. Kieckhoefer [the active, correct man] and his family reached here Sunday. He has hired a house in the neighborhood of the office.*
>
> *Yours in haste,*

On November 10, Elisha reports more of the same:

> *I have been so busily employed for the last few days as to have been altogether unable to answer*

> your several private favors. And even now must
> defer particulars with regard to the subjects on
> which you questioned me, until I shall be able to visit
> with you.... We are running off our Stock for
> Europe rapidly and shall probably send about five
> hundred thousand per the next Boston steamer. I
> want you to get Mr. Bolton to make me out a
> statement of our Joint a/c with George Peabody and
> forward the same immediately, as I want to compare
> it with our books, rectify differences if any exist and
> advise George Peabody of the balance remaining to
> be disposed of.... I have been able to see but little
> of Joe [a brother] as he keeps in the country amusing
> himself with hunting and fishing and I am in the
> office most of the time in daylight.
>
> In haste,

Poetically, for our purposes at least, in the final letter for the year, dated November 29, after some commiseration with his father he closes on a note of optimism:

> I am sorry to perceive from your letter of this
> morning that you have been suffering from Influenza
> which appears at present an epidemic, and am
> rather unwell from an attack of it myself.
> Since the arrival of Mr. Kieckhoefer we have been
> busily engaged with the books and will strike a
> balance sheet at the end of the month....

In respect to George Riggs, Jr. and his wife, Janet, and their little family, we have glimpses of them also via letters. Remarkably enough, among the items obtained from the genial Syracuse physician were two letters from Janet Riggs to her father-in-law, penned in a beautiful hand and in the style and language befitting one raised in her mother's "seminary for young ladies".

The earlier of these two letters was written from Fairfield, Connecticut, only six weeks after her husband's withdrawal from the firm and reads as follows:

CHAPTER 10

Fairfield Hotel,
Monday, August 14, 1848

Thank you my dear Father, for your kind letter & the papers which I gladly received. . . . George writes me daily but cannot as yet say when I may look for him, so I can form no exact idea as to the day of our leaving this place, which has been quite full since our arrival, tho some parties are leaving this week. Our quarters are spacious and comfortable, and the host anxious to do everything in his power for us. Ma [Mrs. Shedden] has not entirely recovered but is doing as well as we can expect for one so delicate in health. The children enjoy the bathing exceedingly, particularly Cecelia [age 4] who never tires; all five go in with us, tho little baby [Mary Griffith, 19 mos.] seems as pleased as any one. Hope ere this you might have heard by telegraph of Lawrason's & Fanny's safe return to St. Louis. [Frances "Fanny" Clapp Riggs, Lawrason's second wife, was expecting her third child]. Many persons stop here on their way to Saratoga; should you make your intended trip there, during our sojourn, pray give us a few hours at least.

In writing to Mrs. Riggs, do remember us most kindly. I hear she is quite well and happy at Lebanon and the children, too [William Henry, 11, and Mary Alice, 9].

We shall probably be in New York a few days on our return to 'Corn Rigs' but I am really afraid the noise of five children will distract you. Ma & Mrs. Cooper [her sister] desire their warm regards, the young ladies send kisses in abundance, while I remain,

Yr. affectionate & grateful
Daughter,
Janet M. C. Riggs.

I shall try to send this by the Norwalk route & beg you will put the enclosed in the Post Office in time for the Southern mail.

J.R.

The fine, slanted scrawl of George Riggs, Jr. was also represented in the Syracuse letters. Near the close of 1848, alarmed by news of his father's health, he wrote as follows:

> *My dear Father*
>
> *I am sorry to hear of your illness. I sent you a telegraphic dispatch to say I would meet you in Phila. or Balt. if you could say when you might come on. No doubt a few days in the country released from the cares of business, might do you much good. If you do not feel able enough to come on here I will make you a visit. I wish you might be induced to keep out of Wall Street a little. Let your money be invested in such way as to give you no trouble and take your comfort for the rest of your life. You have worked long enough.* [Elisha had passed his Sixty-ninth birthday but there was more than just his age on George's mind — he was worried about one of his recent investments.]
>
> *Mr. Rives has just been here and he is going out to my house, the weather being remarkably fine, and I close this to go home to meet him.*
>
> > *Yr. affectionate son,*
> > *Geo. W. Riggs, Jr.*

He wrote his father again the day after Christmas:

> *We are all quite well in the country and glad to hear you are better.*
>
> *Yesterday, being Christmas Day, we all dined with our good friends and neighbors, the Aggs.* [A part of Corn Rigs was purchased from the Aggs.]
>
> *Hope you will soon come to see us. I have a bagatelle table to amuse you on which . . . . Janet plays already pretty well.*
>
> *With the compliments of the Season, I am, affectionately,*
>
> > *Your son,*
> > *George W. Riggs, Jr.*

Twelve days later, George Riggs, catching up his correspondence, wrote to his former partner, Samuel Taylor, then living on his large mill property near Madison, Wisconsin:

CHAPTER 10

Washington,
7th Jan, 1849

My dear Sir:
    I am heartily sorry my neglect in not writing has made you think I was displeased with you. I have for a long time intended writing but have become (as to writing) one of the laziest mortals alive.
    I am very sorry to hear of more trouble with the mill [another miller upstream had in true 'wild west style' diverted the water for his own purposes]. I have always. . thought of you as the merry miller, turning out flour and heaping up his tolls.
    I hope you will not think of selling or giving up your farm. Keep that, if possible. It will be worth more by and by and is always a home. How far is your home from the mill? Your plan of encouraging the growth of a village on your property I like. It will cost nothing and improve what you have left. Let me know what is done by the court [about the damming of the stream] this month.
    I am engaged in winding up my affairs with Corcoran & Riggs, in which I had an interest. After that is over, I shall have my whole time to devote to my family and my little farm. I have not the large fortune that the public give me but I have enough to live on if I live moderately and I want to try to do so. [George Riggs was being modest here about his fortune; for a young man of thirty-five, his net worth must already have exceeded $200,000 — a very large figure for his day.] My experience in business in New York has made me anxious not (by continuing in business) to lose what I have and I am confident I have adopted the prudent and wise course in withdrawing. I am a happier, if poorer man. Contentment is, after all, riches, not possession of money.

Following this bit of philosophy, George Riggs writes of another tragedy that had befallen Lawrason and his family:

    I have just received by telegraph from St. Louis news of the death of my brother, Lawrason's wife. He has been very unfortunate — young as he is, he has lost two wives. [Fanny Riggs bore a son, duly

named George Washington Riggs, on December 22,
1848, and died thirteen days later on January 4,
1849 — by a tragic irony, eight years to the identical
day of the identical month after Lawrason lost his
first wife, Sophia Theresa Cruttenden on January 4,
1841.]

George Riggs goes on to mention his father's health and states:

> The old gentleman is a good deal broken. I was in
> New York several times during the summer and
> about two weeks ago, hearing such accounts of his
> health as to alarm me, I went on again. I left him
> much better but he appears quite feeble.
>
> My family, thank God, enjoy good health . . . I
> would like to see you and show you my little flock of
> daughters.
>
> Present my kindest regards to your wife and
> believe me very faithfully yours,
>
> Geo. W. Riggs, Jr.

Unfortunately, for some months prior to this correspondence Elisha, the much respected Montgomery County native millionaire, had begun to invest in the Collins line of steamships. After a long life of frugality and conservatism, he sudduenly regarded himself as an "insider" at the coming of a new age of steamship technology which, he believed, would make the United States supreme on the high seas and would make Collins and himself and their associates a great deal of money. This was partially an extension of the "Manifest Destiny" and "wave of the future" philosophies which had swept the young nation along to unbelievable conquests and expansion in the 1840's.

The story of this challenge to old-world sea supremacy, and its climatic outcome, is one of the more obscure episodes of American history, as well as a little-known portion of the Riggs family history.

Chapter 11

Edward Knight Collins was an outstanding example of the American success story. He was descended from Joseph Collins, son of a starch maker, who had come from Ireland in 1635 and settled in Lynn, Massachusetts. One of this forebear's sons moved to Cape Cod, from where his descendants followed the sea for several generations.

Around 1800, we learn from the Encyclopaedia *Britannica*, Captian Israel Gross Collins, on a trip to England, married Mary Ann Knight and brought her back to Truro on Cape Cod. She died there five months after the birth of her only son, Edward Knight Collins, who was to become the leader of the most spectacular attempt by the American merchant marine to challenge British supremacy.

Collins went to New York when he was fifteen and served an apprenticeship as a clerk in a mercantile house and later went to sea as a supercargo. He tried the commision business with his father before finally settling into his important life work — the management of packet lines. He took over and re organized several coastal lines, including those to Vera Cruz and New Orleans.

In 1836, he founded a line of swift, square-rigged sailing ships which soon dominated the trade between New York and European ports. The line became known as the "Dramatic Line" — the ships being named for famous actors. *Shakespeare, Garrick, Siddons* and *Roscius,* were some of the names on the bows of these sleek-hulled vessels.

His continued success soon brought him a reputation for outstanding ability and he became one of the wealthiest men in New York. There Elisha met him and a mutual kinship developed between the two self-made tycoons, who were soon discussing the possibilities of steam propulsion which they recognized would soon replace sails. They and other Americans in the shipping industry were goaded into action when in 1838, Samuel Cunard, a Nova Scotian whose parents had emigrated from Pennsylvania after the Revolutionary War, obtained a contract from the British Admiralty to carry the mails on a regular steamship schedule.

Cunard began a new and revolutionary policy in shipbuilding when he constructed four "sister ships" to begin regularly scheduled trans-atlantic operations. His service was inaugurated (ironically enough) on July 4, 1840, when the *Britannia,* a wooden, 207-foot paddle-wheel steamer sailed from Liverpool to Halifax and Boston. The sister ships were the *Acadia, Columbia* and *Caledonia.*

The line prospered from the beginning. It was on the *Britannia* Corcoran had his "long passage home" after selling the 1848 stock in London. Elisha, Jr. referred to the Cunard Line when he wrote his father on November 10, 1848, that C & R was running off their stock for Europe rapidly "and should probably send about five hundred thousand per the next Boston Steamer".

Congress, convinced American subsidies were necessary to combat this "monopoly" (Cunard had both the British and American mail contracts), in 1845 authorized government aid through mail contracts to lines "which would build potential steam warships". On November 1, 1847, Collins and his associates, James and Stewart Brown, received a most significant contract "to build under naval supervision, five steamers of specified size which were to make twenty round trips annually, carrying mail between New York and Liverpool". For this they would receive $385,000 annually for ten years. They hastily organized the U.S. Mail Steamship Company, generally known as the "Collins Line", in which they sold stock to a number of eager subscribers, including Elisha.

Collins spent more than two years building four ships which were to surpass in size, speed and splendor, anything afloat. But he proved a poor corporate administrator. (The corporate form of business enterprise was very little known or understood by most of these early individual entrepreneurs.) Collins spared no expense and exceeded all government requirements (and budgets). He was building elegant ships at enormous cost, carried along by his enthusiasm and the hopeful philosophy that in so grand a venture, all eventually must end well.

But it would be another year before his first vessel would be launched and the story of the Collins Line would begin to unfold in dramatic scope and intensity far beyond anything dreamed of when the early popular lable had been applied to the line.

Meanwhile, on March 4, 1849, the Mexican War hero, Zachary Taylor, was inaugurated as the nation's twelfth chief executive.[1]

Taylor's secretary, Lucien Powell, opened an account at Corcoran & Riggs in his own name shortly after the November, 1848 election, and subsequently opened a "President's a/c" — the crusty old Army commander being indisposed to bother with financial details. The new Vice President, Millard Fillmore, also opened an account a short time later. The firm's business was growing rapidly and it was becoming entrenched as a comfortable, handsome and, not only convenient, but fashionable place to do business.

On June 6, 1849, W. W. Corcoran, still rising in the world, bought the former residence of Daniel Webster, located on the north side of Lafayette Square, at the corner of H Street and Connecticut Avenue (now the site of the United States Chamber of Commerce).[2] He refurbished it lavishly and later enlarged it to include a conservatory and a gallery for his growing art collection, part of which he had acquired on his London trip. He also had a formal garden laid out which extended through to Eye Street. Under his ownership the residence became one of the finest and best known in the capital.

While things continued to go well for Mr. Corcoran, the lives of George Riggs, Jr. and Janet suffered a cruel blow when their fifth little daughter, Mary Griffith, aged two years, six months, died at Corn Rigs of convulsions on August 2, 1849.

For the new partner, Elisha, Jr., however, romance had come along. How it developed and prospered one is perplexed to know, but it is obvious that this haughty young man must have used a totally different personality toward his young love — which is probably the nature of things, in any case.

Mary Keene Boswell was twenty - three years younger than Elisha, the only daughter of a well-known Lexington, Kentucky couple, but an orphan. Her mother had died shortly after her birth and her father only a few years later. At his death a friend, Benjamin Gratz of Lexington, was appointed guardian for the daughter. He was a member of the wealthy and influential Gratz family of Philadelphia and his sister, Rebecca Gratz, was a widely known social reformer and philanthropist. Mary Boswell was educated in Philadelphia and raised like a daughter of this family.

It was fashionable at that time, of course, for young ladies to make their debuts abroad at one of the royal courts. And it is possible that Mary Boswell had done so, through the standing and connections of the Gratz family. And in those glamorous circles she might have met Elisha, Jr. on one of his Heidelberg holidays visiting the American colony, not quite "a student prince," but at least the eligible son of a rich and powerful New York banker. They may have fallen immediately into a recollection of Philadelphia, where Elisha, Jr. was born and she had gone to school. And not unnaturally, when their minds were made up, they were married in that city at St. Stephens Church on November 20, 1849, where, incidentally, Mary was given in marriage by that perennial bride-giver, Henry Clay, said to have been a life-long friend of her family.

In the absence of any other listing for Elisha, Jr. in the Washington directory of that time, it is presumed he brought his bride home to the "rooms in the neighborhood of the office" he had reported to his father. He was to build a fine house nearby in the next few years.

CHAPTER 11

We can also happily report that the year ended on a joyous note for George, Jr. and Janet, when, after five daughters, their first son was born on Christmas day in 1849, at Corn Rigs, and named for him and Janet's mother, George Shedden Riggs. This assuaged, temporarily at least, the deep longing George Riggs harbored for a son to carry on after him in the tradition of his family.

And so the New Year, 1850, dawned, bringing, like its predecessors, a mixture of good tidings and bad, as all the years had done down through the ages.

In early 1850, Mr. Corcoran had written his old friend, Daniel Webster, applauding one of his speeches in the Senate and enclosing a gift for the old gentleman. Webster, like Clay, had opposed the Mexican War but had sent his only son to fight and die in that bloody conflict, as did Henry Clay also. Webster suffered a second crushing blow when his only daughter died shortly after her brother. His stoical reply to Corcoran reads as follows:

> *Louisiana Avenue,*
> *Mar. 9, 1850*
>
> My dear Sir:
> In all sincerity, I am proud of your approbation of my speech, as I feel you are a competent judge, and one who can have no wish but for the preservation of the Government and the safety and security of private rights.
> For what else I received with your note I pray you to receive my thanks. If there be a man in the country who either doubts your liberality or envies your prosperity, be assured I am not that man.
>
> With cordial regard,
> Yours,
> Daniel Webster.

Good news came on April 27, 1850, when the Collins Line steamer, *Atlantic,* sailed on her maiden voyage from New York, to be followed in the course of the year by the *Pacific* and the *Arctic.* Their superior speed was at once apparent and periodicals across the nation proudly published statistics showing that their average runs were shorter by a full day then those of the Cunard Line.

Their luxurious accomodations were also highly publicized — "the double-bed staterooms for newly married couples who wish to spend their first fortnight of their honeymoon on the Atlantic; the first liners to be steam heated, and to offer a system by which a passenger could press a button in his cabin for a steward, and also the first to have 'grand, sea-green, shell-shaped spittoons, and a barbershop'."

The latter received extra coverage, especially the barber's chair. A "comfortable, well-stuffed seat with an inclined back, and, in front, a stuffed trestle on which to rest the feet and legs, and behind, a little stuffed apparatus . . . on which to rest the head."[3]

Collins and his associates were heartened by the favorable publicity but, it was immediately apparent that the line, which was in debt when the ships were launched, was losing money on every trip. It was further apparent that the costs of operating and maintaining steamships, as opposed to sailing vessels, had been grossly underestimated, even under the supervision of naval observers. Already it was realized that the only solution lay in a radical increase in the government subsidy, something all parties knew would not be quick or easy of accomplishment, if it could be done at all, in any amount substantial enough to save this errant attempt to build "potential steam warships" with private capital.

The firm of Corcoran & Riggs would soon be a close and interested spectator of this battle which would take place in the months ahead in the halls of Congress to search for a compromise between the interests of American sea supremacy and the high-minded, albeit woefully, mismanaged private investment for that purpose.

In the interim the nation had been distracted by the sudden death of President Zachary Taylor on July 9, 1850, after one year and four months in office. His death resulted from a heat stroke which aggravated an attack of typhus fever. With the swearing in of Fillmore, the ten-year-old firm of Corcoran & Riggs found itself with another chief executive as a client.

James Buchanan, writing to Corcoran from his home, Wheatland, in Pennsylvania on July 15, comments:

CHAPTER 11

> The death of General Taylor was sudden and alarming, and has inspired universal regret among the people. He was brave and honest, and the true hero of the Mexican War. Should Mr. Fillmore be a man equal to his high position, and act an independent part as a Whig, he may give the Democratic party trouble. For me, it is a melancholy spectacle to witness men of three score and ten and upwards still struggling in the political arena with all the ardor of youthful ambition, as though the earth was destined to be their eternal home. I trust in Heaven that I may never present such a spectacle.

This is a puzzling comment from Buchanan, since Zachary Taylor was in his sixty-sixth year and Buchanan was then fifty-nine. By a quirk of fate, Buchanan would be sixty-six when sworn in at his own inauguration seven years later.

Joshua Bates of Baring Brothers in London also wrote Corcoran on July 30, having made an inquiry concerning the new President: "Many thanks for your note of the 15th. The change of Administration will, as you suppose, do no harm to the Mexican business.... All that I hear of Mr. Fillmore is in his favor, so I hope things will now go ahead at Washington...."

Two weeks later Mr. Bates wrote again, and the first part of his letter contains a most prophetic paragraph: "When the passage across the Atlantic is reduced to seven days, I shall pay you another visit, and that will be before ten years. The Collins Line will quicken the Cunards, and they will be running against icebergs and Cape Race".

In the last part of this letter he makes a delightful change of subject matter as follows: "I shall take the liberty to give a letter to you to Mad'lle Jenny Lind. She is a great personage, although small in stature, and knows as well as any of 'Sam Slick's' family on which side her bread it buttered."[4]

This letter was dated August 16, 1850, and Jenny Lind was then embarking on a tour of the United States, which would begin with her appearance at the New National Hall in Washington (later the National Theatre). Corcoran was obviously pleased and flattered by his coming introduction to this glorious "Swedish Nightingale."[5] He most certainly was present for her opening performance which was attended by the President, the Cabinet and the members of the Supreme Court. Also present was the American composer, John Howard Payne. It was reported that, as an encore number, Jenny sang his composition, *Home Sweet Home* looking directly at him. When she finished, amid enthusiastic applause, Daniel Webster rose, bowed to her and then to the composer, making it a great moment in Payne's life.

The admiring Mr. Corcoran must have found additional satisfaction in the knowledge that the composer of the current "hit tune" was a customer of his firm, even if a modest one. His account is listed in beautiful Spencerian script at the very top of a page in one of the huge Corcoran & Riggs ledgers. In the same ledger is the account of Francis Scott Key, author of *The Star Spangled Banner*. Both are treasured items in the bank's records.

One can guess that Corcoran gave an appropriate reception for this charming little songstress at his newly decorated residence across Lafayette Square from the White House. And who knows — perhaps even the President came across the park for the festivities.

Toward the end of September, 1850, a letter was written in New York which was almost like the drawing of the curtain on the drama of the Mexican War financing.

A copy of this unique document, from sources unknown, reposes in the historical files of the Riggs National Bank, and appears to set the record straight for all time as to the charges and counter charges relating to that financing. The letter is signed by that diminutive and controversial but able former Secretary of the Treasury, the honorable Robert J. Walker, of Pennsylvania and Mississippi, and reads as follows:

> N. York,
> September 24, 1850
>
> Hon. Msrs.
>   Houston & Rusk
>   *of the Senate*
>   and Kaufman & Howard
>   *of the House*
>
> *Gentlemen: I have been requested to suggest the name of W. W. Corcoran, Esq., of Washington City as*

a suitable agent to be selected by the Executive of Texas, in connection with the recent act of Congress in regard to the debt of that State.

It gives me pleasure to comply with that request and to say that I regard W. W. Corcoran as a gentleman of high character and integrity and of great experience, knowledge and ability in all financial affairs. To him, more than to any other man, do I feel indebted for most zealous and efficient service to the Government during my term in the Treasury Department. During the late war with Mexico, the U. S. loans were mainly sustained, at and above par, by his zeal and energy, and but for him, instead of realizing large premiums, for the Government, heavy loss in the way of discounts would in all probability have been sustained & I might have been forced to offer a seven per cent stock.

This he always joined me in opposing, altho his pecuniary interest would have seemed to have dictated a different course. Indeed, throughout that whole period, he proved himself not only a most able financier, but a devoted patriot, always advising such counsel as was best calculated to promote the interest of the Government. In truth he appeared always to act upon the opinion, that, in promoting the interest of the Government he was best advancing his own. These were liberal and enlightened views, and were followed by results alike beneficial to himself & to the country.

Very truly & respectfully,
Your friend,
R. A. Walker.

Out at Corn Rigs in the colorful fall of the year, George Riggs was writing again to his old friend and former partner, Samuel Taylor, of Madison, Wisconsin. One can almost see the late candle and hear the scratch of the quill pen as he writes in the silence of the country night:

Washington,
27th October, 1850

My dear Sir:
I commence this letter late at night, expecting to start for Phila. tomorrow morning to meet and to return here with my wife's mother and sister who, with one of my children, have been at the North for some time.

I am living quietly in the country, out of business entirely, excepting the charge of the books of the old firm of Corcoran & Riggs.

My family numbers now four daughters and one son, the youngest, born last Christmas Day. Their education is already a subject of conversation with us . . . . so far we teach the two oldest at home. I take my share of the tuition as professor of writing and mathematics. My brother, Lawrason, ... has left his children in Georgetown. He was here in the summer and expects to return to visit his little ones next month.

Write me your whereabouts and your what abouts . . . . Are you still at the mill, or farming? I hope you are getting along better than your last letters make you appear to be expecting at the time.

My father enjoys good health. He is largely interested in the Collins Line of Steamers and busily engaged in seeing them fitted out.

Hoping to hear from you,
I am, faithfully,
Geo. W. Riggs.

Chapter Notes

[1] Zachary Taylor was a transplanted Virginian, born in Orange County, November 24, 1764, and a relative of Madison. He had followed a long military career before the conflict with Mexico, including twenty years of garrison life, varied by occasional Indian expeditions. In 1846, he was ordered to the Rio Grande and placed by Polk in temporary command of the Mexican campaign. There followed stirring victories at Buena Vista, Monterey and elsewhere, as a result of which he became a popular hero. At the Whig convention of 1848, Taylor won the nomination from Clay, Webster and Winfield Scott, the other great hero of the war.

[2] A group of Webster's friends had bought the handsome old house in 1841 and presented it to Webster upon his appointment as Secretary of State in the cabinet of William Henry Harrison and subsequently in that of John Tyler. Webster gave up the place when he returned to Massachusetts and it was sold to other owners from whom Corcoran made the purchase.

[3] Frank O. Braynard, "Age of the Superliner", *Modern Maturity*, Aug./September, 1970.

[4] This references by Mr. Bates to "Sam Slick's family" relates to a series of popular letters entitled "Samuel Slick of Slickville," published in 1843-44 and written around a shrewd, ingenious Yankee peddler.

[5] Jenny Lind had made her first appearance in England on May 4, 1847 and created a "prodigious furore." Then only 26, her success was said to be due not only to the glory of her voice and the beauty and charm of her person, but to her superior musicianship and the "naive simplicity of her acting in her favorite roles". No less than P. T. Barnum recognized her magnetic appeal as a concert artist and arranged for her a two-year tour of America, which ultimately netted this tiny daughter of a Swedish lace manufacturer a tidy $120,000.

Chapter 12

The years 1851-53 were restless, uncertain and unsettled for George Riggs, Jr. and his family. He had already discovered he was too much of a banker and businessman to remain inactive, but he was in a genuine quandary as to where and how he should reenter business. And, as often happens, he was the target of much gratuitous advice from well-meaning members of the family and friends.

When he wrote his father on January 13, 1851, he and Janet had evidently rented a place in town, perhaps because Corn Rigs was a little haunted for them since the death of their youngest daughter. They might also have felt that the comfort and convenience of the city would be more beneficial to their children, especially to their little son and namesake, who had just passed his first Christmas-Day birthday. In any case, at the close of the letter George Riggs states: "The weather is so warm [January 13] that we feel as if we would be more comfortable at home than we are in this small house we now occupy."

Just where that small house was located is unknown.

In the preceding portion of his letter he may have been attempting to give his father a signal concerning his heavy investment in the Collins Line, when he wrote:

> I have received your letter in regard to the sale of the Michigan R. Road Bonds . . . . I would rather sell some of my steamer [Collins Line] stock at par and lend the money to Lawrason. It will make him easy in his business and it will reduce my interest in the Steamers which is now too large in proportion to my means.

Elisha, however, was probably too heavily involved to attempt a withdrawal and, furthermore, like many lifelong successful investors (and we have seen some in recent decades), he was overwhelmingly convinced of the infallibility of his own judgment.

In a letter of March 7, 1851, brother Elisha, Jr. sent his father another kind of signal, which was, characteristically, unpleasant. In speaking of a claim he was apparently handling for his father at the Land Office, he writes:

> I have received this morning your favor of the 5th Inst. & noted contents. In it you state, 'If you fully recover I will pay you for the cost of your lot [a building lot on Eye Street].' But as by reference to your letter of the 25th of November last, you will perceive that you promised to make my wife & self a present of the same after the 1st of January. I consider such compensation for my services as entirely out of the question.
>
> Your present claim is a matter that requires attention, diplomacy and influence . . . all of which in Washington must be paid for. And the position of certainty in which it is my intention to place it, will require no little time and labor on my part . . which I am not willing to undertake in the case of a person as well able to pay for them as yourself save for a fair remuneration . . . and which, as it depends entirely upon the contingency of your claim being paid, costs you nothing.
>
> My estimates are that the whole costs of the matter, including my own commission will amount to about 25% of the sum awarded. If you are willing that I should proceed under these considerations, say so . . . & your matter shall not fail for want of

management or attention. But, if you think you are paying too much, let me know and I will be guided by your directions. The amount I shall probably obtain for you will be your original debt with interest at the rate of 5%.

I am sorry you put in a claim for 15% interest, as these unreasonable demands are calculated to prejudice the board in the case of an otherwise just claim.

My wife & son are both well. Cousin Margaret dined with us yesterday.

Yr. affect. Son,
E. Riggs, Jr.

We would like to have witnessed the senior Elisha's reaction to this communication from his imperious twenty-four year old son and namesake he had recently sent through the finest and most expensive university in Europe.

Fortunately Elisha Jr.'s next letter changes direction in subject matter and shifts over to the house he is erecting on lots adjoining those owned by George, Jr. These lots were located on what is now the corner of Farragut Square and Eye Street (the present site of the Army & Navy Club). Not wishing to be overly agreeable, he opens this portion of the letter as follows:

I have not the leisure at present to write you at length about my building.

The lots are those I purchased of George & Suter ... costing me $1,000 & I have since purchased for like amount the lot & frame house between George's property & my own.

I did this for the sake of having a fine garden, guarding against any nuisance and connecting George's property and my own. The lots you promised to present to Mary & I hope when you do so you will include the latter portion of the purchase.

The dimensions of my house are 48 x 55 ft., and it is to be 3 stories high. It will be impossible for me at present to give you any further details as the specifications of the house & stable cover no less than forty pages of foolscap. It is to have all modern conveniences .. gas & water & to be constructed in the best manner. The contractor is the carpenter of the Smithsonian Institute.

> *My little boy has been rather unwell for the last few days; Mary is quite well and desires you & mother her best love.*
>
> Yr. affect. Son,
> E. Riggs, Jr.

On May 23, 1851, George Peabody wrote Mr. Corcoran from London regretting that, "your business will not permit you to come to London this season. The Exhibition is worth coming for . . . it is becoming more interesting every day . . . ."

Mr. Peabody was referring to what was called "the greatest industrial world's fair of its time", housed in a magnificent cast-iron-and-glass structure known popularly as the "Great Crystal Palace Exposition."[1]

He went on to report that: "My proposition to give a splendid flag was accepted by the American Commission and sanctioned by the Royal Commission, but subsequently refused by the latter."

The American Commission had little reason to regret the absence of Mr. Peabody's "splendid flag," for the U.S. section had come up belatedly with the sensation of the fair.

The year 1851 was the pivot of the century and Queen Victoria herself had opened the exhibition amid great pomp and ceremony. It was whispered that the jewel of the American section had been discreetly curtained until the royal party had passed. For the great attraction of the American pavillion was the statue of a demure and naked maiden in chains, carved in unblemished white marble by the American sculpture, Hiram Powers, who kept a popular studio in Florence.

The Greek Slave, as it was titled, was hailed by Londoners as the "one work of art by an American that did credit to America."[2]

A last minute surprise entry, the sculpture had saved the U.S. section from probable disaster. In their fine arts section the Americans had been scheduled to exhibit, among other things, "a group of daguerreotypes and a cathedral window made of colored soap".[3]

When it was finally realized that the statue which had made a sensational tour of American a few years before, was right there in the nearby English countryside, the owner was hastily and hopefully contacted. Permission was graciously granted and *The Greek Slave* was on station on her revolving pedestal (a sop to the purpose of the fair) to greet the hordes of gentleman and long-skirted ladies and their escorts, who came in ever-increasing numbers to gape at the maiden's almost unprecedented bareness . . . billed with tongue-in-cheek as . . . "inspired by the heroic struggle of the Greek people to throw off the yoke of their Turkish masters in the war that had ended in 1830."

Corcoran had really no need to go to London to see the statue. He had seen it in New York at the beginning of its American tour and fallen in love with it. What Mr. Corcoran now wanted, he bought, and he must have made an immediate resolve to one day obtain a copy of this incredibly beautiful and life-like figure.

We cannot say for certain when he placed his order, but it was probably related to a cryptic letter in *A Grandfather's Legacy* dated June 6, 1851, and written from Paris by Dudley Selden, a retired New York lawyer and former Congressman, who appears to have been Corcoran's agent in collecting works of art. The date is two weeks after Mr. Peabody's letter and possibly reflects a rekindling of Corcoran's fascination with the statue caused by the news of its display and the accompanying furor at the great fair.

The pertinent parts of the letter are as follows:

> Paris, June 6, 1851
>
> My Dear Corcoran:
> A few days ago I received yours of May 5th and it was indeed pleasant to see your handwriting once again.
> I certainly should not have written you in relation to the small matters I sent you from Rome, except to assure for them the necessary care on arrival . . . .
> There is more than one original Greek Slave. The original is probably in England, belonging to a Mr. Grant, I think; the true original, after all, is the model in clay or plaster. Good copies can be made equally good as long as the model remains. The occupation of selecting the marble may require some peculiar talent . . . but that of cutting the marble into the lines and form of the original is, with the

> *necessary instruments, purely mechanical....*
> *Indeed, an author of a work in sculpture scarcely ever strikes a hammer, unless in retouching a copy of a living face.*
>
> *I shall be glad to see you in Europe, and, if not there, every or any where else.*
>
> Yours truly,
Dudley Selden.

One can guess that Mr. Corcoran placed his order for the statue through Mr. Selden after receiving these assurances.

Research discloses that Hiram Powers started work at his Florence studio in October of 1842, "on the statue that was to establish him, according to his contemporaries, as the greatest American sculptor of all time."[4]

The original Greek Slave was sold while only partially blocked out to the waist to a retired British Army officer, Captain John Grant, of London, precisely as the astute Mr. Selden had suggested. Grant desired the statue by the following August and promised to exhibit it in London at his own expense, which he did, at Graves in Pall Mall.

After the exhibition in Pall Mall an order arrived in the spring of 1845 from Lord Ward of England for a duplicate of the *Greek Slave*.

The significant accomplishment of the 1847 season at Florence was the final completion of the second copy of the statue for Lord Ward. He then allowed Powers to use it for an exhibition tour while awaiting the cutting of a third that would contain some slight changes he now preferred.

Early in July, 1847, the *Greek Slave* was shipped from Leghorn to New York, where under the supervision of a Barnum-like promoter named Kellog, it began its American tour. Meanwhile, an order for still another copy had been received from one James Robb, a banker in New Orleans who, not surprisingly, was also an art lover. All of these sales were made for a price of $4,000 with, presumabely, one half in advance.

One historian has stated that "before The Greek Slave could repeat in America its London triumph, it had to pass a purity test." Powers had carefully sent along with the sculpture a supply of pamphlets calculated to appease puritan shock at its

CHAPTER 12

nudity. He declared the naked figure represented "the fortitude and resignation of a Christian supported by her faith in the goodness of God; leaving no room for shame." He also included a sonnet poured forth after having viewed the statue by none other than Elizabeth Barrett Browning. The concluding lines were:[5]

> *Catch up in thy divine face not alone*
> *East's griefs, but West's, and strike and shame*
> *By thunder of white silence overthrown.*

Nevertheless, in many American towns and cities public prudery as well as honest embarrassment were only accomodated "by admitting groups of each sex alternately into the small gallery selected for the exhition." The tour, which was extended over more than three years, was a financial success and the small admission fees of five, ten and twenty-five cents eventually added up to twenty-three thousand dollars, split between Powers and the sponsors.

Three additional orders for copies of the "Slave" had been received, making a total of six in all. The last three came from Sir Charles Coote of England, Prince Anatol Demidov, of Paris, and Mr. Corcoran. Some uncertainty exists as to whether Corcoran received the copy he ordered or the one which had made the grand tour of the U.S.A. A violent controversary had arisen between banker Robb, of New Orleans, and the sculptor, mainly over the lengthy extention of the American tour. Other problems arose when some of Robb's drafts for payment were dishonored. In any case, it is stated flatly by one authority that: "The second [statue] brought to America in 1847, which attracted great attention when exhibited. . .is now in the Corcoran Gallery of Art in Washington". Since the same source adds that the statue "was the center of interest at the first World's Fair in New York in 1853," it appears that, following its tour of the country, the promotors had made an additional financial arrangement for it to be shown in New York, after which, with the default of banker Robb, it was to be delivered to Mr. Corcoran in Washington.[1]

Meanwhile, back in Corcoran's elegant mansion opposite Jackson Square in the summer of 1851, he had received from an old friend and longtime client of the bank, and now the recipient of a special Congressional Gold Medal, the following impromptu invitation:

> *My Dear Corcoran:*
> *Having just become possessed of a fine green turtle, I would beg you to waive ceremony and join me in a "hasty plate of soup" today at five o'clock.*
>
> *Very truly yours,*
> *Winfield Scott.*

And thus was W. W. Corcoran continuing to qualify eminently for the definition of bon vivant: "a person who enjoys good food and other pleasant things".

Such as his eagerly anticipated ownerships of the Greek Slave!

Chapter Notes

[1]"Neglected works of a once-famous Yankee artist comes to Washington". by Robert Hilton Simmons, Smithsonian Magazine, November. 1972.
[2] *Ibid.*
[3] *Ibid.*
[4] Lorado Taft. *The History of American Sculpture*, The McMillan Co., N.Y. 1903.
[5] Sylvia E. Crane *White Silence*, Miami 1972. p.
[6] Mrs. Clara (Erskin) Clement Waters 1894, *Artists of The Nineteenth Century*, Houghton-Miflin, N.Y.

Chapter 13

In early 1852, the crucial debate in Congress on the additional subsidy for the Collins Line was heating up and tempers were fraying.

This was illustrated by a letter from Elisha, Jr. dated February 24, 1852, in which he scolded his anxious father for daring to suggest the names of lobbyists who might help the company's cause. Elisha, Jr. was no doubt prodded into his comments by Corcoran, who was the Line's principal representative on Capitol Hill.

With his cutsomary "Dear Father," he launches forthwith into the subject:

> Your letter of yesterday to the firm was duly received and contents noted. As we do not like to put these matters before the clerks, Mr. Corcoran has desired me to say to you privately that we are well acquainted with the merits and influence of both parties you mention. They are of that class that magnify their importance exceedingly & if we undertook to pay them in accordance with their representations we should all be ruined and our cause but little assisted....

> We know the calibre of such gentlemen better
> than you do & if you leave them to us they will get
> their deserts & nothing more. We feel as much
> anxiety as yourself to assure every chance of
> success and being on the spot are better judges of
> the means to be employed.

Then young Elisha abruptly changes the subject and announces:

> Corcoran had a magnificent ball last . . . though
> excessively crowded. I suppose there must have
> been invited from twelve to fifteen hundred.
> Mary and the children are both well . . . .
>
> Yr. affec. Son,
E. Riggs, Jr.

The accidental omission of a word after "last," leaves us to suppose this was a Washington's birthday ball on February 22 given by Corcoran, since the date of Elisha's letter was February 24.

On March 4, 1852, George Riggs, Jr. wrote again to his long-time friend, Samuel Taylor, in Wisconsin, to advise him of a substantial change in his situation:

> My dear Sir:
> I have had your letter on my desk too long
> unanswered . . . .
> This last winter I sold my country place to the
> Government for a site for a military asylum. I did it
> at the earnest request and advice of my father &
> brother, Lawrason, both of whom are desirous to
> have me remove to New York or the vicinity. I am
> now in this city with my family; it is my intention in
> a short time to go on to New York to look out for a
> place suitable for my family for the summer and then
> make up my mind where to locate for the future.
> Perhaps I may live in New York for a while . . . .
> My brother, Lawrason, intends to make New York
> his home although he still remains in business in
> St. Louis.
> My father paid us a visit about a fort night ago.
> Although the number of his years is now large
> [he was 72], he is still quite active in body and mind.

CHAPTER 13

I shall be glad at all times to hear from you. Don't suppose if you don't get an immediate reply that you are forgotten.
  With kind regards to your wife,

Yours very faithfully,
George W. Riggs, Jr.

The Government had purchased Riggs' home and his 256 acres for $58,111.75, — part of the prize money General Scott had levied on Mexico City. For a time, pending the erection of the main building which was to be named the Scott Building, the few members present lived in the Riggs house. It was subsequently the summer residence of several Presidents, including Lincoln.

It soon becomes evident that George Riggs, Jr. and his family had moved into what is now known as the Clarke-Ashburton house at 1525 H Street, N.W., presently the Parish House of historic St. Johns Church. Elisha, Jr. and his wife and children had apparently been living there while awaiting completion of their new home on Eye Street. The two families must have decided to share the same huge structure for a time, with, one hopes, reasonable tranquility.

At this time our file of family letters obtained from the good doctor in Syracuse contains the only letter we possess of Elisha's fourth son, Joseph Karrick Riggs, two years younger than Elisha, Jr. The letter is dated March 31, 1852, at which time he was apparently representing his father at the Collins Line hearings in Congress. His letter is written in a beautifully readable hand and appears to reflect an intelligent and pleasing personality, Karrick blood or no. The contents are as follows:

Washington, D.C.,
Wednesday,
March 31st, 1852

My Dear Father:
  I am this morning in receipt of yours of yesterday and note its contents. Having come through from New York direct, I reached here Saturday evening at 9 o'clock. Both Elisha's & George's families, with

themselves, are well, with the exception of Alice &
Kate, who have the "mumps" but not at all severely.
Yesterday I called to see Grandma! She is very well
and active, as are Uncle Joe & Mr. Burche's
children.[1]

Our appropriation will probably be reached bv the
Senate this week, as an amendement to the Deficiency Bill. Mr. Corcoran has just gone to the Capitol
where he spends most of the morning. I have been
there and shall go again as soon as this letter is written. Mr. C. thinks that our chance is good, but fears
the consequence of the opposition of Western &
Internal men to the Seaborad ones, and vice versa.
He says also as everyone has told me with whom I
have spoken on the matter, that Mr. Collins has done
us a deal of harm by his pompous manner and total
want of discretion. He is as much disliked here as in
New York! Mr. Wetmore will be gladly received . . . .

Our demands seem large when placed on paper!
Mr. Corcoran has taken with him a statement of
deficiency received from Mr. Collins this morning,
showing the indebtedness to us of $255,750 for extra
service from July, 1851 to Jan'y, 1852 and compensation of $33,000 a voyage from Jan'y, 1852 to July,
1852. This will be an appropriation in addition to that
of $385,000, already made by Congress. A large sum
per annum is $858,000; if we do get it, we shall have
to change entirely the "Modus Operandi" of the
Steamers' business, and make a general curtailment.
I see letters here now addressed to Wetmore and
consequently presume that his presence is expected.

George is undecided as to his future place of residence. Janet very naturally prefers remaining in
Washington. George will very probably return with
me. Astaburuaga will be in New York in a week
enroute to Chile. I have invited him to stay with us.
His government has signified their desire to confer
honors on him.[2]

My best love to mother, Mary Alice and all at
home.

Your affectionate son,
Joseph K. Riggs.

CHAPTER 13

On April 1, Elisha, Jr. was getting off another letter to his father, advising him he had made two monthly payments as directed and had charged them to his account.[3]

After reporting these matters, Elisha, Jr. continued with the all-engrossing subject of the Collins appropriation:

> The appropriation the steamers want, upwards of $800,000 per annum, is such an enormous sum that I consider its passage extremely doubtful. About $650,000 would stand a fine chance. We are doing all that can be done & should we be defeated, must take a smaller sum. It is better to take less & see what can be done, than to give up the contract.
> The matter will come up in the Senate next week.
>
> Yr. affco. son,
> E. Riggs, Jr.

On May 1st, the matter was still very much uncertain in both houses of Congress:

> Dear Father:
> In answer to yours of the 30th inst...I cannot tell you when the debate on the Collins Line will cease in the Senate — or when the question will be decided in the House. We had expected it would have left the Senate ere this but from present indications the debate will in all probability be prolonged throughout the ensuing week.

Then, reverting to personal matters, Elisha tells his father:

> We slept in our new house last night and are beginning to get things somewhat to rights... Say to George... the children are all well & Jess just recovering from her attack of measles which was extremely light. The others have all escaped.
>
> Love to all and believe me,
> Yr. affect. Son,
> E. Riggs, Jr.

By May 11th, Elisha was quite discouraged:

> The inteminable debate in the Senate appears to be lessening our chances of success daily....

Geyer from Missouri with whom Lawrason is well acquainted and on whom we had counted, yesterday made a speech against us. He had previously expressed himself our friend as also Wade of Ohio. . . . If we gain the Senate it will be by an exceedingly close vote.

In haste,
Yr. son,
E. Riggs, Jr.

P.S. Mr. Clay is failing so rapidly & seems to depend so much upon seeing Mary daily that she will not be able to leave him at present.[4]

By a curious circumstance our next bulletin on the Collins bill comes not from Elisha, Jr. but from Lawrason in New York. On July 14, writing to his father at his favorite watering place, United States Hotel, Saratoga Springs, N.Y., he states:

New York, July 14, 1852

My Dear Father:
   You did no doubt see all about the Collins steamers by the newspapers — we hope to hear tomorrow of the final passage of the bill.
   I have been at Rockaway with my children for a week & came up this morning for the purpose of meeting George & family. They were to have left Washington yesterday morning & we expect them here today at 1 o'clock — they will stop to dine at your house & proceed this evening to Rockaway. I think that decidedly the best place for George's children he could have selected. The sea bathing is fine & my children enjoy it very much.
   I will meet George at the boat & show him your letter.

Your affectionate Son,
Lawrason Riggs.

In Lawrason's second letter, dated almost two weeks later, he makes no mention of the Collins Line and we can assume the news is still encouraging or the bill has passed.

CHAPTER 13

The most interesting part of this letter refers to George's situation in Washington:

> George, having sold his place in the country & having given up Mr. Corcoran's house in Washington, leaves his family in a very unsettled way, which I regret very much as his children ought to be permanently located. Unless he wishes to go into business in New York, I think he would be better satisfied to remain in Washington — I have, however, offered to him the house I occupy until the time I have taken it expires — two years from last May. If he intends to live in New York I think it his best plan to take my house. I want to remain in St. Louis for 6 months at least, and if he will take my house, I would take my children there with me & if suitable arrangements can be made, will . . . leave them in St. Louis altogether. I find it very inconvenient to be away from my business so long as I have been & will either have to give up business or remain most of the time there.
>
> I shall go to Rockaway again tomorrow & will be glad to hear from you. Hoping you may continue to enjoy yourself, I remain,
>
> Your affectionate Son,
> Lawrason Riggs.

The matter of George's "giving up Corcoran's house in Washington" is amplified by the August 12, 1852 letter from Elisha, Jr. to his father. That letter also confirms that the long battle is over and the Collins bill has passed. The actual news of that momentous event was probably transmitted by telegraph.

His father, in an expansive mood, has made $5,000 available to him — presumably covering the disputed commission and the payment toward his new house. Elisha, Jr., with surprising graciousness, expressed his thanks but declined to accept the money for the present. (Maybe Junior is growing up!)

This interesting letter reads as follows:

12 August, 1852

Dear Father:
I received a letter yesterday from Mr. Bolton stating he held $5,000 subject to my order should I

need it.... As I found I should not require it at present, I this morning answered him to that effect & have to thank you for your kindness in meeting my views....

I shall if possible make you a visit with my family in the fall for the benefit of the change of air.

Mr. Wetmore left this morning, having been busily occupied with matters connected with the passage of the Collins amendment.

I hear that Mr. Corcoran has sold the Clarke property to Commodore Stockton for $25,000. This will oblige George to come on shortly and look after his furniture....

My best love to mother & Mary Alice [his younger sister], who, I hope are enjoying themselves, and Believe

>Me Ever,
>Yr. affec Son,
>E. Riggs, Jr.

And so, the long seige had ended and the Collins Line had obtained a reprieve and a chance of salvation. Once again, Mr. Corcoran had shown himself to be one of the most influential figures in the capital and the nation.

Almost as if in tribute to its sponsors, on August 18, four days after Elisha's last letter, the Collins steamer *Baltic* came bell ringing and horn-tooting into New York harbor to claim the mythical Blue Ribbon of the Atlantic for a new east-west record — nine days, eighteen hours — from Liverpool. Since the *Pacific* held the record in the opposite direction, the Collins Line now appeared to be at the zenith of its power and prestige.

This splendid moment was savored by Congress and the American people, and gave no hint of the overwhelming disasters which lay ahead and would bring tragedy to the line and its backers.

On this great day, the Collins fleet was the finest afloat and the United States seemed close to surpassing the longtime sea supremacy of Great Britain.

But to return to less dramatic matters, we come to the question of the Clarke-Ashburton house, still standing today at 1525 H Street, northwest, and now the Parish House of St. Johns Church.

The fact is well known in local historical circles that this handsome old mansion was built by Mathew St. Clair Clarke, clerk of the House of Representatives in 1839. At that time it was said to be one of the finest in the city.[5]

The summit of importance to the structure came in 1842 with its selection as the British legation when Lord Ashburton was sent to the United States to handle the troublesome northeastern boundary problem. He and our Secretary of State, Daniel Webster, worked out a compromise which was embodied in the Webster-Ashburton treaty. Hence, the name Clarke-Ashburton house.

The next tenant was Sir Henry Bulwer who was appointed to work out the more complex Oregon boundary dispute. This mission, although more difficult and extending over a longer period, was also successful and was resolved by the Clayton-Bulwer treaty passed in 1850.

Thereafter, according to the *Washington Star* of February 24, 1924, "the next tenant was the family of George Riggs, the banker, who lived there while waiting for their own new house around the corner to be finished."

Well, we can recognize an honest mistake here. The "Riggs family awaiting completion of the house around the corner," was that of Elisha, Jr. — not George's. But George's family also moved in, as we have noted, after he sold Corn Rigs to the government.

But what of it being "Mr. Corcoran's house," and of Mr. Corcoran having "sold the Clarke house to Commodore Stockton," as reported by both Lawrason and Elisha, Jr.?

Another hasty excursion into the city's old real estate records finally revealed that W. W. Corcoran apparently signed a five-year lease for the property with an option to buy it when it was foreclosed by the Patriotic Bank in July of 1848. A notation in connection therewith states that Clarke was indebted to Patriotic Bank in "large amount."

Mr. Corcoran, who was then still residing a block to the east, on the north side of H Street between Vermont Avenue and 15th Street, was anxious to locate on Jackson Square, and concluded the Clarke property suitable as soon as the British finished their temporary occupancy, which was, as it turned out, in 1850.

Meanwhile, the Webster house on the corner of H Street and Connecticut Avenue had become available after the retirement of Daniel Webster to Massachusetts and Corcoran, who considered it even more desirable, was able to purchase it on June 4, 1849 — less than a year after he had leased the Clarke house.

His young partner, Elisha, Jr. and Mary Boswell were married in Philadelphia on November 28, 1849, and we can conclude, Corcoran was willing for them to move in when the British moved out. He was also aware they were planning to build a new house around the corner on Eye Street. And after George, Jr. sold his country place, he was also agreeable to the family renting one-half of the building. The tradition of renting half of the huge (for its day) structure had been established when Clarke first suffered reverses and, according to the *Star*: "leased one-half of its spaciousness to the editor of the *National Intelligencer*, where the lovely Mrs. Gales started her weekly 'crushes' to which all society floundered."

As to what happened to the sale to Commodore Stockton for $25,000, we can assume that distinguished officer changed his mind, for he eventually bought, perhaps out of sentiment, in the same block as the Decatur house, at 722 Jackson Place. As usual, Corcoran profited from the Commodore's change of mind; he exercised his option to buy the Clarke house from the trustees on September 21, 1852 for $22,000 and sold it the next year for $30,000. And the change might also have permitted George, Jr. and family to remain a while longer.[6]

The new purchaser was Sarah H. Coleman, and, according to the *Star*, "a few months later her sister and brother-in-law, Colonel and Mrs. William Grigsby Freeman, (here we go again) purchased one-half of it, and they and their descendants have owned and occupied it continuously ever since [1924]."

CHAPTER 13

Chapter Notes

[1]"Uncle Joe" refers to Joseph Augustus Karrick, the youngest brother of Elisha's wife and the eighth child of the family. The reference to "Mr. Burche's children," refers to the children of Eleanor Jones Karrick, her youngest sister, and the ninth and last child of the family. She married John Covington Burche, but was evidently now deceased. "Grandma" was, of course, Rebecca Ord Karrick, the mother of Mary Ann Karrick, and the widow of Joseph, who died in 1829.

[2]This was Don Francisco de Astaburuaga, Secretary of Legation of Chile, and apparently a close friend of the Riggs family.

[3]Elisha was apparently making a payment of thirty dollars per month to his mother-in-law to help her with the Burche children. Burche was listed in the Washington Directory as a clerk in the Interior Department. Elisha's second payment for thirty-three dollars and seventy-one cents was to his niece, Paulina (Gaither) Ould, the daughter of his oldest sister, Henrietta. She and her Husband, Robert Ould, had eleven children before he died in Georgetown in 1840.

[4]Henry Clay was confined to his room by illness at the National Hotel at sixth and Pennsylvania Ave, where he died on June 30, 1852.

[5]*The Sunday Star*, February 24, 1924, by Edna M. Colman, on the Clarke-Ashburton house.

[6]Liber Deed JAS 91-89 (64).

Chapter 14

With the Collins debate concluded, Congress speedily finished its remaining business, and on August 31, 1852, Elisha, Jr. was able to report to his father that, "Congress has just adjourned & we have the Office full of members arranging their many matters."

He goes on to state:

> I received your favor of the 29th Inst. announcing your return home & the improvement in your general health from your summer excursion. As in New York, we have been visited with a violent storm which appears, however, to have purified the atmosphere and occasioned the phenomenon of a couple of fair days — quite an unusual occurrence after the constant inclement weather of the last two weeks.
>
> Mary is improving & I think a change of air will be beneficial — but shall not be able to leave Washington myself before the return of Mr. Corcoran who will probably start in a few days.

> Mr. Ingersoll, our new minister to London,
> informed me this morning that he intended sailing in
> the Collins steamer of the 18th & will write from
> Phila. for a stateroom. He goes alone & is desirous if
> possible to have a stateroom to himself & I told him
> I would see if it could be accomplished & write you
> now for that purpose. Mr. Ingersoll is a warm friend
> of the Line & assisted the passage of our bill & as he
> will possess much influence abroad it will be to the
> interest of the company to make him as comfortable
> as possible.
>
> >   Believe me,
> >   Yr. affec. Son,
> >   E. Riggs, Jr.

On October 10, 1852, Lawrason en route back to St. Louis, wrote his father a most informative letter on the printed and embossed stationery of Burnet House in Cincinnati, Ohio:

> >   Sunday, Oct. 10, 1852
>
> Dear Father:
>
> After leaving New York Wednesday evening, I
> passed through Philadelphia & left there at 11
> o'clock at night. The distance to Pittsburgh, 363
> miles, we made by 12 o'clock next night. The road
> from Philadelphia is owned by the state — the
> company that has it do not appear to be on good
> terms with the Central R.R. Co., which put the
> passengers to the trouble of looking to their baggage
> in transferring from one road to the other about
> 3 o'clock in the morning. I could not help thinking
> that a good example of Pennsylvania dutch
> obstinacy . . . .
>
> I leave here this morning by steam boat for
> Madison, Indiana & tomorrow go from there to
> Terre Haute via Indianapolis.
>
> The Rail Road system in this country is astonishing. I have traveled to this point 845 miles by Rail
> Road, with the exception of 10 miles by stage. There
> is no estimating the increase of wealth which is to
> be developed in this country by the rail road
> facilities, and New York will derive benefit from the
> whole of it.

CHAPTER 14

> *John Elliott has not arrived here yet. I saw a letter from his brother addressed to him at this house. I suppose he must be stuck on the Ohio River somewhere. [John Elliott was a long-time associate of Elisha in his New York office].*
>
> > *Your affect. Son,*
> > *Lawrason Riggs.*

On October 29, George W. Riggs, Jr. wrote again to his friend, Samuel Taylor, in Madison, Wisconsin, advising him of his imminent return to business in New York, and closing with a farewell before embarking for London:

> *New York, 29th Oct., 1852*
>
> My Dear Sir:—
> I have contracted to make this my residence and have made an arrangement with my cousin, Samuel Riggs, formerly of Baltimore, to join him in a Banking and General Commission business in Wall St.
> For business purposes, I sail for England tomorrow morning hoping to be back here by the 1st of January next. . . .
> My family will, after I sail return to Washington to spend the winter and will join me here next Spring.
> I write you late at night, having just packed my trunk and written farewell to Lawrason who is now in St. Louis.
> Goodbye, God bless you and your family. My kindest regards to Mrs. Taylor.
>
> > *Yours very faithfully,*
> > *George W. Riggs.*

It might be noted here that Samuel Riggs, the cousin with whom George, Jr. was launching a new "banking and general commission business" had deep roots and crossroots in the Riggs family, plus a long and distinguished business career.

To begin with, his father was Elisha's oldest brother, Thomas, the third child of Samuel and Amelia Dorsey Riggs. He was, therefore, a nephew of Elisha and a first cousin of George, Jr.

Thomas, it will be recalled, had stayed at Brookeville as a planter and operated his big farm adjacent to "Pleasant Hill." His original stone house, still standing today and much enlarged, fromerly housed the "new" Brookeville Academy after the Civil War. He had been a founding trustee of the old academy in 1815. Furthermore, Thomas had married a Riggs girl, Mary Hammond Riggs, a daughter of old Samuel's brother, Captain Elisha Riggs and his wife, and therefore, *his first cousin*

Young Samuel was born on August 20, 1800 on Thomas's plantation and married January 18, 1927, in Baltimore, Margaret Norris, born April 27, 1808, in Baltimore. To further complicate matters, she was the daughter of Rebecca (Smith) Norris, who, after the death of her husband, was "the comely Norris widow" who became the second wife of old George Washington Riggs in 1820.

Samuel had begun his business career at age fifteen when he entered Elisha's mercantile establishment in Georgetown. About the year 1820, the firm, then Riggs and Peabody, moved its main office to Baltimore. The name was subsequently changed to Riggs, Peabody and Company and Samuel became a partner. Branches were soon established in Philadelphia and New York and Elisha withdrew in 1829. When Peabody also withdrew, Samuel Riggs found himself "at the head of one of the largest mercantile firms in the country." After the year 1850, he moved to New York and purchased a large residence on Fifth Avenue where he was living at the time of the contemplated formation of the new firm with George, Jr.[1]

Samuel was then fifty-two and George, Jr. thirty-nine. The merger of these two experienced and highly successful merchant bankers appeared to hold much promise of success.

George's letter to Samuel Taylor in Wisconsin announcing his entry into business with his cousin Samuel, is followed chronologically by a long and affectionate letter from Janet Riggs to her father-in-law, Elisha, touching on George's uncomfortable trip across the Atlantic and her own family's safe return to Washington:

Washington,
Nov. 26, 1852

I am truly glad my dear Father to learn by your affectionate dispatch of Sunday last, that you got

CHAPTER 14

home safely & today my heart is lightened by letters from my dear husband, at same time, 12th November, he wrote you & Cousin Samuel & I suppose told you everything of interest. His passage out was stormy, or rather rainy & disagreeable as might have been expected — I trust it may be safe one home. I am happy to hear Lawrason's litte ones are well — my sister still continues delicate & I find my time fully occupied putting things to rights after so long an absence. [Presumably, the family was still occupying the Clarke house on H Street].

Tis fortunate we left New York just when we did for we have had no weather since that would have been suitable for our trip. I had a cold when I started & have suffered so much with it I have not been out at all. However, it is nothing serious & in fact wearing away.

Georgie has just been in the highest state of delight, caused by a visit from our old coachman, Joe Simms; the child scarcely knew how to show his joy — he danced, marched & jumped by turns. Your namesake, [Elisha Francis, 13 months] is bright and gay as possible. Mary, Elisha & their children have all been to see us.

As to my wants, my dear Father, I should like to have, tea, candles & brandy, quarter of a chest, I suppose, would do of good black breakfast tea, with good black tea flavour, not green; a dozen or two of Lawry's famous brandy & three boxes of Judd's patent Sperm candles (four to the pound), also three boxes of Lawrason's best St. Louis candles — he had some in your office I think. I send for these six boxes because if I should not need them all, they can readily be disposed of when we break up. All these matters can be sent by Geo. Town Packet & the sooner the better on account of danger of the river freezing.

Ma & My Sister join me in love to you & Mrs. Riggs. Whenever you can spare time I shall be delighted to hear from you, my dear Father, mean while believe me,

> Always Yr. affectionate daughter,
> Janet M. C. Riggs

PS: I sent a letter to Joseph yesterday for George. If you think best send a firkin of good butter or anything else of that kind & let me have the bill for all.

On December 17, 1852, Elisha Jr. wrote his father that he was giving a party in his new home and would soon want to replenish his stock of champagne.

"I want only the best", he added characteristically, "as an inferior article costs nearly as much & is never liked." He then continued:

Please send me a dozen baskets — four of them pints — & have them forwarded by vessel to Georgetown — also a small quantity of fine old rum — and a few gallons of good whiskey.

I am having an impromptu party which promises to become a ball, as it is impossible to give an entertainment of under three hundred in Washington.

It is given to the Princes of Nassau & Weid, who brought letters of introduction to me & they will come to my house after dining with Corcoran [a convenient arrangement since Corcoran's garden backed up to Elisha's house across Eye Street].

As everybody in society here has to give one large party during the winter, I thought it best to get it off my hands on this occasion & leave myself at liberty afterwards to invite a select few.

Mary & the children are well. In Janet's family, however, there continues to be considerable sickness — Mrs. Cooper being still confined to her room & Kathy [a daughter] to bed with a severe influenza."

Thus were things progressing with the Riggs family. Meanwhile, on the national scene, Democrat Franklin Pierce had overwhelmed his Whig opponent and former commanding officer, Winfield Scott, in the November election to become the nation's fourteenth President.

President Pierce opened his account with Corcoran & Riggs on March 16, 1853, shortly after his inauguration, becoming the fifth chief executive to maintain an account with the firm. At forty-eight he was then the youngest President in our history.

CHAPTER 14

And so the firm of Corcoran & Riggs continued to flourish. But the close of the year 1852 had brought tragedy to the Riggs family and ruin to the plans for which George Riggs, Jr. was then in London.

On Christmas Eve, Samuel Riggs, returning from a genial celebration of the anticipated new affiliation, suffered a bad fall alighting from his carriage before the door of his home at 124 Fifth Avenue, resulting in a severe fracture of his leg. The injury proved fatal when blood-posioning set in. [it would probably be termed a blood clot today] and Samuel succumbed at his residence on December 26, 1852.

Fate seemed inexorably pushing George Washington Riggs, Jr. back toward his namesake city and first love — the capital of the nation.

Chapter Notes

[1] *The Riggs Family of Maryland*, p. 237.

Chapter 15

Franz von Recum, our great grandson chronicler of the Riggs family, has described Samuel's death as having ruined "grandiose plans the family had been making for an extended banking operation, including Washington, Baltimore, St. Louis, New York and London".

"It appears", he wrote, "that when Elisha was growing old, his son, George W., Jr., having retired from Corcoran & Riggs. intended to start a banking operation in New York with his cousin, Samuel, taking over much of Elisha's business in New York. Lawrason was to do the St. Louis operation and Joseph Karrick Riggs, fourth son of Elisha, was to join Mr. Peabody in London."

We are left to conclude from bits and pieces not made clear, that Samuel's son, William T., was to establish a branch in Baltimore, and Elisha, Jr. was to represent the firm in some capacity in Washington. Romulus, having died in Philadelphia on October 2, 1846, and none of his heirs being interested, that city had been left out of the plans.

These plans were never really tested for many reasons — the death of Samuel, and the fact that Joseph Karrick Riggs, with wedding bells about to ring for his February 15, 1853 marriage to Rosalie Van Zandt (she was 18 and he 24), was reluctant, despite the Collins Line advertisements, to embark for Europe with his dark-haired bride, or perhaps it was vice versa.

Eventually, a family friend, Junius S. Morgan, was sent to London to handle the English business of Elisha. Born in 1813, he was then forty, the same age as George, Jr., and had started his career at age sixteen in a Boston mercantile firm. Junius Morgan became a partner in George Peabody and Company in 1854, and, as is well-known, after the death of Peabody, the business eventually descended to his son — J. Pierpont Morgan.

George W. Riggs, Jr. takes a somewhat more philosophical view of his cousin's death. In writing to Samuel Taylor again, he says:

> New York, 23 March, 1853
>
> My Dear Sir:
> Ever since my return from England I have been intending to write you, but the duties that devolved upon me, and traveling backward and forward between this city and Washington to attend to business here and visit my family there, have made me neglect my private correspondence.
>
> When my plans for business were knocked in the head by the death of my cousin, we had already embarked on some operations which have required my attention here. I shall not act on the business that it was our intention to have done. Samuel's son, William, and myself have taken an office and will do a little business together. We have hardly embarked in business yet. If I had to have assistance, I should be happy to have you with us, but for some time our business will be so trifling that we shall keep up the appearance of an establishment only.
>
> Mr. Peabody was very kind to me when I was in London and was to have been our correspondent but I shall not embark in such a large foreign business as if my cousin had lived. I have been so long idle

CHAPTER 15

> that I have grown rusty — it will take some time to acquaint myself with the standing of parties here. Names that I used to be familiar with have disappeared & new houses have sprung up. There has been a very great change here. The place and the trade of the city have increased wonderfully. I feel lost where I used to be at home.
>
> My brother Lawrason has taken his children back to St. Louis.
>
> I shall be glad to hear more cheering accounts from you The county in which you live must be improving rapidly.
>
> I leave tonight for Washington. I travel all night, spend a day or two with my family and come back here early next week. I hope to move on my family some time during the next month. My wife's sister is very ill, otherwise, I should begin moving at once for I hate the vibrating life I now lead.
>
> With kind regards to Mrs. Taylor and my best wishes for your health and prosperity, I am,
>
>   Very faithfully yours,
>   George W. Riggs, Jr.

And so we return to Elisha, Jr. in Washington who was about to undertake what was probably the major adventure of his life. And a seemingly less likely candidate for the role is hard to imagine.

In his mammoth volume, *The Riggs Family of Maryland*, John Beverly Riggs, after describing the new house of Elisha, Jr. on Eye Street as "built in the Gothic style and . . of yellow stucco," states in the next paragraph, without further ado:

> On May 1, 1853, he and his brother, William Henry Riggs, left Washington for California, in the Benton-Beal Expedition. They explored the Rocky Mountains and much of the Far West. They returned home in September of the same year.

So what have we here — the harassed, overworked partner in a banking firm, having just finished building a fine home during the preceding year, and having a wife and two children and expecting a third, suddenly taking off on a junket to explore the still wild West with his sixteen-year-old brother, as

145

members of an expedition described only by the hyphenated title "Benton-Beal."

A quick glance at J. B. R.'s biography of the brother, William Henry Riggs .. gives a bit more information, but not much.

> William Henry Riggs, son of Elisha and Mary (Karrick) Riggs was born March 22, 1837, at No. 6 Bowling Green, New York. He began his career as a collector at an early date. As a boy he arranged and labeled specimens of things and had his own museum on the top floor of the large Bowling Green house.
>
> About 1852 he commenced to collect Indian arms and costumes. He accompanied his brother, Elisha Riggs, Jr. on the Benton-Beal Expedition to the West, and in 1853 he sent a large collection of Indian weapons and other things from the eastern slopes of the Rocky Mountains to his home in New York. At one time on the journey he had the choice of the arms of eight hundred war painted Pawnees. The trip was a dangerous one and his quest for knowledge often led him into dangerous places; on one occasion he was nearly lost in a herd of buffaloes.

No further information on the expedition was given by J.B.R.

We were suddenly aware that we had carefully culled all but two of the "Dear Father" letters, and they both proved to have been written in April, 1853, less than a month before Elisha, Jr.'s stated departure. They suddenly took on added significance. Did they give any news or hints of the trip he was undertaking? We had skimmed through them lightly before but could recall no such reference. The answer supplied by another hasty examination was — absolutely none!

The first was dated April 2, 1853, and opened with an advice to his father that $10,000 of San Francisco bonds had been received for his account. Also, that C & R had received an allotment of $100,000 of North Carolina five percent state bonds at 105.02, which he considered a "good purchase." Turning to family matters, he states:

> I hear from John Clarke that Mrs. Cooper's condition is still without change. This I should think

> *impossible to continue much longer. My wife was quite unwell all last night but is better this morning. I thought at first that her time had come.*

The second letter is dated April 13 - 18 days before J.B.R. reports he left for the West. In its, Elisha, Jr. states:

> *I have as yet no augmentation in my family to chronicle although in constant expectation. The health of my little ones & their mother continues good — although the latter is rather feeble. My own I regret to say is unpromising and symptoms that I have watched for some time with anxiety have assumed such character as to render me uneasy and induce me to consult my physician, whose opinion has been far from relieving me.*
>
> > Yr. affec. Son,
> > E. Riggs, Jr.

Our young aristocrat, with these symptoms, whatever they were, was about to set forth on a dangerous mission to the far West. If John Beverly Riggs had not told us he left on May 1, 1853, we would think the whole matter incredulous.

Information on the character and scope of the expedition proved difficult to come by, but eventually we learned that it was one of four or five engineer companies organized by Secretary of War, Jefferson Davis, "to explore routes for railroads from the Mississippi River to the Pacific coast." The first half of the name was supplied by the surname of Senator Thomas Hart Benton of Missouri, who introduced legislation authorizing the trips, and whose name was, in all cases, coupled with that of the leader of the party.

Beale (spelled with a final "e") turned out to be a much less well-known figure, but, nevertheless, possessed of considerable stature as a leader of western exploration. Edward Fitzgerald Beale was a junior officer on the frigate *Congress* when that vessel reached Monterey in 1846 and he also took part in the annexation of California. He was with a detachment that reached General Kearny just before Kearny's forces were surrounded by Mexicans in the battle of San Pasqual. With Kit Carson, Beale made his way through enemy lines to summon reinforcements resulting in a victory. Later he and Carson were sent overland to Washington with dispatches.

He was evidently a captain in the Army Topograpical Corps, when chosen to direct the expedition which Elisha, Jr. and his brother were to join.

The question arises as to how Elisha, Jr., a graduate of Heidelberg, with five years expereince as a junior partner in a banking firm, ever obtained permission for himself and his brother to go on one of these expeditions so obviously under the supervision of the U. S. Army. The question was a good one, but there was also a ready answer.

Corcoran & Riggs had become the Army bank after the Mexican War, and W. W. Corcoran, himself, one of the greattest non-military heroes. It was common knowledge that the banking house had largely financed the war with its purchases of government notes.

Old "Fuss 'n Feathers," General Winfield Scott, had ordered a huge collection of Mexican coins melted down and crafted into a handsome set of silver goblets which he presented, with appropriate ceremony, to the bank as a token of the gratitude and appreciation of himself and his staff.[1]

If any civilian could join one of the railroad exploring groups, it was a member of Corcoran & Riggs.

Beyond what was mentioned by John Beverly Riggs, we never found any particulars on the personal experiences of Elisha, Jr. and his brother. Senator Benton quoted from Capt. Beale's journal in a speech addressed to the people of Missouri, but his reference were largely to topographical features, mountains, valleys, streams, etc., and to glorious stands of timber which must have whetted the appetites of all eastern loggers.

He did finally make a specific reference to the party when he quoted the following piece of information: We [the members of the party] had our horses shod at a small Mormon settlement at Little Salt Lake [260 miles south of Great Salt Lake].

Perhaps any person of that day whose head was on straight knew that explorers of the West rode horses, but we were glad to find some confirmation of that fact.

In the rare book section of the Library of Congress, in a small colume written by one Edwin F. Johnson and entitled

CHAPTER 15

Railroad to the Pacific, we did find some brief, hurried excerpts from the Beale party journal. These entries cover the very last stages of their journey, as follows:

> On the 15th [August] the heat was intense . . . .
> On the 17th [Aug], during the night, we had a heavy storm, the howling wind was hot and filled with sand, and the rain fell in large drops.
> Aug. 19th — The road was through heavy sand . . .
> On the 20th crossed the Mojave . . .
> The distance reached from Westport, Mo., this day was, by estimate, 1,772 miles.
> The next day the party reached Cajon Pass and descended to Los Angeles.

The author, Johnson, then explains that an accident had befallen Capt. Beale's party and forced them to alter their final route and plans:

> In consequence of the detention for some days of Capt. Beale and party at the Grand (Colorado) River, where they were so unfortunate as to lose their arms and provisions by the upsetting of a canoe, and the slow progress made over the sandy and heated surface west of the Colorado, and the necessity of making direct for Los Angeles, their friends from San Francisco who designed to meet them at Walkers' Pass, were disappointed.

And that, apparently, was the somewhat inglorious end of the Benton-Beale expedition. It was also the end of our knowledge on the subject, and so we took leave of Capt. Beale and his party and also of the "Dear Father" series of letters. This last we did with considerable reluctance.

Back in Washington, Elisha's third child, another son, had been born on April 18, 1853, just thirteen days before he left on his trip, and was duly christened Francis Blair Riggs. This naming was presumably for the distinguished Francis Preston Blair (1791-1876), a longtime client of the bank who lived on President's Square diagonally west of the White House, and it probably indicated an intimacy between the two families. Blair had been a member of Andrew Jackson's "Kitchen Cabinet" and was editor of the *Globe.*

Janet Riggs's long-suffering, fourty-five-year-old sister, Jane Agnes Cooper, died on April 23, 1853, and was buried in the Riggs family plot in Rock Creek Church cemetery.

Meanwhile, early in May, Mr. Corcoran had received a letter from George Peabody in London, in which he inquired, "Are you not coming out to see us this summer?," obviously unaware that his old Georgetown friend was trapped for the summer by his youthful partner's reconnaisance of the Rockies.

George Riggs and family had apparently moved to New York after the death of Mrs. Cooper, where, von Recum reports, they lived at 25 East 22nd Street, presumably the house Lawrason had been renting.

Their old friend and neighbor at Corn Rigs, John Agg, wrote them there on July 27th, 1853, as follows:

> *Everything here remains about the same. The Asylum [Soldiers Home] buildings go on slowly ... The farm which Boyle sold is wonderfully changed. A great deal must have been expended there, to fit it for a cemetery; from fifteen to twenty men having been steadily at work for months. We have our new road marked out through the ravine between the church [Rock Creek] and the parsonage, and are only waiting for the next meeting of the Levy Court before we commence selling ... There are numerous inquiries about lots in our cemetery, and once commenced, I think it will go pretty well.*
>
> *The city is rapidly going ahead. I think I have never seen so many buildings in progress as now. The Metropolitan railroad will be commenced speedily, and the water works for the supply of the city will employ a great number of hands. Property has risen in value astonishingly.*

This last paragraph recalls that the construction of the Acqueduct to bring water to the capital from the Great Falls of the Potomac, fourteen miles upstream, was under the supervision of Captain Montgomery C. Meigs, U. S. Army, Corps of Engineers. He had opened under his signature at Corcoran & Riggs the "Washington Acqueduct Account," from which he disbursed funds appropriated for the project.

CHAPTER 15

At about the same time, Meigs opened the "Extension of the Capitol Account," to accomodate funds for the enlargement of the Capitol — erecting the new House and Senate wings, and adding the present great dome. And thus did the bank play a small part in the very building of the Capitol itself.

Mr. Agg closed his letter by stating:

> New York must be thronged with strangers at this time to see the great exhibition. I suppose you are there frequently.
>
> Health, happiness and prosperity be with you all and believe me always,
>
> Yours very sincerely,
> John Agg.

Perhaps the Riggs family had been to the Great New York World's Fair and been entranced at its brilliance and excitement. But they soon had other and more somber matters on their minds.

If Elisha Jr.'s letter of April 13, was not the last letter he wrote his father, it was certainly one of the last.

The senior Elisha died at his residence at No. 6 Bowling Green, on August 3, 1853, and was buried in vault No. 35 in New York Marble Cemetery on Second Ave in that city, while his third and fifth sons were still somewhere in the West.

Chapter Notes

[1] We have been told that there were fourty-eight of these goblets, and they were found in the Riggs mansion at 1617 Eye Street by the McMullens after the death of Miss Jane Riggs. We further understand they are now in the possession of Mr. John Beverly Riggs of Wilmington, Delaware and Mr. Richard C. Riggs of Baltimore, a great grandson of Lawrason by his marriage to Mary Turpin (Bright) Riggs, his third wife.

Chapter
16

After his father's death George W. Riggs continued to live in New York, where on October 28, 1853, his eighth child, a daughter, was born and promplty christened for Janet's late sister, Jane Agnes Riggs — balancing temporarily once again the family ledger of births and deaths. Von Recum recalls that, "being born at their home on East 22nd Street, she was the only 'Yankee' among the children".

George Riggs was engaged in the banking business with his cousin, Thomas, son of Samuel, and also in the settlement of his father's estate. The latter task was complicated, of course, by Elisha's large investment in the Collins Line stock, for which no buyer could be found. (The company was paying interest on an issue of bonds, but had never paid a dividend on its stock.) The amount of his investment has variously been estimated at from $1,000,000 to $1,500,000 out of his total estate of roundly $3,000,000.

A Collins Line family historian has reported that, "As finally constituted there was a controlling board of five men: Collins, James and Stewart Brown, partners in Brown Brothers, bankers, 59 Wall Street, Elisha Riggs and William Shepard Wetmore of Rhode Island. James Brown, the youngest of the four Brown brothers, became president of the company, and Collins, its general manager. The paid-in cash capital initially amounted to $1,200,000, contributed by these men and smaller stock-holders, but this by no means provided sufficient funds even with the fairly liberal subsidy by the government."[1]

The average cost of the first four Collins liners was the spectacular sum of $650,000, or $2,600,000 for the fleet. The fifth and largest vessel, the *Adriatic,* launched after Elisha's death, but contracted for during his lifetime, cost $1,200,000, bringing the total expenditures for ships alone to $3,800,000. When the fact is recalled that the line never made a profit, even with the government subsidy, but had accumulated a substantial deficit, we can accept the estimate that Elisha, as one of the wealthier directors, had contributed in excess of $1,000,000. Therefore his eldest son and executor had a king-size headache in the settlement of his estate.

Sometime in September, Elisha, Jr. and his youngest brother returned from the West and undoubtedly rushed to New York to join the family and learn the news of the estate. It should be remembered, however, that even if one-half of Elisha's assets were tied up in the Collins Line, his estate had a balance remaining of $1,500,000 — an enormous sum for that day — equivalent, probably, to twenty times the purchasing power of today's dollar, or $30,000,000.

It will be recalled that his nephew, Samuel, who had been fatally injured the previous Christmas Eve in a carriage accident, and was considered a most substantial and successful financier, had left $500,000.

It was obvious, therefor, that Elisha's widow and six children would all be handsomely provided for, assuming that he slighted none of them in his will, which, from all indications, he apparently did not.

Back in Washington, at some time in the long summer or fall, W. W. Corcoran decided to retire from business. He might have been influenced by Elisha's death, or by the sudden illness at about the same time of his old friend, George Peabody, in London.

CHAPTER 16

Peabody's illness was variously described as gout, rheumatism, and serious intestinal disorders. In any case, his indisposition was genuine enough for the old tycoon to issue a formal denial, fearful that news of his health might affect the standing of his firm.

"We are asked to say", the *New York Times* reported, "that Duncan, Sherman and Company have received a letter written by George Peabody himself saying he is not in ill-health. Ogden Haggarty came over on the *Artic* and states he left Mr. Peabody in perfect health."[2]

Corcoran might have seen a warning in some of this, or he might have been uncommonly inconvenienced by the long absence of Elisha, Jr. It is also possible to conclude he was influenced by all of these factors, along with the new development of George Riggs's imminent inheritance which placed him in a position to work out a satisfactory deal for the firm, and, at the same time, to gratify the fond wishes of his wife and family, and probably himself, to return permanently to the capital.

Our first formal word of Mr. Corcoran's decision is contained (ironically enough) in a letter from George Peabody to him dated six months later, January 13, 1854. In alluding to his illness, Peabody states:

> *My illness last summer, and consequent accumulation of correspondence and business, has kept me constantly engaged to bring [it] up.*
>
> *My health, I am happy to say, seems quite restored, and I feel as well as I have done for many years; but experience warns me to be cautions, and to avoid those causes which have heretofore affected my constitution, and I shall try to do so.*

Mr. Peabody then reports:

> *I find your friend, Mr. Buchanan, a very agreeable companion and ... he seems greatly attached to you, and regrets that you have made up your mind to leave business ... as he thinks as I think, that you should not break up a house, the establishment of which has done you so much honor.*
>
> *It is true you don't want more money; but if you retire, I think you will sigh for that particular*

> occupation and excitement which both you and myself have been accustomed to all our business lives. Why, if no other way, do you not continie the house, and remain a limited partner, putting in half a million capital?.

Mr. Peabody goes on to comment:

> I suppose you will not give up your splendid entertaining business. By the by, the Archdeacon of Middlesex was greatly pleased with your attention ...I enclose a note to me from him, and also from his talented sister.

The letter from the Archdeacon's sister, Catharine Sinclair, contains the following:

> Hopetoun House,
> South Queensferry, N.B.
>
> Dear Sir:
> Allow me to trouble you with a single line to mention how much my brother has been benefitted by the friendly introduction with which you favored him in America, where he says that his tour has been beyond measure delightful, and the scenery far exceeded his utmost anticipations. He writes to me, in a letter received this morning from New York and dated 3rd October, 'Mr. Peabody had given me an introduction to Mr. Corcoran, and at his house I had the grandest dinner I ever partook of on either side of the Atlantic. He has a fine gallery of pictures, the original Greek Slave, etc....

Catharine Sinclair's reference to her brother's letter of October 3, 1853, is our first definite confirmation that Mr. Corcoran now has the Greek Slave in his collection of fine arts. So perhaps the statue was sent to him after creating a sensation at the Great New York World's Fair of 1853.

In the files of Riggs Bank the first news of Corcoran's impending retirement is contained in an ordinary correspondent letter dated March 15, 1854, from E. S. Whalen & Co., Philadelphia, in which the opening sentence reads: "We have received your circular letter of the 1st Inst. apprising us of your intention of closing your business on the 1st April next."

CHAPTER 16

There must have been many such acknowledgments of the circular letter sent out to all correspondents and clients, but only one other acknowledgment remains in its entirety. And that, we have discovered, on making another belated and careful examination, contains a wealth of contemporary history and, to our amazement, reopens completely our speculations on Elisha, Jr.'s trek to the Pacific with the Benton-Beale expedition.

This letter, which is from the Banking House of James King, of William, San Francisco, dated April 29, 1854, reads as follows:

> Messrs. Corcoran & Riggs,
> Washington, D.C.
> Dear Sirs:
>
> I have received your favor of 18th March. The draft for $100 is paid and at your debit. Referring to my request of 1 April, in which I allude to a draft for $500 not yet presented, I have now to request that in case you have not forwarded any coupons or other collections, you will please deposit with Messrs. Riggs & Co. [the new name of the firm] any balance to my credit with you to the end that our old a/c be finally closed. After which I will remit for deposit for any collections you may hereafter forward me.
>
> I trust I shall hereafter have the pleasure of hearing from you frequently, but as you have now published your dissolution it would seem as though this were the last business letter I shall address you and with this feeling I beg to return you my warmest thanks for the many favors received from you and which by no means have stopped short at any point bounded by the courtesies of business correspondence, but have extended to personal favors that I had no right to expect.
>
> Most sincerely wishing that the full enjoyment of your ample fortune may equal your success in business,
>
> > I remain,
> > Very truly & very
> > respectfully, Yours,
> > James King of W

However, it was the footnote of this letter which startled us into a complete reappraisal of Elisha's trip of the previous year and our conclusions with regard to it.

> My family leave on Monday the 1st June on a visit to the District. One of my clerks accompanies them. Fremont is here, but I have not called on him. I am expecting your Mr. Riggs shortly, & will do nothing further until I see him. I incline to the opinion the S.C. [Supreme Court] of the U. S. will confirm the Mariposa.

Now, "your Mr. Riggs" is obviously Elisha, Jr., since the letter is addressed to Corcoran & Riggs. So here we find our young worldly aristocrat headed for the second time toward California, and probably traveling as James King of William had — via the Isthmus of Panama.

King, a native of Georgetown, had gone West for his health in 1848 and embarked from New York for the West Coast via Panama, hoping also to meet an older brother who had been a member of the famous Fremont expedition of 1846.

That expedition, with Kit Carson as guide, played a part in bringing California into the Union after war broke out with Mexico. James C. Fremont appears to have been operating as a sort of "one-man CIA", with secret orders and finances from the government and President Polk. He was later the temporary governor of California and one of its first two senators.

Fremont was a customer of Corcoran & Riggs and the bank possesses a letter from him written from St. Louis, Missouri, on June 3, 1845, when he was outfitting his expedition:

> Messrs Corcoran & Riggs,
> Gentlemen:
>   I have this day drawn on you for the sum of six thousand dollars in favor of Messrs. H. V. A. Campbell & Co., of Philadelphia, and I will beg of you the favor to have the draft paid at that city.
>
>   Very respectfully,
>   Your Obdt. Servt.,
>   J. C. Fremont.

Elisha, Jr.'s younger brother, aged sixteen, might have been seeking Indian weapons and costumes on the Benton-Beale expedition, but Elisha himself might have been on the trail of gold. Either for Corcoran, the firm or himself, he was apparently headed for San Francisco with that ill-fated expedition the year before.

We recall starkly now, the author of *Railroad to the Pacific* telling of the "upsetting of a canoe and the loss of weapons and supplies which forced Beale's party to hurry toward Los Angeles, and thus their friends from San Francisco who designed to meet them at Walker's Pass, were disappointed"

Evidently, "their friends from San Francisco" meant probably James King of William and Fremont, who hoped to meet and escort Elisha, Jr. or perhaps the whole Benton-Beale party, back to San Francisco.

Fremont was very much involved in the California "gold-rush" scene. The "Mariposa" mentioned in James King of William's footnote, was his 44,000-acre Rancho de las Mariposas (ranch of the butterflies) in the San Joaquin Valley he had bought in 1847 for $3,000. Discovery of gold the next year in the foothills to the east of his property put Fremont in line to become a rich man. "From a place within pistol shot of his ranch, in 1851, $200,000 of gold had been taken in four month".[3] And as suggested by the astute Mr. King, the Supreme Court soon confirmed his disputed ownership of the property.

But Fremont was in debt by reason of the long, drawn-out litigation and the conversion of his ranch to mining purposes. In April of 1852, when Fremont and his wife, Jesse (she was the daughter of Senator Thomas Hart Benton of Missouri) were in London trying to raise funds for his Mariposa venture, he was ignominiously thrown in prison by some of his creditors, whereupon, he hastily called Mr. Peabody to bail him out. Undoubtedly he had carried an introduction from Corcoran & Riggs to his benefactor.[4]

There seems every liklihood that Elisha, Jr. had intended to visit San Francisco the previous year to acquire a first hand knowledge of the Mariposa situation for Corcoran or the firm or possibly even for George Peabody. But on this second occasion he arrived too late.

"In 1854, "says one authority, "the Great Bonanza suddenly slackened. Fortunes large and small collapsed. Disillusioned miners drifted up and down the State. Added to their numbers were the wagon trains and boatloads of new immigrants arriving to homestead Uncle Sam's new fertile acres."[5]

The results, or even the purpose, of Elisha's visit are conjectural. No evidence exists that he or Corcoran or Peabody ever made any loans or investments in the Mariposa venture. The signs of imminent collapse were overwhelming. And despite Fremont's expensive investment in stamp mills, tunnels, and shafts, it soon became painfully clear that the ore from the tantalizingly close gold-bearing foothills, did not extend below his ranch.

This was a bitter financial tragedy for the Great Pathfinder. Intrepid soldier, leader, explorer and discoverer, personally bold and brave, he was totally lacking in business acumen. Eventually, he was to say, "When I came to California I hadn't a cent. Now I owe two million dollars."

Eventually, we were to understand the reason for the laying aside and preservation of the James King of William letter so long ago. That was the subsequent tragic history of King himself. This had all the trappings of a genuine westerner, except that the good guy was done in by the bad guys, albeit through his courage and self sacrifice, justice eventually prevailed.

King seems to have lost his own fortune and banking business shortly after Elisha's arrival, when "he entrusted large sums to an agent for the purchase of gold which, without King's authorization, the agent had used to purchase stock in a mining venture. The investment was disastrous and King sacrificed his personal fortune to make good the deficits of his bank."[6]

In 1855, he returned to Journalism, having worked as a youth on the Washington *Globe*. With one C. O. Geberding as a partner, he founded the San Francisco *Daily Evening Bulletin*, of which he became editor and publisher. He began immediately to expose and condemn lawlessness and civic corruption. His paper expanded rapidly and in six months the daily edition had grown to the unexampled circulation of 7,000.

He singled out an individual named Cora, accused of the murder of Federal Marshal Richardson. A corrupt city official, James P. Casey, defended Cora and King later exposed

> Great Salt Lake City
> Augt. 9th 1864
>
> Messrs Riggs & Co.
> Bankers, New York
> Gentlemen:
>
> I herewith send you my draft no. 497, for £850.0.0, upon D. H. Wells, my Agent, Liverpool, which please sell and place to my credit.
>
> I have this day drawn upon you my draft no. 498, for $10,000 00/100 in U.S. Currency, favor of McCann and Metcalf, which please honor on presentation.
>
> Respectfully Yours,
>
> Brigham Young

Above, a letter to Riggs & Co., from Brigham Young, dated August 9, 1864. *Below,* the signature of Sam Houston, reproduced in actual size. Letter closes with, "Thine Truly".

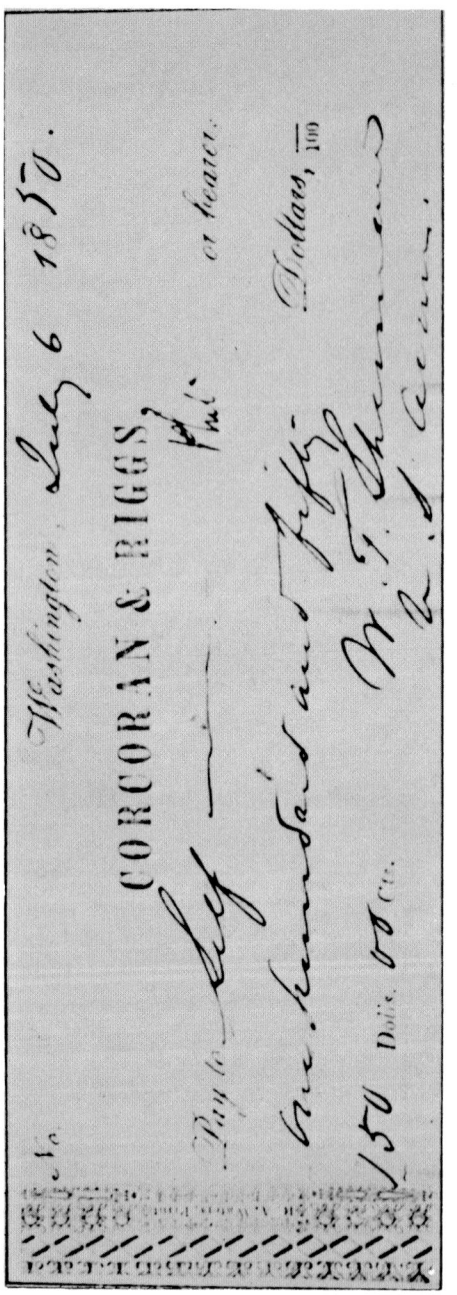

Check of William Tecumseh Sherman on Corcoran & Riggs, drawn shortly after his marriage.

Lincoln's check payable to "William", with no last name, which might have been to his son Willie who died in the White House.

heck payable to Dr. Gurley, pastor of New
ork Avenue Presbyterian Church.

One of the President's earlier checks payable to "Mr. Johns (a sick Man)" for three dollars.

Lincoln's most famous check payable to "Colored man, with one leg".

Ole Bull. From a Daguerreotype taken in 1852.

Christmas card showing old Riggs & Co. Building and stating it was "The first Home of the Armed Forces Institute of Pathology, 1862-64". This card sent out by the Institute in 1949, was adapted from a Riggs National Bank Christmas card.

The First Home of The Armed Forces Institute of Pathology, 1862-64
Riggs Bank Building, 1503 Pennsylvania Ave. N.W.
Washington, D.C.

Christmas Greetings

Left, view of the ARCTIC leaving her pier at the foot of Canal Street, New York. Captain Luce is one of two figures on top of starboard paddle box. From woodcut in Harper's New Monthly Magazine, June, 1852., U.S. Library of Congress. *Below*, Home of Elisha Riggs, Jr., located on what is now the corner of The Army & Navy Club . Darker structure beside it on Eye Street was the mansion of George W. Riggs, Jr. That site is now covered by the Cafritz Building.

wrason Riggs and his third wife, Mary Turpin Bright.

Above, the entrance foyer of the Riggs Mansion at 1617 Eye Street, NW *Right*, Photograph of George W. Riggs, Jr., from the files of Mount Vernon Ladies Association

Library in The Riggs house showing the Emperors Bowl at right and the desk, center, on which the Alaska Papers were signed.

The Lincoln Monument towers precariously above the steps of City Hall. This building is now the Superior Court of the District of Columbia at 451 D Street, Northwest. The statue has been lowered to a small pedestal on approximately the same site.

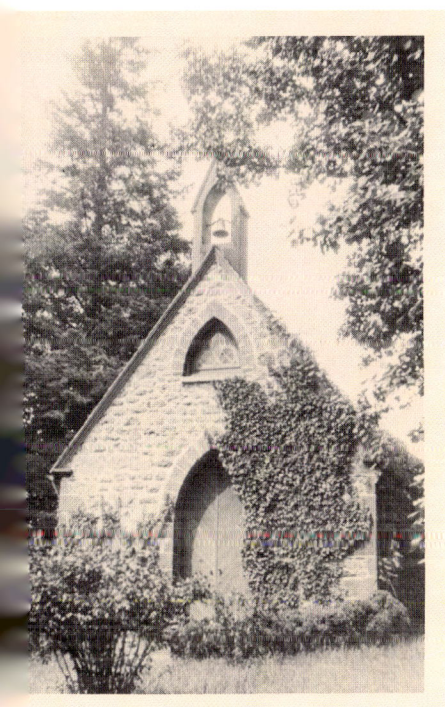

Chapel of Saint Cecelia, Green Hill.

William W. Corcoran
(c. 1868)
Courtesy Columbia Historical Society

CHAPTER 16

him as a former inmate of Sing Sing. And thus the die was cast. Casey waylaid King on his way home from work and mortally wounded him.

As 2,600 vigilantes mobilized and took Casey and gambler Cora from jail, King lingered for five days. "Two days later, while King's two-mile funeral procession was wending to Lone Mountain, Casey and Cora, quickly tried and convicted, were hanged at Fort Vigilance. A plaque now marks the site on Sacramento Street between Davis and Front."[7]

And so did James King of William, a native son of Georgetown, D. C., sacrifice his life and inspire the very crystalization and real beginning of law and order in the Golden State.

Chapter Notes

[1] Alexander Crosby Brown, *Women and Children Last*, 1961.
[2] *George Peabody, A Biography*, Franklin Parker. p. 65. Vanderbilt University Press, 1971.
[3] *California, The American Guide Book Series.*
[4] *George Peabody, A Biography*, pp. 61-62.
[5] *California, American Guide Book Series.*
[6] *The Call Bulletin*, San Francisco, Letter E. D. Coblentz, Feb. 7, 1951.
[7] *Ibid.*

Chapter 17

We have noted that the firm of Riggs & Co. succeeded that of Corcoran & Riggs on April 1, 1854. We have no direct accounts of the return of George Riggs and family to Washington from New York, but we can be sure that whenever the move, or moves, occurred, they were joyous ones. George and Janet were natives of the District (Janet was born in Newark but brought to Georgetown at age two). Their seven children, five daughters and two sons, ranging in age from thirteen to a few months, had all been born there except the baby. They were a happy young Washington-oriented family.

George Riggs at forty-one, was relieved to have the direction of his life and career resolved and must have moved into Corcoran's office in architect George Hadfield's elegant structure (which he himself had helped to purchase in 1845) with a great deal of satisfaction and contentment. Destiny had finally brought him securely to anchor in the Nation's capital.

Through a coincidence, the 1855 directory of Washington and Georgetown, one of the most comprehensive and unique volumes on the city ever published, fills us in on the family's return and the makeup of the new firm.

This book is entitled *Ten Eyck's Washington and Georgetown Directory* . . . compiled and published by L. Ten Eyck, Contractor for Numbering the cities of Washington and Georgetown.

Now, just what was meant by "numbering the cities of Washington and Georgetown?" Well, although we of this age would never guess it, the houses in Washington and Georgetown had never had any street addresses before 1854. Everyone knew where the houses were and in previous directories they had been referred to by their location on their street. For example, George Riggs first lived on New York Avenue in a house described as, "between 13th and 14th, south side, nearer 14th." Corcoran's first house on H Street was described as "north side of H Street, between Vermont Ave and 15th, near center of block." But finally the city fathers had decided the towns were growing up and needed street addresses. Under date of May 18, 1854, they promulgated the necessary ordinances for that purpose. That for Washington read as follows:

Numbering Houses.

1. The dwelling houses, shops, stores, and all places of business fronting on the streets of the city of Washington shall be numbered after the manner hereinafter designated by this Act.

The order of arrangement of said numbering shall be as follows, viz; the western extremity of each street on the boundary of the city (Rock Creek) shall be the starting point for numbering the streets running easterly; and the northern extremity of each street on the boundary line of the same (the Boundary, long known as Georgetown — Bladensburg Road, now Florida Avenue) for numbering from their northern extremity. Every street or avenue shall be numbered by itself, and on each side of the same .. thus placing the odd numbers on one side (right) and the even on the other (left), and allowing a number for every twenty-two feet . . . in all cases of open spaces. . . .

2. The smallest number permitted to designate any building . . . shall be a properly painted figure on a tin plate of a different color, of not less than

CHAPTER 17

> *two-and-a-half inches square, the price of which to be paid by the householder or owners in all cases . . . Provided, Nothing in this act shall . . prevent any owner or occupant . . . to procure at his own expense, larger or more desirable plates or numbers.*
>
> *Those persons refusing to designate their houses by numbers . . . after they have been notified of the proper number . . . for four days thereafter, shall have a number furnished by the city at their expense to be levied . . together with the penalty of five dollars . . to be collected as other penalties.*
> Act of May 18, 1854.

The remarkable Mr. Ten Eyck precedes his directory listings with a Preface, so precise and interesting as to seem worthy of reproduction in full.

> PREFACE
>
> Having numbered the cities of Washington and Georgetown, under contracts with the corporate authorities, and being compelled to visit every house in these cities for the purpose of designating and placing the numbers thereon — and believing a complete Directory of the Cities are universally needed, I have endeavored to present to the citizens one of the most complete works of the kind, in every respect, that has ever been published in this city. It will contain more than double the number of names than any similar work ever published in Washington.
>
> My thanks are due to the officers of the General Government, and to the citizens generally, for the courteous manner they treated my agents, and the promptness manifested in giving them the information they desired in the discharge of their duty.
>
> Being fully aware that it is impossible to get up a work of this character without misspelling some of the names — and as a part of this work was done during the summer months when a portion of our citizens were absent from the city, and my agents had to rely on those who were left in charge of the property for their information they required — but we have endeavored, and I trust succeeded, in

making this book as complete as a work of this kind can be by publishing an ADDENDA containing the names omitted and a correction of the errors in the names misspelled, with changes, removals, etc., to this date.
January 1, 1855.

This *Addenda* immediately proved its importance to us. In one of his letters, Franz von Recum had said that with the help of John Beverly Riggs he had learned that "George W. Riggs lived at 218 Eye Street when he returned to Washington (1855 directory)." That address on Eye Street was just off Pennsylvania Avenue between 20th and 19th streets, on the north side. In the block to the west, fronting on Pennsylvania Avenue, is the old James Monroe house, now the proud home of the Arts Club of Washington. We puzzled about the location as being somewhat distant from the bank, although old plats showed two large houses in the center of the block having stables in the rear, which might have been suitable for the family. But the listing itself was reported as "Riggs, ---, banker, 218 Eye." It had seemed strange indeed that a well-known banker should be so listed and we began to wonder about the source of the information. Obviously it had not come from any member of the family or the firm.

Now, suddenly, leafing through the *Addenda* of the 1855 directory, courtesy of one of the astute Curators of the Columbia Historical Society, we came across a corrected listing for Mr. Riggs. It read, "Riggs, George, banker, 273 Vermont Avenue," and we had a totally different situation.

That address was on the west side of Vermont Avenue between H and Eye streets, near the center of the block, just above Lafayette Square and around the corner from the Clarke-Ashburton house where the family had lived after selling Corn Rigs. (The site is now covered by the Veterans Administration.) Furthermore, the lots on which George Riggs would soon build his splendid new home on Eye Street, next door to Elisha, Jr., were also "right around the corner," where he could conveniently scrutinize the progress of construction.

But what of 218 Eye Street? Perhaps the family had lived there briefly after their return, or had indicated an interest in the property, or the family had been away on vacation when

CHAPTER 17

the agent sought information. In any case, the *Addenda* had brought the matter nicely into perspective.

But the 1855 directory did much more. It gave us the original address of the firm on President's Square — No. 32.

This stretch of the avenue from 15th to 17th streets had been known familiarly as President's Square for many years (the term had first appeared in the original L'Enfant Plan for the city) and it continued to be so known and listed for some years following the Civil War. However, many historians have overlooked that fact, and simply referred to the famous three blocks by their much later designation as a part of Pennsylvania Avenue.[1]

Many great things had happened at 32 President's Square before the number went up and many more would happen after it was in place. It was an address of destiny in the "city of magnificent distances" which was rapidly growing into its role as the capital of one of the future great nations of the world.

Our story continues henceforth behind a proud plaque of "not less than two-and-a-half inches square" . . . . but . . "larger and more desirable at owner's expense" . . . and reading — No. 32.

The Riggs Family of Maryland states that when "George Riggs . . . returned to the firm now named, Riggs & Co., Elisha, Jr. remained the junior partner, [but] . . . Elisha, Jr. later withdrew from the firm and it continued thereafter under the sole control of George W. Riggs." Evidence furnished in the 1855 directory appears to refute this contention. Near the latter part of the book, in a section on banks which preceded a listing of government offices, we discovered the following:

Banking House of Riggs & Co.

Geo. W. Riggs, Jr.
John G. Clarke, Teller
Charles H. James
Bookkeeper

A. T. Kicckhoefer
Wm. C. Corcoran,
Collection Clerk
C. L. Chapman
Runner

Thomas Hyde, Runner

167

We know that Elisha, Jr. was absent when the firm started in business and, for some time thereafter, while visiting San Francisco and enroute home. We also know the information for the directory was gathered in the early and late summer of 1854. Elisha, Jr. is listed in the directory at his home, 278 Eye Street, but not otherwise. A. T. Kieckhoever, who was the "active, correct man" sent to the firm by Elisha, Sr. from New York in 1848, had apparently been taken in by George Riggs as a partner, as shown by his listing to the right of Riggs's name at the top of the writeup for the firm. He is also listed under his home address at 319 G north, (between 13th and 12th, south side). Thus, for whatever reasons, Elisha, Jr. seems not to have joined his half-brother in the firm.

Of the other names in the bank listing, only the last, Thomas Hyde, is known to us as the son of Anthony Hyde, Corcoran's longtime secretary and accountant. We assume the Wm. C. Corcoran shown was a nephew of W. W. Corcoran, but he was evidently with the firm only briefly. Thomas Hyde eventually became a partner in the firm and a vice president of Riggs National Bank.

There was one other important partner in Riggs & Company, and that was John Elliott, his father's close friend and associate, who became manager of the New York branch George Riggs had established in Wall Street for the numerous and distinguished clients of his late father. It was located at No. 56, situated on the north side of Wall Street between William and Pearl Streets, and faced Hanover which cuts into the south side of Wall Street at that point. It was only a short distance eastward of the old Sub-Treasury Building where George Washington accepted his commission as Commander of the Revolutionary Armies.

Diagonally across the street was the banking house of Brown Brothers Company at 59 Wall Street, and the two families were close friends. The youngest of the four brothers, we have pointed out, was president of the Collins Line and it may have been the interest of the Brown Brothers as backers of Collins's venture that led Elisha to begin his fateful association with the company.

This cordial and close family relationship would bring the two families into mutual grief and suffering in the dire days

CHAPTER 17

toward the close of the otherwise happy and promising year of 1854.

The tragedy began to unfold in October's bright blue weather.

George W. Riggs, like most substantial and well-informed citizens probably read the newspaper, *The National Intelligencer*, regularly.

He must have been made uncomfortable by the issue of October 6, 1854, where under Telegraphic Correspondence appeared the following:

> *New York, Oct. 5. We are still without tidings of the Artic, and some fears are beginning to be entertained. She is thought to have about 200 passengers on board. We have nothing from Halifax since Thursday, and there was a violent gale on the coast that night.*

Now George Riggs was close enough to the Brown and Collins families and to the general operations of the Collins Line itself, to have known that the *Artic* was overdue. But to have seen the fact published in the *Intelligencer* must have caused him additional uneasiness and a growing sense of apprehension. His New York partner, John Elliott, must have sent him word received from the Brown Brothers across Wall Street that young James Brown's family had been scheduled to return from Europe in the *Artic*, as also the family of Mr. Collins. Financial considerations concerning his father's estate and the prosperity of the line were one thing; the even remote possibility of loss of the two families was staggering.

The near panic in Washington and New York must have been amplified by the article of October 9 in the *Intelligencer* headlined "The Missing Steamer *Artic*."

> *The steamer Canada brings intelligence that the steamer Artic sailed from Liverpool on the 20th of September, her regular day, and is accordingly now nineteen days out. (Since the Arctic's usual crossing time was nine days, this meant she was then ten days overdue.) No one, however, yet despairs of her safety, the New York Courier says.*

> There can be no doubt that some derangement of the machinery must be the occasion of such an unusual delay. She has on board a large number of passengers including Mr. Collins's family; but those who have friends on board should not permit their minds to be disturbed by any apprehension as to the entire safety of the vessel and her freight. There would be no uneasiness in regard to a packetship sixteen [sic] days out (mariners preferred the expression "out" instead of "overdue"), and it must be remembered that while the Arctic is stronger than any packetship [sailing ship], the failure of a single piece of metal would reduce her powers of locomotion below those of an ordinary sailing vessel.
> Another editor remarks that the Arctic is so strongly constructed as to defy any tempest ever seen in the North Atlantic, while her safeguards against fire are perfect, and danger from icebergs is unknown at this season.
> The Atlantic was once twenty-eight days without being heard from owing to the breaking of her machineryl [This was the burning out of a bearing, after which the Atlantic returned to Liverpool under sail.]

But all these speculations and reassurances were swept away on October 12th when a three-column *Intelligencer* article reported a few survivors had reached port and disclosed that the *Arctic* was in collision with another vessel and sank with heavy loss of life.

The record of this grim tragedy was not set straight for more than a century when finally, in 1961, a dedicated descendant of the Brown family published the full story under the shameful but appropriate title, *Women and Children Last*.

As indicated by this carefully researched volume, the *Artic* cast off her mooring lines at precisely noon on Wednesday, September 20, 1854, and sailed out of Liverpool harbor for New York. By a coincidence, that date was also the twenty-first birthday of James Brown's favorite daughter, Millie. Her eldest brother, Bill, recently made a partner in Brown Brothers, was also aboard with his pert French wife and their small daughter, not quite two. Millie's older sister, Grace, was also in the party with her husband, George Allen, an associate in the firm that had built the *Arctic's* engines. And with them was their little son, (they had previously lost two children in infancy) who was one week shy of his first birthday, which the family planned to celebrate on September 27th. Both the Brown children were accompanied by their nurses.

The Collins family, too, were looking forward eagerly to getting home to Larchmont. Their group included Mrs. Collins and two of the Collins children, Mary Ann, aged nineteen, and named for her mother, and Henry, aged fifteen. Mrs. Collins's brother, a New York attorney, and his wife also accompanied them.

The ship was crowded with 282 passengers, "including a French duke with entourage, a learned professor or two, and a few New York millionaires, and other assorted passengers of note." The *Arctic*, a 260-foot side-wheel steamer, was one of the queens of the transtlantic fleets of her day. She had already set a record for the fastest west-east crossing, averaging more than nine knots, and she "commanded the elite of transoceanic travelers."

Her seaboard routine revolved around the lavish schedule of meals: breakfast at eight o'clock, lunch at noon, dinner, very sumptuously at half-past three, tea at seven, and final supper at ten o'clock. A special attraction was the "patient Alderney cow 'Bossie' in her stall on deck. She and her sisters were carried back and forth across the Atlantic to provide milk for youngsters on board."[6]

The *Arctic* was commanded by her veteran skipper, forty-nine-year-old Capt. James C. Luce, who had been aboard her since she entered service in 1850.

Her return trip was uneventful until her seventh day, Wednesday, September 27, the birthday of the little Brown grandson. The weather that morning had been foggy, opening occasionally for visibility of half to three-quarters of a mile, but closing in suddenly for moments of very dense fog. The ship was running at full speed with two lookouts on the forecastle head and an officer at the command post which was on one or the other of the huge, half-moon-shaped paddle boxes covering the revolving side-wheels. Despite the weather, the skipper had not come topside.

The *Arctic* had not yet been equipped with the new-fangled steam whistle, but when occasions warranted, in working up a narrow channel or congested harbor, a sailor was stationed on the bow to toot on a tin horn. But on this day she was running at top speed (speed seemed to be a major consideration of the Collins Line) with no alarm bell, whistle or other signal being sounded, as she sped across a supposedly empty ocean.

And then, of course, the unexpected happened. Out of the fog emerged the dark shape of a smaller steamer at an acute angle off the starboard bow. "Steamer ahead," came the chilling cry from the lookouts, followed by "hard a-starboard" and, finally, "stop" from the command post. But the collision was inevitable. The bow of the smaller vessel rammed the starboard side of the *Arctic* near the bow, after which she caromed off the paddle guard, and passed astern. To those on the deck of the *Arctic* the smaller vessel's bow appeared completely shattered and exposed.

The first reaction of Capt. Luce was to put a boat over to pick up survivors of the smaller vessel he presumed to be sinking. A second boat was being lowered when the Captain received a stunningly revised damage report indicating that his own ship was leaking "fearfully." She was also settling slightly by the starboard head. "Hoist up that boat", the Captain shouted, as all available passengers were ordered to the port quarterdeck and the anchor chains and all other heavy objects on the bow were jettisoned in an attempt to elevate the bow.

Then, making an irreversible decision, the skipper called for full speed in a desperate attempt to reach the coast of Newfoundaland believed to be forty or fifty miles distant. He thus abandoned the first of his six lifeboats (capacity thirty persons) leaving behind his capable first officer, the chief boatswain's mate, and five of his best seamen.

Very soon it became obvious that the *Arctic* would not proceed very far. Her pumps were working furiously, but the ship was still settling and the side wheels were slowing perceptibly.

Although there was no way the fact could have been made known to Capt. Luce, the small ship with which the *Arctic* had collided was the modern, 152-foot, stern-propelled and bark rigged, *Vesta*, launched the year before at Nantes, and whose hull was constructed entirely of thick iron plates and fashioned into three water-tight compartments. As later revealed,

CHAPTER 17

her remaining two compartments held securely and she made port safely. The sad conclusion is inevitable that she might have taken off some of the *Arctic's* passengers.

By contrast, although the much larger *Arctic* had been hailed as having the latest and best of ship construction (she had been certified at her East River launching in October, 1850, by none other than the illustrious Commodore Perry, U.S.N. as "of first class, and acceptable to the terms of the Navy contract"), she had a wooden hull, lined at the bottom with copper sheathing, but "she was as open from stem to stern as a canoe."[3]

Once the iron prow of the *Vesta* penetrated the *Arctic's* hull below the water line, accompanied, as it turned out, by jagged portions of her broken-off iron anchor stock, the *Arctic* was doomed. And all activity aboard the vessel soon confirmed that fact.

Practically stopped, she lowered a second boat containing twenty-seven or twenty-eight passengers with a quartermaster in charge, and the boat quickly fell astern and was never heard from again.

A dozen women and four or five male passengers had been embarked in the third boat, when a horde of firemen jumped aboard and so overloaded the craft that one of the falls parted, dropping the boat down perpendicularly and spilling its screaming occupants into the sea.

Mutiny is defined in *Webster's New World Dictionary* as "a revolt against constituted authority - especially of soldiers or sailors against their officers." Captain Luce now had a mutiny on his hands. He threatened and shouted himself hoarse eventually being barely able to make himself heard. He sorely missed the services of his efficient first officer whom the crew was accustomed to obeying.

On the other side, another partially filled boat had been launched when crewmen and male passengers started jumping in wholesale numbers from the deck and either slammed into it or splashed into the water and were mostly lost.

The skipper had desperately conferred with his second mate, Baalham, indicating that he, himself, would stay with the ship but he wanted him to launch the fifth boat and bring it around under the stern to take off the women and children of the Collins and Brown parties. With Baalham and two or three seamen the falls were cast off, dropping the boat precipitously with a resounding splash, but it had hardly struck the water and begun to move, before a dozen frantic males hurled themselves toward it from the railing twenty feet above, many of them again landing in the water. But officer Baalham defied his skipper's orders to stay close astern, claiming lamely at a later hearing he was afraid the boat would be swamped.

With the *Arctic* now wallowing helplessly, her engines stopped, panicky efforts were made by the Captain to hold the last boat for women and children. He waited as long as he could, but, when it was finally launched, none came — they had been brutally thrust aside by able-bodied coal-heavers, firemen, waiters, and sailors who piled into it helter-skelter.

And with the last boat gone there were still more than 200 passengers aboard. Millie Brown had proved "a tower of strength," leading the singing of familiar hymns. Her brother-in-law, George Allen, saw to it that all had life preservers. On the forward deck, apprentice seaman, Stewart Holland, was faithfully firing a signal gun at intervals of one minute in the forlorn hope that someone out there in the fog might hear it and come to the resuce. He was the son of the Assistant U. S. Senate Sargeant-at-arms, Isaac Holland, and had signed on for one trip as an adventure.

The skipper bade farewell to the sobbing passengers and climbed the catwalk to the top of the paddle box that served as his bridge, taking with him his crippled 11-year-old son who had been brought on the trip with the hope it might do him some good. The bearing of those aboard throughout their long ordeal had been admirable, but they were now reduced to a tearful, stunned and despairing acceptance of the inevitable. During the last minutes the ship was afloat, George Allen was holding his year-old son in his arms, when his wife, Grace, reached for the baby herself.

At a quarter to five, four and one-half hours from the time of the collision, the *Arctic*'s stern dipped under — the bow rose in the air and, stern-first, she began her final plunge.

One survivor who was clinging to a piece of wreckage nearby, reported that at the last moment when air from below decks was forced through the smokestack, there was created an eerie and almost human-sounding wail that mingled with the cries of the doomed.

CHAPTER 17

Capt. Luce was one of the survivors. He had surfaced from an almost fatal immersion when the ship sank and found himself beside one of the upside down paddle boxes, from which he was later rescued by a passing vessel. In a report he later prepared, he denounced the conduct of his men as "most infamous." In his opinion, two-thirds of those on board could have been saved had he been able to control them. George Allen, also finally surfacing from the interminable plunge, crawled aboard some wreckage and was spotted and picked up.

Of the 153 crewmen aboard, 92 were lost and 61 survived. Of the 282 passengers, 258 were lost and 24 survived — with not one woman or child among the survivors. The American Merchant Marine, seemingly so near its pinnacle, had suffered one of its blackest moments — "a bitter descent from Olympus," as characterized by author, Alexander Crosby Brown.

An effort was made to raise funds for a memorial to Stewart Holland and an account for that purpose was opened at Riggs & Co., but nothing came of it. Americans, generally, while admiring the brave conduct of the young man, did not wish to perpetuate in any form the horror of the *Arctic*. They even appeared relieved when the overwhelming events of the Civil War pushed it for the balance of their lives into the forgotten background of history.

The story is told that the Brown family gathered to hear George Allen's story and thereafter invoked a rule of silence toward the tragedy.

James Brown erected in beautiful Greenwood Cemetery over in Brooklyn a soaring, many-faceted monument to the six members of his family lost in the sinking — one son, two daughters, one daughter-in-law, and two grandchildren.

Chapter Notes

[1] References to President's Square in the *Washington and Georgetown City Directories:*

1855
Riggs & Co., bankers, 32 President's Square.

1860
President's Square - from 15th to 17th west, on Pennsylvania Avenue.

1867
Madison Pl. (or 15½ and 16½ west), on both sides Lafayette sq, from President's sq. to H North.

President's Square - from 15th to 17th west, on Pennsylvania Avenue.

[2] The three quotations in the foregoing two paragraphs are from pages 35, 11 and 39 of the fascinating epic by Alexander Crosby Brown, *Women and Children Last*, S. P. Putnams' Sons, New York 1961.

[3] *Ibid.*, p. 49.

Chapter 18

The *Arctic* disaster was not the end of the Collins Line, but it was most certainly the beginning of the end.

A wave of revulsion and anger had swept through Congress and the nation as the harrowing details of the shipwreck emerged. New York City was draped in mourning for days. Ministers made the *Arctic* the subject of impassioned sermons. Strong sentiment in Congress to revoke the subsidy was only blocked by a natural sympathy for the cruel loss of life suffered by the families of top management. But the position of the line's enemies in Congress had been irretrievably strengthened.

Desperate efforts were made to meet the required schedule of sailings with the three remaining vessels, but some dates were missed and the number of passengers declined drastically. Company officials clung to the vague hope that things would improve when the much larger *Adriatic* was launched later in 1855.

George W. Riggs, as executor of Elisha's estate, had always taken a conservative and pessimistic view of the value of his father's enormous investment in the line. But so long as they continued to operate he had to hold the estate open.

The family's attention was diverted temporarily by the death of Janet's mother on January 19, 1855. This doughty Irish lady, Matilda Cecilia (Dowdall) Shedden, born in County Meath, Ireland, was in her seventy-fourth year. She succumbed to what was described on her death certificate as "senile debility" and was buried in the Riggs family plot in Rock Creek cemetery.

Elisha, Jr. was soon to make some news of his own when on June 25, 1855, he purchased what was known as the Washington house on the Georgetown Heights. This old mansion with its beautiful parklike grounds had been the home of Hon. George Corbin Washington, the great nephew of the first President, who had served with Romulus Riggs during the War of 1812 on the board of the Farmers and Mechanics Bank. The house, situated at the southeast corner of 30th and R streets is now the home of Mrs. Katharine Graham of *The Washington Post*.

The purchase price, though not shown in the transfer of title, is estimated at $8,000. A later transfer of ownership in the 1860's, following the Civil War, and after considerable inflation in prices, showed a price of $12,500.[1]

We can presume that, inasmuch as the purchase was made on June 25th, the place might originally have been intended as a summer home for Elisha, Jr. and his family. He had complained bitterly in some of his letters of the gaseous humidity of the Washington flats in summer, and brother George had already remodeled and enlarged a summer residence in Prince Georges County. This property, formerly part of the great Digges estate known as "Chillum Castle Manor," had come into the Riggs family back in 1824 when Elisha had purchased it at a mortgage sale.[2]

Nevertheless, it seems strange that Elisha, Jr., owning a spanking new residence described by one authority in late 1851, as "the most prominent — of various substantial buildings erected [in 1851]", should now feel it necessary to invest in a second house — even one located on the "Heights" of Georgetown and probably commanding at that time an unobstructed, beautiful and refreshing prospect of the unspoiled Potomac.[3]

CHAPTER 18

The suspicion exists that the two half brothers had experienced some disagreement over their father's estate or the composition of the new partnership or some other matter, that would eventually render their soon-to-be "next door" status on Eye Street uncomfortable — a circumstance that has occurred in many families.

In that connection, we might also note that the fourth and last child (a son) of Elisha, Jr. and Mary Boswell Riggs, born the preceding September of 1854 at Berkley Springs, Va., after the formation of the new Riggs & Company firm, had been named for Elisha's former partner, William Corcoran Riggs.

Meanwhile at Riggs & Company's brand new address, No. 32 President's Square, matters were proceeding smoothly. Prior to his withdrawal from the firm in 1848, George Riggs had been very close to many of the depositors, as a result of Mr. Corcoran's frequent and lengthy absences from the bank in connection with his outside activities, largely on Capitol Hill. and Elisha, Jr.'s autocratic and somewhat haughty bearing had not endeared him to the general clientele. Consequently, George Riggs had been welcomed back enthusiastically by both local and national friends as well as by those of the diplomatic corps to whom he and his family were widely known.

In early 1855, he had received a letter from the "Legation of the United States in London," in the careful, erudite script of our minister, James Buchanan, reading as follows:

> *I have this day given a check in duplicate upon you ...for $968. If I mistake not, you have more than this amount of mine on hand; but whether or not, I rely upon your friendship to pay the amount of this check.*
>
> *I would thank you to inform me of the state of my account with you*
>
> With my kindest regards...
> Yours very respectfully,
> James Buchanan.

A penciled notation on the letter in the handwriting of a bookkeeper states the balance is $1,221.61, thus leaving $254.61 remaining after payment of the check.

Mr. Riggs would soon find himself closer than ever to this distinguished Pennsylvanian who would be accorded his party's nomination for President in the summer of the following year, 1856, and soon thereafter, as the fifteenth President, would become the sixth consecutive Chief Executive to carry his account with the firm.

The reaction to the *Arctic* disaster had barely subsided, when, fourteen months later on January 23, 1856, the *Pacific* left Liverpool and was never heard from again.

Now, this could have been a blameless accident caused by freak winter weather conditions producing a huge "rogue wave" such as almost swamped the gigantic *Queen Mary* nearly a century later toward the close of World War II. But the wolves in Congress were in full cry. After a sufficient interval of silence, and following payment to the company of the marine insurance, Congress withdrew its subsidy, with the predictable result that the company was soon forced into bankruptcy. The new *Adriatic* had made one round trip half empty. When the three remaining "queens" were sold at auction to satisfy creditors, they brought the grand total of $50,000.

George Riggs could finally close the books on his father's estate by entering a final "0" for the value of his stock. And the family and the nation could get on with trying to forget the heartache of the ill-fated Collins Line and its two major catastrophes.

The wave of the future in ship propulsion, as foreseen by Elisha, was indeed steam as opposed to sail. But many years would pass, "before experience made clear that hulls similar to the old clipper ships and driven by stern propellers were necessary for seaworthiness."[6] Meanwhile many tragedies would occur such as those of the Collins Line, and some real curiosities in ship construction would be produced.

The biggest monster of all was the British ship *Great Eastern* built on the Clyde in 1851 and dubbed in its own day "an historic failure." This behemoth was 692 feet in length, had two paddle wheels with 3,411 horse power engines, a stern propeller with 4,886 horse power engines, and carried 6,500 square yards of sail set on her six masts. In the twilight of her career the huge misfit distinguished herself as the "work ship" in the successful laying of the Atlantic cable in the late 1860's.

CHAPTER 18

Personal tragedy struck the family of George and Janet Riggs again on May 20, 1856, when their first and favorite son, George Shedden, aged six years, five months, died of a rheumatic heart condition. Having a son to succeed him, as had his father and his grandfather and his uncles, had been one of George Riggs's fondest dreams. Now of his six remaining children, five were girls and his one son, Elisha Francis, second youngest in the group, was four and a half. Approaching forty-three, George Riggs was an affectionate father and family man and he adored his daughters, but Little Georgie had been something special, handsome, bright and gay, and one of his great hopes for the future. With heavy hearts, the family had made another sad pilgrimage to Rock Creek cemetery.

Perhaps on their way out of the cemetery George and Janet had paused at the grave of their old friend and neighbor, John Agg, who the year before on April 19 had died at age 75. As a longtime and faithful parishioner, he had been buried in the yard close to the old church. His stone bore the inscription "of The Vineyard" (the name of his farm) and "Evesham, England," his birthplace.

A great many gaps had appeared in their lives in the past few years — Janet's sister, his father, her mother, an old neighbor, and now a young son. Time was voracious, but they could still count their blessings.

Seeming to give credence to the possibility of a rift between the two half brothers, Elisha, Jr. and Mary moved out of their Eye Street residence on July 14, 1856 and sold it to George Riggs for $19,000. Thereafter, they made their home at the old Washington house in Georgetown.

They may have been prodded by the remarkable progress being made in the construction of George's large and elaborate new house under the supervision of the brilliant young architect, Richard Snowden Andrews (1830-1903). Andrews, a Washington native, had studied architecture and building with a prominent Baltimore firm, and later practiced there as a partner in Faxon and Andrews. Architectural opportunities in Baltimore greatly exceeded those in Washington, since the bustling port city had exploded to a population of 109,000 compared to Washington's 58,000. Several sources give the year of the construction and/or completion of George Riggs's house as 1858, but that date appears erroneous.

In an historic interview with the only two surviving granddaughters of George Riggs in January of 1949 at the Hotel Gramercy Park in New York City, these still alert ladies, Baroness Marie Ernestine Howard von Recum, 81, and her sister Lady Jessie Howard, seventy-nine, remembered emphatically that the house had been built in 1856. This fact is corroborated by the "Sessford Annals," published on January 1, 1857 in the *National Intelligencer*. This curious set of statistics was compiled annually by an employee of the Treasury Department, principally for his own satisfaction at seeing his name in print, but they also contained amazingly reliable and painstakingly gathered data on the number of new structures built during the year, streets paved, walkways laid, sewers and pipes installed, etc. In the issue of January 1, 1857, cited above, appears the statement:

> *Mr. Riggs' elegant building on I Street is nearly completed. It has a front of about 60 feet and is fitted up with all the modern improvements.*

In speaking of their grandfather's house the two granddaughters had said that "it had five bathrooms at a time when there was not a single bathroom in the White House. The bathrooms were all equipped with hot and cold running water and the walls of the house were of double thickness of imported English brick." Thus it seems apparent that George Riggs and his family occupied their new home in middle or late 1857.

As for Elisha's house, real estate records disclose that George Riggs sold it on November 2, 1857 to Eliza Stoeckl, wife of the Russian minister, Baron Edward de Stoeckl, for $20,000. It thus became the Russian legation and this marked the beginning of a long and close relationship between the two families. Down the road of history it would also bring de Stoeckl and George Riggs together as principals in a most important drama that would have immense bearing on the future of the nation.

While George Riggs had been quietly and steadily reestablishing himself in the bank and renewing old friendships and contacts, fateful events had been taking place nearby which would soon lead to another drama along the Potomac in which he would play a prominent part.

This revolved around a prominent young woman from Rosemont plantation in South Carolina — Ann Pamela Cunningham. As a young girl, she had been thrown from her horse and suffered serious spinal injuries which left her a lifelong invalid. Her life, thereafter, had been a constant search for relief from the pain caused by the accident, and she spent much time in Philadelphia under the care of a specialist, Dr. Hugh I. Hodge. A part of her journey to that city each year took her up the Potomac to Washington.

On the return portion of one such trip in 1853, after leaving Ann Pamela in Philadelphia, Mrs. Robert Cunningham went on deck as the bells of the little river steamer tolled the passing of Mount Vernon, where she had made several happy visits in her childhood. The sky was clear and the moon full and she stared in amazement and disbelief at the scene thus revealed.

Gray and ghostly on its eminence, the old mansion towered above wild gardens and overgrown thickets, its windows cracked and broken, shutters hanging askew, the once-proud portico sagging ominously and propped up in places by the masts of riverboats.

A mere fifty-four years after the death of the first President, George Washington's home was falling into ruin.

Mrs. Cunningham was aghast. Writing to her daughter she expostulated, "If the men could not do it . . . why was it that the women of the country did not try to keep it in repair?" And suddenly Ann Pamela Cunningham had a unique and magnificent crusade and (what her mother had most hoped for) a new meaning to her pain-filled life.

Her first appeal addressed "To the Ladies of the South", was published on December 2, 1853 in the *Charleston Mercury* and signed, "A Southern Matron." One paragraph alone paraphrases the entire two-column, eight paragraph appeal:

> *Believing this, one of your countrywomen feels emboldened to appeal in the name of the Mother of Washington, and of southern feeling and honor, to all that is sympathetic and generous in your nature, to exert itself and by your combined effort now, in village and country, town and city, the means may be raised from the mites of thousands of gentle hearts, upon whom his name has yet a magic spell, which will suffice to secure and retain his home and grave as a SACRED SPOT for all coming time.*

The response was instantaneous and widespread, but one very serious obstacle immediately arose. John Augustine Washington, who had inherited the mansion from his mother the year before, was barely able to support his wife and seven children, but he had sworn to sell Mount Vernon only to the State of Virginia or the Federal government, in accordance with the longtime wishes of his family. He had received numerous offers, from "speculators, charlatans and thieves," as one source reported, who wished to do everything from subdividing the estate, to transforming it into a resort or carnival area. In a letter of October 28, 1854, to Miss Cummingham he sent his polite, thankful but firm regrets. But this served to delay the campaign only momentarily, if at all.

His asking price for the two-hundred-acre tract, including the mansion, the tomb, the gardens, grounds and wharf, was $200,000. The state of Virginia had no speical appetite for the proposition since they regarded the price as excessive and also felt the purchase and preservation should be a national matter.

Congress, on the other hand, torn with regional dissensions and mounting unrest, was not anxious to commit for the purchase at a price they also considered out of line, but many members felt that in any case the timing was wrong. So all fiddled, in a sense, while Rome burned.

John Augustine Washington was incensed at what had transpired and wrote Miss Cunningham on March 13, 1858, changing his position, as follows:

> *The events of the past few years .. seem to indicate that neither Virginia nor the United States wish to acquire the place. Under the circumstances, and believing that after the two highest powers in our country, the Women of the land will probably be the safest as they will certainly be the purest guardians of a national shrine, I am willing to comply with your request...*

An Act incorporating the Mount Vernon Ladies Association, which provided for a regent to coordinate the campaign in every state of the Union, speedily passed the General Assembly of Virginia on March 19, 1858.

CHAPTER 18

The Articles of Agreement, between John Augustine Washington and the Mount Vernon Ladies Association, Ann Pamela Cunningham, Regent, were signed on April 6, 1858.

And so it transpired that Miss Cunningham wrote to George Riggs as follows, on May 5, 1858:

>Richmond, May 5, 1858

George Riggs, Esq.

Dear Sir,
You are doubtless aware from the public journals that the Mount Vernon Ladies Association, incorporated by the Legislature of Virginia, has assumed a National and permanent form.

This being the case it is thought necessary to have a Treasurer for the Association at a central point, and for obvious reasons, the City of Washington presents itself as the most suitable. It is also necessary that the Treasurer should be a man whose name is so well known, and whose credit is so firm as to command the confidence of the entire Union. And as there is no one in the District who possesses these requisites in a higher degree than yourself — at the suggestion of the Hon. Edward Everett, we would be happy to learn if it would be agreeable to you to assume the duties of this office.

We enclose to you a Bill of incorporation and the Constitution of the Association — also an appeal.

>Very respectfully yours,
>Ann Pamela Cunningham,
>by
>Christie Johnson
>Private Sec. of Regent,
>Mt. V.L. Asso.

George Riggs answered very promptly on May 7, 1858, with the following letter:

My dear Madam,
It would give me great pleasure to do anything in my power to promote the success of the Mount Vernon Ladies Association, and, if as you intimate

in your letter, you wish my services, I shall be happy to perform the duties of Treasurer of the Association, with the understanding that there is to be no compensation or salary attached to the office.

> *With great respect,*
> *Madam, Your faithful*
> *Servant,*
> *Geo. W. Riggs.*

This appointment must have been the culmination of a happy spring at No. 32 President's Square, where during the preceding month, on April 11th, an ebulient George Riggs had passed out fine cigars to celebrate the birth of another son, named for his father's eldest brother, and his own brother, Thomas Lawrason Riggs.

At their beautiful mansion, too, at 280 Eye Street, where decorations and furnishings were gradually being installed and completed, George and Janet Riggs must have touched glasses, smilingly and happily under their gleaming chandeliers, in a toast to their new home, to their wonderful new son, and to this rewarding opportunity to serve in a national crusade to restore and preserve the home and tomb of the first President and George's namesake.

Chapter Notes

[1] Deed JAS 100 - 281

[2] *The Riggs Family of Maryland*, p. 330.

[3] The authority quoted in this paragraph is The Sessford Annals, p. 350, Vol. Xi, *Records of Columbia Historical Society.*

[4] Quotation is from Vice Admiral K. K. Cowart, USCG (Ret), in a letter to the author, April 16, 1978.

Chapter 19

In reviewing and bringing up to date the affairs of W. W. Corcoran and his overseas friend, George Peabody, we discovered quite unexpectedly that the principal reason for Corcoran's retirement and the sale of the firm to George Riggs as of April 1, 1854, was the health of his only daughter, Louise, or Louly, as he fondly called her.

Sometime prior to the sale of the firm, Corcoran's doctors had apparently advised him discreetly that Louly's health was unsatisfactory and she needed to go abroad for the benefit of the sea air and a change of scenery, as well as for the English climate and countryside and its magnificent beaches, all of which, it was hoped, would be helpful to her.

And for some months following his withdrawal, Corcoran had been extricating himself from his multiplicity of responsibilities and involvements in preparation for the trip. It is believed these plans had been purposely delayed after the *Arctic* loss to push away and diminish as far as possible the impact of that disaster. Eventually, their schedule called for them to embark in mid-July of 1855 — Corcoran, Louly, and her governess of some years, Miss Yardley.

Through all of the preparations for this trip, this man of diverse destinies must have been haunted by the specter of the dread disease which had robbed him of his young bride, leaving only little Louly, now grown to be the jewel of his middle years. It will be recalled that Corcoran's bride of seventeen, Louise Amory Morris, had succumbed to consumption four years after their marriage at age twenty-one. She had born three children, of whom only the middle one, Louise, had survived. Now, on March 29, 1855, Louly had just turned seventeen and in the intervening years Corcoran's fortunes had soared to heights beyond the wildest imaginings of most successful men.

To add to his complications, Corcoran had originally planned to tour Europe with ex-President Millard Fillmore, of Buffalo, who had been widowed shortly after going out of office on March 4, 1853. Not wishing to say too much about his daughter's health, Corcoran had tried patiently and delicately to suggest that Fillmore should go on earlier with another congenial traveling companion. At one point the ex-President, a neophyte, never having been abroad, and writing, "*between you and me, as a profound secret,*" must have horrified the worried and urbane Mr. Corcoran when he suggested:

> *I should like to go prepared to visit England, Scotland, and Ireland, France, Germany, and Italy in the south, and possibly Alexandria and Cairo and Constantinople, and return to the north of Europe, and visit the principal countries bordering on the Baltic, as far east as St. Petersburg.*

Eventually, with many misgivings, Fillmore was persuaded to sail on May 16, 1855, with one Mr. H. E. Davies as a companion, and was soon reporting enthusiastically to Corcoran:

> *We arrived at Liverpool on Sunday evening the 27th, and reached London via Chester, Shrewsbury, Warwick, Stratford-on-Avon, and Oxford, on Saturday, June 2nd, where we found an invitation from that prince of good fellows, your hospitable friend, Peabody, awaiting our arrival.*

In early June, Corcoran received a letter from his longtime friend and client of the banking firm, Edward Everett, who had

CHAPTER 19

been minister to London under Tyler, and later, had succeeded Webster as Secretary of State in Fillmore's cabinet. The letter reads as follows:

> Boston, 11th June, 1855
>
> My Dear Corcoran:
> The time for your contemplated departure for Europe is, I believe, approaching . . . I have [enclosed] a letter to Lord Ashburton, a very amiable and intelligent person, more quiet and retiring than his father, but like him, of solid worth. His wife is one of the cleverest women in England; her health not good and, unhappily, no living children. I should like very much to have you and Louly visit them at Grange, in Hampshire.
> If you or the young lady should need medical advice, you will find Sir Henry Holland, of Brook Street, an excellent physician. He is one of the Queen's physicians, and is very much my friend. Mr. Stokes, of Brook Street, is a good dentist. It is well to know such things in a strange place.
> I hope dear Louly's health will be entirely confirmed by the voyage and journey; and, wishing you much enjoyment yourself,
>
> I remain, my dear
> Corcoran,
> Sincerely yours,
> Edward Everett.

Corcoran carried a letter from Mr. Joseph Henry, Secretary of the Smithsonian Institution, reading as follows:

> Smithsonian Institution,
> July, 1855
>
> The bearer of this letter, Mr. W. W. Corcoran, a gentleman of wealth and influence, a warm friend of the Smithsonian Institution, and to whom has been entrusted the management of a part of its funds, visits Europe as a recreation and in behalf of the regents. I beg to commend him to the attention of the

> libraries and officers of the societies in correspondence with the Smithsonian Institution which he may visit in the course of his tour.
>
> > Joseph Henry,
> > Secretary, Smithsonian
> > Institution.

The Corcoran party sailed on or about July 12, 1855, and found a letter from George Peabody awaiting their arrival, as follows:

> I trust this will reach you on Sunday, and find you and your daughter in good health and spirits after a pleasant voyage. I assure you it will give me great pleasure to again meet you after a lapse of several years.
>
> I have invited some friends to meet you at dinner at the Star and Garter, Richmond, on Friday, 27th, and shall also arrange to give you places at opera on Thursday evening, 26th.
>
> If you wish accomodations for yourself and daughter, write me and I will obtain such apartments as you may require.
>
> > Sincerely yours,
> > George Peabody.

Despite the nightmare of the *Arctic*, Corcoran evidently sailed via the Collins Line, out of a sense of loyalty or patriotism or, perhaps, with a feeling that the worst was over. This is revealed by a letter from Fillmore, now a seasoned and ardent traveller, reading as follows:

> > Dublin, July 23, 1855
>
> W. W. Corcoran, Esq.
> My Dear Sir:
> I perceive by the paper this morning that the Baltic has arrived, and presume, therefore, that you will be in London today.
> I write, therfore, merely to say that I go to the Lakes of Killarney and shall return by the Menai Strait, and hope to be in London, at Fenton's, on Thursday evening, and shall be ready to go to Paris,

CHAPTER 19

> Friday or Saturday; but should you desire to go
> before, I beg of you not to tarry for me, as I shall
> have Mr. Davies's company.
> I have a good courier who will remain with us.
>
> In haste, truly yours,
> Millard Fillmore.

From Paris on July 30, 1855, Corcoran received a letter from the U. S. Legation stating:-

> Mrs. Mason unites with me in the wish that
> Miss Louly and her governess may be our guests
> while in Paris. It will subject us to no inconvenience,
> but will give us much pleasure, and I hope that it
> will not conflict with your arrangements to gratify
> our wishes.
> Mr. Fillmore wishes to unite with you in your
> lodgings, and arrangement will be made for you
> .. My wife and daughters send kindest regards to
> Louly and yourself.
>
> Very truly, your friend,
> J. Y. Mason.

Then from Berlin arrived a succinct note from the German minister to Washington, reading:

> I leave Berlin tomorrow to return to Washington,
> where I hope to see you also by and by. Enclosed you
> find a letter of introduction to Baron Humboldt,
> who will be happy to see you with Mr. Fillmore, and
> will, no doubt, present you to the King . . .
> I regret very much not to have met you here.
>
> Fr. Geralt.

Not to be outdone in these matters, Fillmore writes Corcoran from The Hague on Oct 31, 1855, stating:

> While at Amsterdam I received a very polite
> invitation from Mr. Belmont to stay with him, which
> I accepted, and arrived here last night . . . .
> I am just going to be presented to the King, and
> have only time to say that I intend to be with you
> on Sunday evening.

> *Make my kindest regards to the ladies, and believe me,*
>
> > *Truly yours,*
> > *Millard Fillmore.*

The foregoing must have been "the barest bones" reporting of the elegant, ostentatious and enthusiastic round of travel and entertainments showered upon Corcoran and Louly and also upon the nimble ex-President, Fillmore, who was making his way gayly and somewhat independently, exactly as had been hoped by his original host. One wonders at times whether Louly's doctors had advised Corcoran to take her abroad for her health or for a last fling. If the latter, she managed to confound the prophets of doom and her diagnosticians, and to survive for at least a few more-than-expected, courageous and rich years for her father and herself.

Finally genial banker, Joshua Bates, of Baring Brothers, joined the hospitality act and wrote Corcoran from his home:

> *Eastsheen, Nov 11, 1855*
>
> *I hope you and Miss Corcoran and the governess will be able to come down and dine, and pass the night with us one day this week — say, Tuesday, Wednesday or Thursday. On either of these days, if you will let me know which, and hour, my carriage will be at the station .. Mrs. Bates is not very well, but cannot allow Miss Corcoran and you to go home without seeing her.*
>
> *Take the Richmond Railway at Waterloo and stop at Mortlake station, where my carriage will take you.*
>
> > *Joshua Bates.*

It appears that W. W. Corcoran, Louly and Miss Yardley made their return voyage late in November (a bad season in the north Atlantic) and, presumably, once again via the Collins Line. The exact vessel is unknown, but, by a quirk of fate, it could have been the *Pacific*, which sailed on another voyage from Liverpool two months later on January 23, 1856, and was never heard from again.

CHAPTER 19

The Corcoran party arrived back in Washington only a short time before the death of Commodore Morris, Corcoran's father-in-law and Louly's grandfather, who passed away on January 27, 1856, in his seventy-second year.

The old seadog, a veteran of an almost unheard-of fifty-five years of active service, of which twenty-one years had been served at sea, succumbed at last to pneumonia, at his residence a few doors from Corcoran's mansion in Lafayette Square. The long years of sea duty evoke the beautiful couplet which appears in Robert Louis Stephenson's epitaph on his grave in Samoa, in the South Pacific:

> "Home is the sailor, home from the sea,
> And the hunter, home from the hill."

Commodore Morris was a national figure, best remembered, perhaps, because of his appointment in 1825 to command the *Brandywine*, the warship which carried Lafayette back to France after his last visit to the United States. He had also received some unwanted publicity in 1846 when his eldest son, a lieutenant in the Navy, was killed in the Mexican War while serving aboard the frigate, *Cumberland*, during the taking of Tabasco. The Commodore's high standing inspired many letters of condolence to Mr. Corcoran and to Louly. Two will have special exposure here, the first to Corcoran and the second to Louly.

Edward Everett, writing from Boston on February 1, 1856, states:

> Dear Mr. Corcoran:
> I duly received yours of the 26th of January. It prepared me for the melancholy event in your family which has since taken place. I had known the Commodore from my entrance into life, and had occasion many times, in connection with my public duties, to consult him on subjects relating to naval affairs. I entertained the highest respect for his character and ever regarded him as one of the very best officers in any branch of the public service. He was especially esteemed in this part of the country, as, indeed, he was throughout the Union.
> I wish, when you see Mrs. Morris, you would

> *assure her of the sincere sympathy of Mrs. Everett and myself.*
>
> *With the kindest rememberances to your daughter, I remain, my dear Mr. C., sincerely yours,*
> *Edward Everett.*

Louly received a long and affectionate letter from an old family friend, Emilie Vail, from Geneva, Switzerland, dated March 11, 1856. After expressing condolences, the letter delves into family recollections as follows:

> *But, independently of this, our share of the national feeling, Mr. Vail — and, by sympathy, myself also — entertained toward Commodore Morris a grateful sense of kind partiality to our family, dating from the early days of his brilliant career, for, even while the laurels of his boyish exploits were yet green on his brow, he had visited Mr. Vail's family — then residing in France — and the name of Commodore Morris and the fame of his youthful heroism had been household words at our fireside through three generations.*

The letter then goes on to recall a visit to the Corcoran home and states:

> *Our imagination often carries us back to the bright days of our visit to Washington, and the splendid hospitality of President's Square. Amid those scenes .. we have often, around our midnight hearth, luxuriated in thought, but, above all, have our cherished fancies drawn us again around the table in the little back room sanctum . . . . Remember us most kindly to your aunt. . . also to Mr. and Mrs. Bright and their sweet daughters, and last, but not least, to kind Miss Yardley, is she be still with you.*
>
> *Now, as ever, very sincerely,*
>
> *Your attached friend,*
> *Emilie L. Vail.*

The introduction here of "Mr. and Mrs. Bright and their sweet daughters," deserves some enlargement and will soon require more. Research discloses that Senator Jesse D. Bright of Indiana, owned a home around the corner from 32 President's Square on 15th Street. The 1855 city directory (the first with street numbers) lists it as "No. 423 15th St., north, west side near center of block." This site is now covered by the American Security Building or the Walker Building. Bright was a two-term senator from the little Ohio River city of Madison, Indiana, midway down river between Cincinnati and Louisville. He had apparently been a customer of the bank since his arrival in Washington, and quite naturally, in living so close by, he was well known to Corcoran and to George Riggs and to Elisha, Jr. As suggested by the Vail's letter, his daughters, especially the eldest, Mary, were close friends of Louly.

In early 1857, Edward Everett, who appears to have had an old man's special affection for Louly, wrote her in Charleston, South Carolina, where she had apparently gone for her health, describing one of her father's lavish parties as follows:

> Having a half hour before breakfast this morning, I thought I could not employ it so agreeably as in giving you a little account of your father's beautiful dinner yesterday . . . It was really the most beautiful and successful dinner at which I have been for a long time, not excepting Lord and Lady Napier's, last Wednesday.
>
> The company consisted principally of the members of the Cabinet and their favorites, with a few others, such as Mr. and Mrs. Reverdy Johnson [senator from Maryland] Mrs. Senator Slidell [Louisiana], Mrs. and Miss Bright — by the way, Miss Bright has a beautiful face, and seems to be a very sensible girl — Mr. Reed, [the new minister to China], my daughter, etc. The flowers were beautiful and your papa made a most liberal distribution of them among the ladies. . . I took Mrs. R. Johnson into dinner, and sat opposite to your father, between her and Mrs. Senator Slidell. . . .

Here again is evidence that the Brights were close to the Corcorans and probably, also, to the Riggs, and that "Miss Bright [doubtless the oldest daughter, Mary Turpin Bright, then nineteen] has a beautiful face — and seems a very sensible girl" — an accolade from old, sophisticated girl-watcher and former minister to London, Edward Everett, that probably meant she was stunning.

And these delightful and distinguished people gathered in Corocran's mansion in these "golden days" when Louisiana and Maryland, Indiana and Massachusetts, and all the other states of the Union could be represented at a sumptuous banquet as friends and neighbors and citizens of the brash and promising United States of America — soon to be torn apart and separated for much of the balance of their lives by one of the most dread and fratricidal wars in history.

The year 1858, as already disclosed, was a most auspicious one for George Riggs, in bringing him a new son and the treasuryship of Mount Vernon Ladies Association, both of which events were celebrated in his handsome new mansion at 280 (later 1617) Eye Street, northwest. The year was also one of profound change for other members of the Riggs family. Lawrason's factory in St. Louis had burned down in early 1858 and he eventually decided to close his business there and come east to settle in New York City with his three children. Undoubtedly, the family had also paid a visit to Washington and were warmly welcomed by George and Janet Riggs and their children and comfortably ensconced in their new thirty-room home which was just across Eye street from the back yard and garden of Corcoran's house. There, George Riggs must have given a reception for his brother, as also, in all probability, did Corcoran. And at one or both of those parties Lawrason must have become reacquainted with the Bright family and been pleasantly surprised at the maturity and beauty of their daughters, especially that of Mary, the eldest, who had so impressed Mr. Everett.

There was no reunion with the family of Elisha, Jr. and Mary Boswell and their children, for the reason that this restless and continental-minded young couple had left the "city of magnificent distances," much of which was still occupied by canals and bogs and planned, but empty, streets, and moved abroad. They were supposedly then living in Germany where Elisha had gone to school. Elisha had sold Washington House to, of all people, Senator and Mrs. Bright, who probably considered its attractive setting and historical background most appropriate for the entertainments of their daughters. The fact cannot be proved, but, it is probable that Lawrason visited their new home before returning to New York.

George Riggs continued to be busily engaged at the bank and some months before had been elected president of the Washington Gas Light Company, one of the city's most exciting and important new industries. This was the beginning of the well-established treadition for the top officials of Riggs Bank to become involved in the city's business and civic affairs.

He must have still recalled with a chuckle an event which took place on the very first business day of 1858 when a courier from the White House presented him with a note from the President on a small, discreet strip of paper which read:

> *Please to send my tin box by the bearer, Lewis Burgdorf, & oblige,*
>
> *Yours tr.*
> *James Buchanan,*
> *2 January, 1858.*

At that time there was no safe deposit department as such, but important personages were often granted the privilege, gratis, of leaving their "strong boxes," properly tagged in the cashier's vault. The phrase "my tin box" probably draws a smile from us, but such products had just come on the market and were superior to anything else available and objects of pride to their possessors.

George Riggs evidently thought so much of this little note from the President that he carefully preserved it and passed it along to his successors and, happily, it still reposes in the bank's historical collection today.

Chapter 20

Early in 1859, Washington society was pleasantly excited by two important marriages which took place within a relatively short period of time.

The first was reported by brief announcements in the local press, giving the information that on Thursday, February 24, 1859, Mr. Lawrason Riggs of New York was married by Rev. Stephen P. Hill, D.D., to Miss Mary T. Bright, eldest daughter of the Hon. Jesse D. Bright, of Indiana.

We know from later information that Rev. Hill was pastor of First Baptist Church on 10th Street and was a brother-in-law of W. W. Corcoran. The property of First Baptist Church was sold later in 1859 to John T. Ford who remodeled it into a theatre — the church apparently having been moved to a new location on the east side of 13th Street, between G and H streets.

The ceremony was probably a simple one and might have taken place in George Riggs's commodious new residence. Lawrason was forty-four and his bride twenty-one. He had been widowed for the second time ten years before, and his three children, two sons and a daughter, were thirteen, twelve and ten — the little girl being the middle child. He was, according to his photograph, a sort of middle-aged Rhett Butler — tall and spare, with a small handle-bar mustache and a shock of well-combed dark hair. He had been a prosperous merchant in the frontier city of St. Louis for twenty years and his financial success there, along with the rich inheritance from his father, made him a most attractive and suitable prospect for marriage with a senator's daughter who was not only beautiful, but also "very sensible." After the wedding the couple left for New York and later embarked for Europe.

The second wedding, which had been preceded some weeks before by the announcement of her engagement, was that of Louise Corcoran (Louly) to the Hon. George Eustis, a member of Congress from Louisiana. This ceremony took place in the elaborate setting of her father's house on April 5, 1859, and was the subject of lengthy coverage in the Washington press and elsewhere.

One society columnist wrote:

> But here I am gossiping, when I sat down to chronicle the wedding last night at the palatial mansion of W. W. Corcoran, Esq., who gave his only child in marriage to Hon. George Eustis, a member of Congress from the New Orleans district in the last two Congresses.
>
> Only a few weeks have elapsed since we received from across the ocean fabulous accounts of a wedding in the Rothschild family at Paris, but none but the members of the family were admitted.
>
> Mr. Corcoran, who may be styled the Rothschild of the United States, as he amassed his collossal fortune by government loans, was more liberal. Nearly 1,500 invitations, gotten up in Broadway, were distributed the Union over.

The groom was the eldest son of the late George Eustis, a member of a prominent Boston family who had settled in New Orleans and become the state's attorney general and later Chief Justice of its Supreme Court. Young George Eustis had been educated at Harvard, but his law career had been interrupted by his election and reelection to Congress. He was described as "dashing and handsome" and was apparently in his middle thirties.

CHAPTER 20

And so these two young neighbors and girlfriends had set out upon the promising but uncertain sea of matrimony in the ominous year of 1859, when war clouds were steadily lowering over the national horizon.

The war clouds actually helped with the Mount Vernon campaign. George Riggs, although busily occupied with his expanding banking firm, was swept along in the activities of the Ladies Association.

On June 7, 1859, he wrote Miss Cunningham in South Carolina as follows:

> I accompanied Miss Hamilton [vice regent from New York and granddaughter of Alexander Hamilton] to Mount Vernon yesterday. We met there Mr. Upton Herbert and took a hurried look at the parts of the house and outbuildings which seem to require immediate repairs.
>
> The roof of the house is in better condition than I anticipated, but the portico is in very bad order — it is propped up with a piece of timber... it may require a new frame for its roof and new columns to support it; the extent of the repairs can only be ascertained by an examination of the timbers, which I could not make. The outhouses, those especially belonging to the gardens, require immediate attention. They should, I think, be repaired at once, retaining in them everything that can be retained and restoring them as nearly as possible to what they were in General Washington's day. Three or four carpenters might be employed under direction of Mr. Herbert to proceed with such repairs as will not inconvenience the family, as soon as possible.
>
> We saw pieces of stone removed from the old vault. Miss Hamilton suggested that it should be surrounded by an iron railing to save it from utter destruction. If not done, the removal of stones will soon cause the arch to fall. I am willing to serve the association but an unable to devote much time to the personal examination of the property. If you wish me to employ Mr. Herbert with whom I am acquainted, please to let me hear from you with instructions to do so.

Miss Cunningham must have complied to the last request at once, for on June 27, three weeks after the above letter, George Riggs advised her that he had made arrangements with John A. Washington to have Mr. Herbert take charge of the property and the interests of the Association on July 4, 1859.

This seemed altogether appropriate, inasmuch as a surprising $150,000 of the purchase price, plus interest, had already been paid by George Riggs, as treasurer, to Mr. Washington and he was making arrangements to move his family to Waveland, his estate in Fauquier County.

On July 25, 1859, Mr. Riggs again wrote Miss Cunningham as follows:

> A few days ago Mr. Herbert came up to see me and I went with him to Mount Vernon to see what had been done. I found that good progress had been made in clearing up the walks which were completely hidden [by the underbrush]. With the kind assistance of Mr. Washington and the memory of an old negro woman on the place the course of the walks had been traced out. Mr. Herbert has had them cleared up and will have them gravelled and returned as nearly as possible to their original condition....
>
> He has carpenters at work at the seed house in the corner of the garden. They will be repaired by putting new timber in place of the damaged ones without any changes of plan or of material where the wood is not rotten .. The garden walks are in very bad condition.
>
> The portico in front of the house will have to be entirely renewed .. the timbers supporting the roof are almost entirely gone... Mr. Washington might consent to have repairs on the portico commence at once. If it be your wish, I will have Mr. Herbert to ask him. A severe storm might blow it down in its present condition.

As shown by the foregoing, a dramatic sense of urgency and haste had been displayed by the quickly recruited corps of female crusaders and their staunch band of male allies, in the collection of substantial sums in an unbelieveably short time.

The contributions came from all over the nation, North, South, and West. They came from school children, Sunday schools and fraternal brotherhoods. They came from visitors to Independence Hall in Philadelphia and from the Superintendent at West Point, enclosing the donations of the staff and 229 cadets at the Academy. Even from across the sea, from the Commandant of the Navy Yard at Gosport, England, came a draft for $229.27 collected from the officers and men of the English garrison.

From California via Wells, Fargo & Company's Express came a "nice little block of virgin gold" as a result of one month's collections from "Generous and Golden California." George Riggs's letter to Miss Cunningham stated he had credited $3,326 from California to the Mount Vernon fund and added, "It [the gold bar] was worth more than it was valued at.[1]

Old Edward Everett, who in addition to his other accomplishments, was one of the most popular orators in the country, had donated $70,000 himself, from the receipts of his oft-repeated speech on "The Character of George Washington." Once, in writing W. W. Corcoran about an appointment for giving the talk in Georgetown, he had chided him gently but certainly with some truth, when he said:

> I have had the curiousity to note on the margin
> of my address, the sums which have accrued at the
> places where it has been repeated. The net amount
> of thirteen repitions is about $12,000, the gross
> amount from 25 to 33 percent more.
> You millionaires don't think much of $15,000 or
> $16,000, but to us small fry it is a considerable sum
> to be raised by a single address.

And all of these contributions, coming directly to, or being receipted for by Riggs & Company, brought the firm nationwide and even overseas publicity.

George Riggs and his partners, Mr. Elliott in New York, and Mr. Kiookhoefer in Washington, carried on a wide and diverse correspondence, which, in many cases, combined both friendship and business. By reason of the ample supply of foreign currencies kept on supply, the firm attracted many foreign luminaries as clients, including, not only diplomats but actors and artists and other important foreign visitors.

The celebrated Norweign violinst, Ole Bull (pronounced o le bull), who made several concert tours of this country, was a client of the bank, and became a close friend of George Riggs as well as of John Elliott in New York. Bull, who often appeared in Europe with Franz Lizst, was immortalized by Longfellow in his "Tales of a Wayside Inn." He was a handsome six-footer whose female audiences reacted in much the same way as some of the present day followers of their own currently favorite entertainers.

In a letter of December 15, 1856, he states, "An antiquated tailor's bill for $160, as also a demand of $60 from a violin maker, I sent down to your consideration, the acceptance of which is duly felt and most gratefully acknowledged." He closes with an apology, "I am sorry, Dear Mr. Elliott, to give you such a lot of troubles [he probably pronounced it 'troobles'] I wish it was rubles instead".

Old account records show that an Irish actor named Tyrone Power was a customer at about the same time, possibly the grandfather of the more recent handsome movie idol of the same name.

But George Riggs was even closer to the renowned Irish playwright and actor, Dion Boucicault who opened his new hit play at The Winter Garden in New York in December of 1859. After the play opened he wrote:

> *My dear Riggs:*
> *I delayed writing until after the Octoroon was out. The play was a great success. I called in at Marly's ... saw ... the clock and he was then going to send it on. I have called twice since, but he, Marly, was not there, so I left a note about sending it on...Marly is uncommonly proud of your purchases, and I believe he kept the clock unnecessarily long that he might be able to say to people who inquired the price of it, 'No, Sir, that clock, sir, is going to Mr. Riggs, sir, in Washington, the great banker, sir -- Ah, there's a gentleman of taste'.*

This clock was probably the handsome wall clock shown in the photograph of the entrance hall of the Riggs Mansion.

CHAPTER 20

To give some idea of the attitude of sophisticated old world visitors toward the struggling metropolis of Washington, Boucicault gayly chides George Riggs:

> Really I admire you for the way you stick up for your forlorn city to which you are tied by business — or else you would be here. It is quite creditable to you, really. And Mrs. Riggs manages to hide her mortification with great success. And now you have succeeded in building a house, just after the fashion of a London Week-End Mansion, so that when you are shut up in it you forget that you are in Washington and fancy yourself in Belgrave Square.

He goes on about his play:

> A tremendous house last night and the promise of the same tonight. If you want a large loan now's the time to apply to Stuart — if the House of Riggs & Co. want support — here is the prop. Stuart is rising barometrically...[William Stuart was the proprietor of The Winter Garden.]

A few days later the chatty Boucicault wrote again, saying:

> The sensation produced in New York by the Drama is intense... If it lasts, there is no doubt that the piece will make $30,000 or $40,000 — that is, if it runs one half the length of time as The American Cousin.[This was playing the night Lincoln was shot].
> I shall call on Marly this afternoon... and row with him about the clock....I saw Mr. Elliott yesterday who immediately greeted me with, 'How gets on the Octoroon' — just conceive how N.Y. must be upheaved when Elliott feels it!
>
> Yours very sincerely,
> Dion Boucicault.[2]

In early 1860, collections had continued to pour into Riggs & Company for the Mount Vernon Ladies Association, and by mid-year, all but a few thousand dollars, plus interest, of the debt to John Augustine Washington had been paid.

Also great progress had been made in repairing, cleaning and restoring the mansion and tomb, and the gardens and outbuildings. This is revealed by the following letter of George Riggs to Miss Cunningham, reporting on a matter about which all Washington was agog — the arrival in early October of 1860 of the nineteen-year-old Prince of Wales. (the future Edward VII). Apparently one of the first places chosen for him to visit was Mount Vernon.

Washington, 6 Oct., 1860

My dear Miss Cunningham:
The trip to Mount Vernon yesterday was in every way successful. Herbert did wonders and though he had difficulty in getting labor the place was looking much better than I have ever seen it.

I understand that the Prince last night expressed himself much gratified — and said the day was the most agreeable one he has spent in the United States.

The President was in a glowing good humor and seemed satisfied with everything. There were very few people invited. We went down in the Cutter Harriet Lane [named for Buchanan's thirty-year-old niece and hostess] and landed in her boats. The Prince steered the first boat in which were the President, Miss Lane and Lord Lyons. The President insisted upon Mrs. Riggs and myself going in the same boat. Herbert was at the head of the wharf. I landed first and waited at the wharf until all the company had landed — Herbert, meanwhile, having led the Prince and President up to the house, Mrs. Riggs with them.

Before leaving, at the request of the Ladies, the Prince planted a horse chestnut near the tomb....
I enclose you extracts from our papers.

Faithfully yours,
George Riggs.

This visit to Mount Vernon was one of the last and most pleasant formalities of Buchanan's administration. Exactly one month following George Riggs's letter, on November 6, 1860, Abraham Lincoln was elected President.

CHAPTER 20

The young banking firm (beginning to be known familiarly as "Riggs bank") had been proud of the accounts of Tyler, Polk, Taylor, Fillmore, Pierce and Buchanan.

The soon-to-be-opened account of President Lincoln was to place it more firmly than ever in the mainstream of American history.

Chapter Notes

[1] From the *Centennial Exhibition Bulletin* of Mount Vernon Ladies Association, 1953.

[2] Copies of these letters of Boucicault were furnished us through the courtesy of Professor F. Theodore Cloak, Bergstron Professor, Theater and Drama, Lawrence University, Appleton, Wisconsin. The originals are said to be at Yale University.

Chapter 21

During the last months of Buchanan's Presidency, he faced a series of critical events which brought the United States to the verge of armed conflict between the rival sections.

On December 20, 1860, South Carolina seceded from the Union and Governor Pickins demanded the withdrawal of the Federal troops from Fort Sumter in Charleston harbor. Buchanan refused this demand. He had already denied the right of secession but was uncertain of his powers of armed coercion. In any case, his fervent desire was to leave the solution to his successor.

Between January 9 and February 1, 1861, six other Southern states followed South Carolina's example. Delegates from those states met at Montgomery, Alabama, and on February 9, 1861, announced the formation of the Confederate States of America, with Jefferson Davis of Mississippi as President, and Alexander H. Stephens of Georgia, Vice President.

In the midst of all this turmoil and excitement, Janet and George Riggs suffered another harsh personal blow when their fourth daughter, fifteen-year-old Janet Madeleine, always known as Jessie, died of diptheria on January 30, 1861, at the Convent of the Sacred Heart in Manhattanville, New York, where she was attending school.

This unexpected loss was especially painful, as things in the family had seemed to be going so well since the birth of little Thomas Lawrason, now almost three.

On Saturday, February 2, Jessie's coffin came into the new Potomac railroad station at 6th Street and Pennsylvania Avenue and was taken to St. Aloysius Church at North Capitol and Eye streets for a brief service before burial in the family plot at Rock Creek Church cemetery.

That desolate winter afternoon probably matched in bitterness the mood that was spreading across the nation.

George Riggs had just about settled down to business again when he received a note from the lonely frustrated occupant of the nation's highest office which read:

> My dear Sir:
> I would thank you to come over for a minute & oblige,
>
> Your friend,
> James Buchanan.
>
> George W. Riggs, Esq.
> Thursday, February 14, 1861.

The harassed banker, hardly recovered from his daughter's death, was most likely as disturbed as the President by the trend of events, being himself a Democrat and treasurer of the national committee whose candidates had been defeated by Lincoln. But he probably hastened to the White House as requested.[1]

Affairs in Washington were proceeding routinely but an air of apprehension hung over the city.

In the realm of business as usual, George Riggs, as president of the Washington Gas Light Company, had been much occupied with having a new plant built at 26th and G streets, northwest, known as the West Station Works. Here, large barges could move along the Potomac and discharge their cargoes of coal directly at the wharves of West Station. This additional capacity soon proved invaluable, with the war-time increase in population and demand.

CHAPTER 21

The *National Intelligencer* had published as customary in its issue of January 1, 1861, the annual report of the "Sessford Annals," regarding construction projects in the city, which included the following:

> The building erected by Mr. W. W. Corcoran for an Art Union [gallery] is a splendid piece of workmanship, lofty with a beautiful carved entrance of light brownstone, window-heads of the same material, the whole resting on a basement story of thick stone walls and iron girders. The exterior of the building is nearly completed; it covers a space of 105 ft. by 125 ft., and is much admired by citizens and strangers, being at the corner opposite the War Office [17th street and President's Square].

It would be many years before this handsome edifice would be used for its original purpose, being destined to be appropriated for the prosecution of the approaching conflict. And Mr. Corcoran, himself, would soon be forced to leave the country as a "southern sympathizer" whose daughter was married to a rebel congressman. Additional suspicion stemmed from his close friendship with Senator John Slidell of Louisiana, who had been Corcoran's next-door-neighbor on H Street for many years and was now being appointed Confederate Commissioner to France.

The final blow came with the naming of Corcoran's son-in-law as Slidell's secretary. His country estate, known as Harewood, adjoining Soldiers Home to the south, was soon to be taken over as a Union hospital. Sentiment on the part of some radicals to confiscate his baronial mansion opposite the White House, was only thwarted by the crafty old banker when he quietly leased the premises to the sympathetic French Minister, the Marquis de Montholon, who exercised his lease in time to forestall threatened seizure.

And so the dreary demise of the "golden days" of Corcoran's regal hospitality and munificence was being signaled even before the outbreak of hostilities.

Lincoln opened his account with Riggs & Company one month after his inauguration as President, when he deposited his first monthly salary warrant of $2,083.33, on April 5, 1861, based on a President's salary of $25,000 a year, and representing his pay for March.

In that connection a letter which turned up in the hands of a Lincoln collector in 1959, sheds new light on the President's scrupulous honesty in financial matters.

The short message, composed by an unindentified clerk in the White House for Lincoln's signature, was written the same morning he opened his account at Riggs & Co. It is headed "Executive Mansion, April 5, 1861," and is addressed to "Hon. S. P. Chase, Secretary of the Treasury."

As written the letter read:

> On today and on the first of each month, please to send me a warrant for the amount of my salary as President of the United States.
>
> Your obt. servt.

But when the letter came to the President's desk, Lincoln reasoned that since he was inaugurated on March 4, 1861, his salary should begin the following day, March 5, his first official day in office. So he crossed out the word "first" in the first line and substituted "fifth", then signed the document with his usual A. Lincoln.[2]

How Lincoln came to have his account with Riggs & Co. is still something of a mystery. The three $100 bank drafts he had in his pocket when he arrived in the capital were drawn on another Washington bank — and incidentally, these drafts, plus $100 in cash, represented a withdrawal from his Springfield, Ill. account, not borrowed money as some legends maintain. By a curious coincidence, Jefferson Davis closed his account on March 5 — Lincoln's first official day in office. But then as now, "The Riggs" was Washington's largest bank and perhaps Secretary Chase himself, who hurried to the White House with the President's first salary warrant, suggested he open an account for him across President's Square, where virtually all the members of the cabinet already had accounts.

Hostilities broke out, of course, when, after Colonel Robert Anderson's refusal to surrender Fort Sumter, the Confederate batteries opened fire at 4:30 a.m. April 12th — one week after the President opened his account at Riggs & Co. At noon on the 14th Anderson evacuated and the Federal flag was lowered.

Virginia seceded on April 17th, to be followed by North Carolina, Arkansas and Tennessee.

But Lincoln's restraint had forced the Confederates to commit the "aggression" against which he had warned them in his Inaugural Address. A wave of anger swept through the North. Democrats joined with Republicans in denouncing this outrageous insult to the flag. And the reaction was also felt in the border states. Eventually Lincoln was able to keep four of them in the Union.

Western Virginia, beyond the Alleghanies, with long-smoldering resentments against the eastern portion of the state, seceded from Virginia and joined the Union. Maryland, after General Butler occupied Baltimore and quelled several riots, followed suit. Kentucky was divided, but a new legislature declared for the North.

The governor of Missouri was violently secessionist, but the convention summoned was overwhelmingly Unionist. A section of those loyal to the government was led by Francis Preston Blair, Jr., a native of the District of Columbia, whose brother, Montgomery Blair, was Postmaster General in Lincoln's cabinet and still resided in the family home at No. 6 President's Square, diagonally across from the White House.[3]

Young Blair raised several regiments, largely of Germans from St. Louis, who were ready to fight violence with violence. Lincoln allowed himself to be guided by the Blairs, and, after a brief civil war within the state, Missouri was saved for the Union. Francis Blair, Jr. was later commissioned a Major General by the President.

The foregoing developments brought George Riggs an anxious inquiry from Miss Cunningham in secessionist South Carolina, to which he replied on May 16, 1861.

> Washington, 16 May, 1861,
>
> My dear Miss Cunningham:
> I have your letter of the 26th & 30th of April.
> I suppose Miss Tracy gives you all the news from Mt. Vernon.
> You must not be concerned about our condition in this city. We have not been shelled by the Southern Army and I don't think there is much chance of their getting near enough to us to do it. We have been

quite comfortable and safe at our house. I have heard stories of letters being opened but I do not believe any have been opened in this city at the Post Office . . . I have not heard of any letters being opened which came to me with any sort of evidence of the fact.

No one regrets more than I do the breaking up of our Union. I think the South has made a mistake; I hoped for a long time that some settlement would be made but I have lost all hope.

There have been reports (without foundation, I hope) that the Virginians have removed from Mt. Vernon the remains of Washington. This report has caused a deal of excitement . . . .

You speak of employing a guard — but I must say that the finances of the association will not admit of this expense. There is no lack of employment here. Those who have no work can easily get into the service of U. States, where the pay is certain. . . . and those who would be fit to guard Mt. Vernon have entered the service or are ready to do so.

There has been no "reign of terror" here, and I go on with my business just as always, and I don't think anyone who does mind his business has ever had the slightest discomfort. We have no riots, & the gov't will not permit one.

I wanted to communicate to Gen'l Scott the subject of making Mt. Vernon sacred ground, excluding all armed men from it, but I am told it is impossible to see him — he is so overwhelmed with business and he has notified the public he has not time to read the letters addressed to him.

If, however, I have a chance of speaking to him I shall do so.

The boats do not run now. There is, however, no difficulty with the mails and I send Miss Tracy all letters that come to my care in that way . . . .

I shall direct this letter to your address in So. Carolina, thinking it just as likely to reach you as otherwise.

Yours faithfully,
Geo. W. Riggs.

CHAPTER 21

The "Miss Tracy" mentioned in Mr. Riggs letter was Sarah Tracy, a lovely, well-educated young lady from Troy, New York, who was serving as secretary of the Association, probably recruited by Miss Hamilton, the vice regent for that state. Originally she had been residing in the Clarendon Hotel in Washington and commuting to Mt. Vernon by the river steamer.

With the rapid deterioration of affairs between the North and the South, Miss Cunningham, determined "not to let an argument between men" spoil her dream, concluded that the best protection for Mount Vernon would be the presence of a woman. Accordingly, Miss Tracy took up residence there, assisted by the faithful visits of Mr. Herbert, managing the small household staff, looking after supplies and finances, and greeting visitors, if any. She also hurried to Washington where she explained to General Scott the neutral position they were attempting to maintain. The general very courteously agreed that no Federal troops would be stationed there, so long as Virginia observed the same neutrality. He also furnished her a pass for crossing Federal lines.

This, however, was before the outbreak of hostilities and apparently the iron-willed Miss Cunningham was seeking additional assurances via George Riggs on this point. The spunky Miss Tracy would play an important part in the dangerous and exciting drama of Mount Vernon throughout the war.

Meanwhile, back on March 27, she had been happy to report to Miss Cunningham that Mrs. Lincoln had accepted the Association's invitation to visit Mt. Vernon, and had come down on the steamer *Thomas Collyer*, with a small party of friends, without government escorts or formality "just like any body else."

On the twenty-eight of August, 1861, Lincoln wrote the first of the checks which would make him one of the most unique and famous check writers in history.

This check was payable to "Mr. Johns (a sick man)" — the amount three dollars.

The disastrous Battle of Bull Run had taken place on July 21, and the tragic fiasco at Ball's Bluff, near Leesburg, was soon to follow.

Contemporary accounts state that Lincoln roamed the neighborhood of Jackson Square (popularly so named because of the rearing horseback statue of "Old Hickory," done by sculptor Clark Mills, which had recently been erected there) seeking relief and escape from the pressures and stifling August heat of the White House.[2] There he must have encountered the payee of the check — a man so obviously sick, afflicted, palsied or pock-marked, that the President felt he would have no difficulty in cashing his check.

The century-old check reposes today in the archives of Riggs National Bank and it shows no endorsement. The payee's appearance apparently supported his description and the check was cashed and spindled. How we wish some alert teller or officer had left us a memo describing Mr. Johns — a man whose identity will never be known, but who will remain in history by reason of the President's description and his charity in giving him three dollars — a generous amount by present day reckoning, and equal to about twenty times the purchasing power of today's dollar, or sixty dollars.

A number of Lincoln's checks seem to have followed bad news at the battlefront and might have been a small offering for better tidings. Some superstitious, but generous, check-givers of today follow the same pattern.

Meanwhile, at Mount Vernon conditions had grown desperate and soon called for courageous action by Miss Tracy which she described in a letter of October 9, 1861, to Mrs. Comegys, vice regent for Delaware, perhaps because she was unable to communicate with the frail spinster in South Carolina.

Sarah Tracy wrote the following lively and intelligent letter in a vivid, direct style that provides an insight into the hazards of trying to cross Federal lines (for which her pass had been declared invalid) and reach Washington to obtain help.

> *The day before I intended to leave, word was brought that the Federal pickets had moved to within three miles of Mt. Vernon and barricaded the road . . . Finally I became desperate, candles and oil disappeared entirely, and many other small things considered the necessaries of life were not to be had. . . . I announced my determination "to run the*

CHAPTER 21

blockade. . . ." I heard of a farmer living some three of four miles west of us who had made himself a way through the woods, so I decided to "take to the woods. . . ." Such a ride! My attendant, a negro of admirable sangfroid and old enough to be reliable; my horses, a pair of mules. . . . For two hours we wandered around but finally saw a fence, then "the bars" and were "out of the woods." I went direct to Washington. . . Gen. Scott was sick but my friend, Col. Townsend, a noble, true-hearted man, listened to my story and requested me to write it down . . . . I did so and received a reply saying Gen. Scott advised me to see Mr. Lincoln. So to Mr. Lincoln I went. He received me very kindly and wrote a note to McClellan requesting him to see me and arrange the matter in the best possible way. . . . He [McClellan] offered to do anything he could for me, would send a steam tug with provisions from time to time, General Scott gave me a new pass rather more positive than the first, and also one for Miss McMakin, that I might not be obliged to go and come alone. . . .

Thus you see we are now quiet . . . I have found the troubles of today so absorbing as to annihilate those of yesterday, and those of tomorrow too far off to command attention.[5]

What a valiant little lady, and what a great boon that she was destined to be the war-time angel at Mount Vernon!

Chapter Notes

[1]This letter from Buchanan is now in the collection of the Riggs National Bank. It was obtained from Franz von Recum, great grandson of George W. Riggs, who had received it from his mother, Baroness Marie Ernestine Howard von Recum. She, in turn, had inherited it from her mother, Ceclia Riggs Howard, the third daughter of George and Janet Riggs. An inscription on the back of the letter reads:

> *Autograph letter from Mr. James Buchanan (President of the U.S.A. from 1857 to March 4, 1861, born 1791, died 1868), dated Feb. 14, 1861, to my father-in-law, Mr. George W. Riggs, of Washington, D.C. U.S.A.*
>
> *Found in the papers of my late wife nee Cecelia Riggs. She passed a summer at a summer resort in Pennsylvania called "Bedford Springs" with Mr. Buchanan & was a favorite of his & it was evidently for this reason her father gave her this letter.*
>
> Henry Howard.
>
> *Ceclia Riggs Howard died Dec. 3, 1908 at the British Legation, The Hague.*

[2]This Lincoln letter was reported in the *New York Times* of August 1, 1959. The letter was acquired by Philip D. Sang, a collector of Americana and a co-founder of Freedom Hall, a museum for the display of historic documents. The letter was to go on display in Freedom Hall in suburban, Oak Park.

[3]Francis Preston Blair, senior, was the owner of the *Washington Globe* and was a member of Jackson's "Kitchen cabinet." It was for him that Elisha Riggs, Jr. named a son. In 1836 he bought the home at No. 6 President's Square which remained in the family until acquired by the U.S. Government in 1942. Most of the members of the family, including Francis Preston Blair, Sr. and Montgomery Blair, were clients of Riggs & Company.

[4]The Jackson statue by Clark Mills was erected in Lafayette Park on January 3, 1853, the thirty-eighth anniversary of the Battle of New Orleans, the orator of the day being Stephen A. Douglas, who had an account at Riggs & Company from 1846 until his untimely death on June 3, 1861, at the age of forty-eight. He had been the nominee of the northern wing of the Democratic Party in 1860 while

Breckenridge of Kentucky was the nominee of the southern wing, both beaten by Lincoln.

Clark Mills, sculpter of the statue, was also a customer of Riggs & Company and the bank possesses two of his original checks in its collection.

[5] This letter from Miss Sarah Tracy is reproduced in the Centennial issue of the *Bulletin* of the Mt. Vernon Ladies Assn. for 1953, p. 66.

Chapter 22

The disgruntled North was suddenly jubilant at the bold action of Capt. Charles Wilkes, the Commander of the U.S. warship, *San Jacinto*, when, on November 8, 1861, he overhauled the British mail packet *Trent* in the Bahama Channel and forcibly removed the Confederate Commissioners, Mason and Slidell, who were enroute to London and Paris.

The headlines did not so state, but Louly's husband, George Eustis, was also taken off the *Trent*. Wilkes sailed north to Boston where the men were jailed as traitors at Fort Warren. Here, the long and influential arm of W. W. Corcoran somehow reached through the maze of official-dom to give aid and comfort to the prisoners.

A letter from Boston dated November 24th, 1861, from Corcoran's friend, William Appleton, states:

> My Dear Sir:
> Mr. Eustis and others will land at the fort this day.
> I wrote him saying anything in the way of warm clothing, bedding, etc., that he might require, to send for me. The physician at the fort, Dr. Green, is a

> *connection of my family; through him I can confer freely as to Mr. Eustis' health ....*
>
> *I understand they have all they wish that can be had in Boston market — their (own) mess, a cook — at their expense of course. I sent Mr. Eustis a box of sherry wine and a hamper of seltzer water. I note what you say as to writing. I am writing this at the post-office.*
>
>
>
> *Your sincerely,*
> *William Appleton.*
>
>

Mr. Appleton had previously advised Mr. Corcoran that George Eustis would not be allowed to write his wife, and requested her address that he might keep her advised from Boston. This would seem to suggest that she was still in Louisiana.

Wilkes' action was in direct violation of International Law and Lincoln suddenly found himself in the midst of an unexpected crisis with England. Montgomery Blair and others had urged him from the very first to disavow Wilkes' action. Lincoln eventually took a similar view, which he outlined as follows:

> *I fear the traitors will prove to be white elephants. We must stick to America's principles concerning the rights of neutrals .... We fought Great Britain for insisting ... on the right to do what Capt. Wilkes has done. If Great britain shall protest ... and demand their release, we must give them up [and] apologize for the act as a violation of our doctrines....*

By Christmas, Her Majesty's government was appeased, largely through the efforts of Secretary of State William Seward, and on New Years Day in 1862, the prisoners were released and proceeded on their mission.[1]

Mr. Corcoran received another letter from Mr. Appleton, written on January 3rd, 1862, from Boston which read:

> *My Dear Sir:*
>
> *I had a very kind note from Mr. Eustis just on departure. He drew on me for $165.86 for his expenses which amount I have drawn on you. I am delighted they are off ....*

CHAPTER 22

> *You cannot conceive of the nonsense there is among our strong-willed women and weak-minded men.*
>
> *I am watched for having been disposed to be kind to . . . Eustis. You know I am not a Republican dyed in the wool, but a Union man and love my friends alike North and South, when they behave equally well.*
>
> *Yours, with love to that little secessionist.*
>
> Wm. Appleton.

W. W. Corcoran, Esq., Washington.

The "little secessionist" was obviously Louly, still living in the Confederacy.

On January 17th, 1862, Corcoran received a brief communication from the British Minister, Lord Lyons, as follows:

> Washington,
> January 17, 1862
>
> My Dear Sir:
> *I have just received intelligence by telegraph from New York that the Rinaldo arrived at Bermuda on the 9th instant, coaled, and sailed on the 10th for St. Thomas.*
>
> Yours faithfully,
> Lyons.

This indicated, apparently, that George Eustis and friends had safely reached Bermuda and were headed for Europe via the southern, January route.

Back in Washington a few weeks later, the entire city was shocked and saddened by the death of the President's son, Willie, on February 20, 1862. The Lincolns had lost their second son, Edward, when he was four years old, eleven years before they left Springfield. Their oldest boy, Robert Todd, eighteen, was at Harvard and he spent little time with his parents. This left eleven-year-old Willie and eight-year-old, Tad, to take over the White House as their personal playground, and they did much, unconsciously, to relieve their father's worry and tension.

225

Although Willie was named William Wallace after Mrs. Lincoln's sister Frances' husband, Dr. William Wallace, he was always referred to as "Willie." Both of the boys had taken cold in the severe February weather, and Willie had developed a high fever. The fever developed into typhoid and Willie's condition became critical and finally hopeless. He died February 20, 1862. Both parents were desolate over the loss of the handsome, blue-eyed boy, and Lincoln gave way to uncontrollable expressions of sorrow, at the same time trying to restrain Mrs. Lincoln, who was prostrated and hysterical with grief. Months later, she was still unable to control her paroxysms of weeping.

The Riggs National Bank owns an original Lincoln check for eight dollars payable to "William," with no last name, which may have been to son, Willie, for it was written prior to his death. Eight dollars was a lot of money in those days, but if Willie had something very special in mind and appealed to the President, it is doubtful that the fond father would have refused him. Willie had five dollars in his pocket when he died and Mrs. Lincoln gave this to New York Avenue Presbyterian Church in his memory. Some historians feel that the check to "William" was actually written to William Johnson, Lincoln's negro valet. On the other hand, another Lincoln check was payable to "William Johnson (colored)." Still another was payable to "Lucy (colored woman)," and the President seemed invariably to add this parenthetical description when appropriate.

This leads to the story of another extraordinary Lincoln check drawn on March 10, 1862, a little over two weeks after Willie's funeral.

In the previous forty-eight hours momentous events had taken place. The *Merrimac*, a grotesque, armored hulk flying the Confederate flag, had shot up the Union fleet of wooden vessels in Hampton Roads, and fought a battle from which she retired with the valiant little turret vessel, *Monitor*, ushering in a new epoch of naval warfare. Secretary of War Edwin M. Stanton, who had visions of the *Merrimac* shelling the War Department and even the White House from the Potomac, was just getting over his hysterics. But Mrs. Lincoln was still prostrated from the loss of Willie. Tad, recovering, but still seriously ill, wouldn't take his medicine. Things got so bad upstairs at the Executive Mansion that Tad's nurse took the problem to John Hay, and Hay interrupted Lincoln in an important White House conference with a group of border-state politicians.

The President walked down the long corridor and said to the young nurse, "You stay here," entering the sickroom and softly closing the door behind him. He soon emerged smiling and announced. "Tad and I have fixed things up."

The nurse found Tad grinning weakly from his pillows and clutching in his hands the bank check reading, "Pay to Tad (when he is well enough to present) — Five dollars."

The Riggs & Co. records show a five dollar withdrawal the next day, and another debit in the same amount three days later so Tad either got well in a hurry or persuaded someone to go to the bank for him.[2]

On the Preceding February 26th, two days following Willie's funeral, George W. Riggs had applied for a military pass for himself and two daughters to go to Mt. Vernon. The winter had been long and bitter and he had probably received some disquieting news from Miss Tracy. The pass read:

> *Pass Mr. G. W. Riggs and two daughters to Mt. Vernon and back. By command of Major General McClellan.*
>
> *S. Williams, Asst. Adj. Gen.*
> *NOT TRANSFERABLE.*

The two daughters who accompanied him were probably his eldest, Alice, twenty, and Kate, nineteen, enlisted to help carry food, supplies and clothing to the beleaguered recluses at Mt. Vernon. Mr. Riggs himself unquestionably was prepared to leave a generous gift of money from his own pocket.

In addition to trying to maintain liaison with the Mt. Vernon ladies, banker Riggs, a charter stockholder and organizer, was much involved with the Washington and Georgetown Railroad Company which was laying a double iron track from Georgetown to the Capitol on which would run horse-drawn vehicles.

Previous efforts to build the railroad had failed on two occasions in the 1850's for lack of interest, but the enormous increase in population and the urgent necessity of obtaining regular transportation for government officials and employees, as well as for civilians, had prompted President Lincoln to intervene personally to have the necessary supply of iron allotted for the tracks.

This street railroad project was of great importance for the bank in providing a boarding and dismounting station at its front door on President's Square, and furnishing much more convenient access to its services for its customers throughout the city, but especially for those on Capitol Hill. The line was popular and profitable from the beginning. This innovation, along with greatly expanded gaslight facilities, was spurred by the war, as was also the employment of some thirty or forty young ladies as clerks in the hard-pressed Treasury Department.

Riggs & Co.'s office was thronged with military personnel who wanted to open accounts or purchase drafts to send funds to their loved ones back home. Despite the war, as also because of it, the bank's volume of business was rising substantially.

Meanwhile, on Capitol Hill in April of 1862, Senator Jesse D. Bright had suffered a cruel blow when the Senate had charged him with disloyalty to the Union. Some of the charges stemmed from the Bright's close friendship with Corcoran and Louly, and also his long friendship with Slidell and Jefferson Davis and numerous other southern politicians who had been frequent guests at Corcoran's banquets. Despite his eloquent and vehement denial of the charges, the Senate expelled him by a majority vote. (He was later exonerated by an investigating committee.) Senator and Mrs. Bright went abroad for much of the balance of the war.

It was the summer of 1862 that the Lincolns first decided to use the Riggs cottage out at Soldiers Home as a summer retreat. They wished not only to avoid the heat of downtown Washington, but also to escape the haunting memories of little Willie at the White House.

The old Riggs "cottage" had been George Riggs's twelve-room country seat known as Corn Rigs, now somewhat

CHAPTER 22

dwarfed by the larger asylum buildings around it. The Lincolns occupied the master bedroom on the second floor from which two large windows opened directly over the porch, providing a splendid view of the city and the Capitol building, where, under General Meigs supervision, and by Lincoln's direction, work was continuing on the new great dome. The parlor below, opening onto the front porch became the President's sitting room.

Lincoln's occupancy of the cottage (which still stands today just inside Eagle Gate, the Upshur Street entrance to Soldiers Home) gave it its greatest historic importance, for it was here in July, 1862, that he prepared the original draft of the Emancipation Proclamation which he issued following the battle of Antietam.

The accuracy of this statement is vouched for in Lincoln's own words when he said, "I put the draft of the proclamation aside, waiting for a victory. . . .Finally came the week of the Battle of Antietam. I decided to wait no longer. The news came, I think, on Wednesday, that the advantage was on our side. I was then staying at the Soldiers Home. Here I finished writing the second draft of the proclamation, and came up on Saturday, calling the cabinet together to hear it, and it was published the following Monday. I made a solemn oath before God that if General Lee was driven back from Maryland I would crown the results with the declaration of freedom of the slaves."

And so the first home of George and Janet Riggs, where five of their children had been born and one had died, was destined to be preserved as the Summer White House of the Civil War President.

By December, 1862, W. W. Corcoran was in London and Louly was in Paris with her husband. Corcoran's delay in leaving Washington might have been necessitated by his transfer in installments (for the sake of safety, and probably through the diplomatic pouch of the helpful Lord Lyons, the British Minister) of a sizeable portion of his cash assets as insurance against eventualities. It is possible he met Louly in Bermuda and embarked with her for Europe.

Their presence abroad is revealed in several letters, including one from Lord Ouseley to Corcoran on December 20, 1862, reading as follows:

> 3 Berkely Square
> Dec. 20, 1862

Dear Mr. Corcoran:
I much regret having missed you yesterday, when you were good enough to call. If you are likely to be home between 10:30 and 11:30 this morning, I will call at your hotel.

The best way of seeing you, without interfering with your arrangements in London, would be for you to come and join our family party (consisting of Lady O. and myself and, perhaps, my son-in-law) at dinner, at or about 7, if that suits you. I hope, if you do not prolong your stay, that you will return to London by the by . . . .

I hope that your daughter is well and likes Paris, as most ladies do . . . .

> Ever, most truly yours,
> W. G. Ousely.

George Peabody, writing to Corcoran from Brighton, where he has gone for his health, invites Corcoran to spend part of the winter with him at Nice, where he hopes to pass about three months. Louly has apparently presented Corcoran with a grandson named for him, and Peabody closes his letter by reminding him to "Kiss the baby — for yourself."

A second letter from Peabody to Corcoran again invites him to Nice and reads as follows:

> Hotel Victoria, Nice,
> France
> Feb. 11, 1863

My Dear Corcoran:
I comply with my promise to write you after I had been a while at this place . . . . I think you will 'tear yourself' from the baby in the course of next week and join me here. It is full of English and Americans, and the climate is most beautiful; there has been no rain for twenty-seven days, and ever since my arrival there has been a hot, sunny, cloudless weather — so much so that no fire has been required, night or day.

CHAPTER 22

Now, my dear Corcoran, I advise you to leave off politics and come and join me without delay; and early in March we will go to Florence together. Affairs seem to be coming to a crisis in our distracted and self-destroying country — exchange on England about seventy per cent! How lucky you were to get to England the $1,600,000 at ten.
With best regards to Louly and Mr. Eustis,
I am, very truly yours,
George Peabody.

Corcoran's correspondence suddenly takes a starkly contrasting turn with a letter from Mr. Joseph Henry, Secretary of the Smithsonian Institution — which letter is a tragic reminder of the carnage on the battlefields back home.

Grisly, but scientific, the subject matter is as follows:

Smithsonian Institution,
February 23, 1863

My Dear Sir:
An enterprise has been started in this city to form a surgical and anatomical museum to which the Smithsonian has given aid and cooperation.
The effort has thus far been very successful, and, through the agency of the present Surgeon-General and his colleagues, the largest and most valuable collection to be found has already been gathered. The only drawback on the establishment is the want of a suitable room in which to exhibit the anatomical specimens, and, therefore the proposition has been made to apply to you for the use of the upper part of the building near Dr. Gurley's church ... I can truly say that it cannot be appropriated to a better purpose for the reputation of the city and the good of humanity than the one mentioned.

I have the honor to remain, very truly, your obedient servant,
Joseph Henry

Mr. Corcoran's reply to this letter is unknown, but it reminds us that "the collection" they were seeking to exhibit was then housed in the upper floor and small back annex of Riggs & Co.'s building at 32 President's Square.

A communication in the bank's historical files from the Surgeon-General's Office on the nintieth Anniversary of the founding of the Armed Forces Institutes of Pathology, May 21, 1852, contains the following:

> I obtained for him [Hospital Steward, Frederick Schafhirt] amputated arms and legs from the Washington hospitals, and afterwards from those in the neighborhood .... These he prepared and mounted and very soon the first specimens... were ready, and made their official appearance on top of my desk and on the shelves put up for that purpose in the rooms of the Surgeon-General's Office ... at Riggs Bank.

An amplification below the foregoing states that this was "a part of the former 'Riggs Bank Building,' being that part above and back of that occupied by the bank itself."

And, therefore, in addition to his other wartime contributions, George W. Riggs was renting space in architect George Hadfield's splendid old building to the Surgeon-General's Office for this great project "for the good of humanity."

The 1954 Christmas card of the Armed Forces Institute of Pathology, employing a sketch of the old bank building previously used on one of the bank's own Christmas cards, contains below the picture the legend: "The first home of the Armed Forces Institute of Pathology, 1862-64."

Chapter Notes

[1] Exactly one month after release of the Confederate prisoners, Lincoln wrote a diplomatic letter to Queen Victoria expressing the nation's sorrow over the death of the Prince Consort. While this was more or less routine, the President was anxious to remain on good terms with England.

[2] In March of 1967, the Riggs National Bank learned through Mr. King Hostick, an energetic Lincolnian and collector of historic documents, of Springfield, Ill., that the check to "Tad (when he is well enough to present)" was being sold at auction in New York City. The bank authorized him to bid up to $2,500 for the check, but did not wish to go higher, since it was felt the check would be sold to some wealthy collector and be preserved in any case. Later information revealed that it was purchased by a Mr. David A. Wolper of Hollywood, California, for $5,500.

Chapter 23

In late 1862 and early 1863, Lincoln tried desperately to find a Commander for the Army of the Potomac who could produce a solid victory for the Union cause. Even when the advantage was temporarily on the Union side, as at Antietam, Lee's outnumbered and will-o-the-wisp armies always slipped away from the slow and bungling Union commanders. The President traveled tirelessly to visit and encourage his generals; to Harpers Ferry, to Antietam, to Belle Plain, Virginia, and to Acquia Creek; to Fredericksburg and Falmouth, Virginia, and back to Acquia Creek. He replaced McClellan with Ambrose Burnside, and Burnside with Joseph Hooker, and finally (and providentially, just before Gettysburg), he relieved Hooker with "Old Snapping Turtle" — Maj. Gen. George Meade.

In between his battlefront visits, Lincoln formed the habit of going to the War Department for the news. An Army Telegraph office had been set up there in the old building occupying the site of the present Executive Office Building. Day and night he crossed the wooded lawn west of the White House, passed through the turnstiles, and followed the path to the side door of the small building at the corner of 17th Street.

Sometimes he went with a secretary or friend, who would be uneasily aware of the target the tall figure in high hat made in the gloom — but more often he went alone across the White House grounds so heavily planted with trees and shrubbery.

As often as possible Lincoln attended church services at the New York Avenue Presbyterian Church. It is said he also frequently attended the weekly prayer meeting at the church, but usually sat alone in the pastor's room from which he could see and hear the service without being seen, thus avoiding the interruption of the many people who gathered to speak to him at its close. He once said he chose the New York Avenue because he had found a minister who preached the gospel and let politics alone. It was Dr. Gurley who had officiated at Willie's funeral in the East Room of the White House.

Although it is certain Lincoln contributed generously to the church, the only check extant on Riggs & Co. supporting that fact is dated June 25, 1863 and payable to "Dr. Gurley (for church) — twenty-five dollars" — again, possibly, written at a time of gloom and uneasiness with the hope of better news to come — which news came swiftly eight days later with the great victory at Gettysburg on July 3, 1863.

The Riggs National Bank possesses a much-prized photoprint of this check, so sharp and readable it also reveals Lincoln's initials on the two cent "war revenue stamp" then required to be affixed to all bank checks and initialed by the drawer.

A few weeks later, perhaps in a related mood of gratitude for the sudden shower of Union victories, including Grant's triumph at Vicksburg (which opened the Mississippi to the Union armies) on Independence Day in 1863, the day following the "high water mark" at Gettsburg, the President wrote one of his most intriguing checks. It was drawn on August 11, 1863 (August being the month in which he drew the check to "Mr. Johns (a sick man)" two years earlier) and was payable to "Colored Man with one leg — five dollars."

And once again he may have been wandering around Jackson Square escaping the heat and pressure of the White House when he encountered this particular colored man.

This check was first reproduced on the cover jacket of an early Lincoln biography published by Ida M. Tarbell in 1895. It

CHAPTER 23

appeared again the following year in a newspaper article by her in the *Denver Republican*. In both instances she merely speculates on the identity of the payee — "An applicant who reached Lincoln as he passed to and from the White House." and "a one-legged colored man, a solider perhaps, seeking the President with his story of woe."

Well, despite Miss Tarbell's musings and imaginings on the subject, no one can say for certain who the "Colored Man with one leg" was. But the most plausible hint of his identity was given us during our memorable interview in January of 1949 with Baroness Marie Ernestine Howard von Recum, the elder of the two last surviving granddaughters of George W. Riggs.

She told a fascinating story of having seen a "colored man with one leg" many times when, as a little girl of five or six, she had walked to the bank with her grandfather from his home on Eye Street.

"He always stood between the Freeman house on H Street (now the church parish house) and St. Johns Church," she related, "and my grandfather spoke to him and gave him something every morning as we passed by."

"He was a fine looking man", she added, "and his beard was turning gray."

Baroness von Recum was born at Green Hill, the country estate of George Riggs, on August 22, 1868. She was, therefore, five and six years old in 1873 and 1874. And her parents were then, and for some years thereafter, residing in the big Riggs town house on Eye Street.

If this "fine looking man" with one leg was a successful beggar in 1863, as the President's check would indicate, he was probably also a successful beggar at the same stand ten years later in 1873.

And what better spot could he have chosen? All the houses around the square were occupied by prominent and well-to-do citizens, and the church had many distinguished parishioners. Between the Freeman house and the church, there was a driveway to the Freeman's large two-story stable on the lot behind the house which extended all the way to 16th Street, north of the church. These excellent stable facilities had been a factor in pursuading Lord Ashburton to lease the property as the British legation back in 1842. There would always be a number of Negro coachmen and hired hands back at the stable who would probably have no objection to the "nice looking man" on crutches or with a peg leg, using their facilities from time to time. And the church itself probably had colored cleaning and maintenance personnel.

As to the length of time the "colored man with one leg" may have stayed at his strategic location, the oldtimers at Riggs Bank have seen in their lifetimes, beggars with one leg and even with no legs on F Street, the "prime territory" for that activity, who solicited there for twenty or thirty years. In some cases, even retiring to Florida with appropriate newspaper publicity.

And so we conclude that, at the very least, Baroness von Recum's story has a marked sense of reasonableness.

As to why Lincoln made out his check as he did, he probably instinctively avoided a name that could bring complications; and perhaps, also, the recipient couldn't write. With the description the President used, the obstacles to encashment were reduced to practically nil. And the man, as a familiar figure in the neighborhood, might have been known to the bank in any case.

On Saturday, October 10, 1863, in the middle of the war but looking forward to better times, the first election of the Metropolitan Club was held to choose a president, 24 governors and a secretary. The election was continued on the following Monday, the twelfth, at which time George W. Riggs, the banker, just having been elected a governor, became also the first treasurer.

The constitution proclaimed as the object of the Club, "to promote social and literary intercourse and enjoyment among the members." And once again, George Riggs added another civic and social responsibility to his already busy schedule.

The first clubhouse was the General Ripley house at the southwest corner of 15th and H streets, on the site now occupied by the Union Trust Building. This house had recently been vacated by the Prussian Minister, Baron Gerolt. In those days and for many years thereafter, it was a purely residential neighborhood.

The Club soon invited its first foreign diplomat to membership, the same Baron Gerolt who had preceded the Club as tenant of the house it had leased. (This was the same Minister who had arranged for Mr. Corcoran and ex-President Fillmore to be presented to the king by Baron Humboldt.) The Prussian legation had purchased its own house near the Club on 15th Street, and was the first foreign mission to own its own real estate in Washington.

And by a coincidence, as shown by the city directory of that era, it was "423 15th St. north, west side near center of block," the former residence of Senator Bright.

The Riggs National Bank has possessed for many years in its file of George W. Riggs's personal correspondence, a cryptic little communication from him to his attorney, James M. Carlisle. It is dated 26 November, and quite uncharacteristically for banker Riggs, no year is indicated.

George Riggs's slanted scrawl was becoming more difficult to read with the years, possibly because of the burden of his drastically increased correspondence. We have no evidence he ever used a scribe. As best we can decipher this letter it reads as follows:

26 Nov.

My dear Carlisle:
I mailed your letter to ——— this morning without any remarks of my own, or changing a word of yours.
I spent the morning in the country, not in church as ordered by the authorities.
Did you get a note I sent you by Bayliss about a deed of trust from Digges? I have received papers, copy of proceedings, from Chew which I will submit to you. They seem all right.

Yours truly,
Geo. W. Riggs.

The second and third paragraphs refer to Mr. Riggs's country estate in Prince Georges County. Known as "Green Hill," as we have previously noted, it had formerly been part of the great Digges' estate, "Chillum Castle Manor," of which Elisha Riggs had obtained a part at a mortgage sale in 1824. George Riggs had enlarged and improved the original stone house and decided to make it his country home. He was also purchasing additional parcels of land from the Digges heirs, whose fortunes had been declining for some years.

But regarding the curious sentence, "I spent the morning in the country, not at church as ordered by the authorities", we had long puzzled over what "day of prayer" it was, and in what year. And almost by accident we stumbled across the answer. In looking up some unrelated facts about Gettysburg we were startled to read "The first national observance of Thanksgiving Day in America was celebrated on November 26, 1863, a week after Lincoln dedicated the Soldiers' National Cemetery at Gettysburg." Here was our November 26, and here was our year — 1863, and perhaps that was why the little document had been preserved.

The "first Thanksgiving" had been called for by Lincoln's Proclamation of October 15, 1863, which contains some of his most haunting phraseology.

With respect to George W. Riggs at Green Hill on November 26, 1863, we can only say in his behalf (as also for many other prominent Americans, especially Democrats) that, implausible as it may appear from this distance, the high-minded, sincere composer of the "first Thanksgiving" proclamation, was still to them the opposition party President. The myth of Abraham Lincoln had not yet begun.

Chapter
24

In late 1863, the gallant Miss Tracy, still struggling to keep Mt. Vernon financially afloat, and possibly prompted by Treasurer George Riggs (who recognized the value of her appeal in behalf of the Ladies Association), wrote to Captain John A. Dahlgren, Commandant of the Washington Navy Yard, requesting his cooperation as follows:

> *Dear Sir:*
> *In consequence of the small means which the Mt. Vernon Association now possesses, it finds difficulty in procuring a sufficient force to protect the grounds at Mt. Vernon from the inconsiderate depredation of visitors. It has therefore become necessary that it should make such arrangements as will prove the most effectual for that purpose. The War Department has kindly issued an order, permitting the Boat now under contract to the Association to commence her regular trips, at the same time prohibiting all other Boats or vessels from landing at Mt. Vernon. This enables the Assoc. to receive a small revenue to aid in preserving Mt. Vernon of which it is deprived by the frequent*

> landing of impromtu parties — at the same time
> affording ample opportunity for those who desire,
> to visit the Sacred place. May I request in the name
> of the Asso. that you will extend the same courtesy
> which it has received from the War Department
> and prevent the Boats from the Navy Yard from
> landing at Mt. Vernon.

The reply to her letter is unknown but doubtless the Navy followed the example of the War Department and issued an order prohibiting the landing of any Navy Yard boats at Mt. Vernon.

Meanwhile, Janet, Mrs. George W. Riggs, had been named Acting Vice Regent for the District of Columbia, there being no provision in the charter for a permanent representative. Miss Tracy was probably helpful in this connection and much pleased with its occurence. She was soon a guest at the Riggs mansion which afforded her a blissful excursion from the strain and boredom of her Mt. Vernon residencey. She gratefully acknowledged "the aid and comfort" she found in the Riggs home.

There might have been other and more surprising visitors to the mansion of George and Janet Riggs during the coming Christmas season. Sometime in late 1862 or early 1863, Elisha, Jr. and Mary Boswell Riggs and their four children had returned from Paris to the United States and settled in New York City. The circumstances of their returning are not known and can only be conjectured. But in the light of more recent history, that speculation takes on a fascinating aspect.

In his comprehensive Riggs family geneology, John Beverly Riggs says simply that, after returning to New York in 1862, Elisha "once again entered the banking business in the firm of Jerome, Riggs & Company." In that context, it should be recalled that this volume was published before World War II in 1939.

We vaguely recalled that Roger Farquahar, in writing about "Washington house, on the heights of Old Georgetown," had reported that "Elisha Riggs, Jr., who married Mary Boswell of Lexington, Kentucky, lived in the house for a short time as a tenant," — obviously not knowing he had owned the house. That inaccuracy had left us somewhat unimpressed by his next statement that "Miss Boswell was a famous beauty . . . .

CHAPTER 24

and a close friend of Lady Randolph Churchill, the mother of Prime Minister Churchill." But suddenly the publication of the best-selling "Jennie" in 1969, revealed to millions of readers that the mother of the great wartime prime minister was an American girl named Jennie Jerome, the daughter of the flamboyant New York financier, sportsman and man-about-town, Leonard Jerome. And here we had Elisha, Jr. in a banking firm in New York having the name "Jerome, Riggs & Company." Could his partner possibly have been Jennie's father?

We fired off a missive to the New York Public Library, asking what the city directories for 1862-65 disclosed in the way of listings for the firm or its principles. Their reply three weeks later was helpful but failed to provide a definite answer. The letter read as follows:

> No. 1. No first name for (any) Riggs was found. New York City directories for the period list a Riggs & Co., bankers, 56 Wall street [This was, of course, the New York branch of Riggs & Co.]
>
> No. 2. Jerome, Riggs & Co., brokers, appears twice in the period 1862-65 in Trow's New York City Directory, compiled by H. Wilson. The volume for 1864-65 lists the address as 46 Exchange Place. The volume for 1865-66 lists it as 48 Exchange Place.

And so our second letter went off asking if they had any "Jerome" listed in connection with the firm. And this time the reply was "yes". They had found listed a "Leonard W. Jerome, at 46 Exchange Place, home 30 west 21 Street," and we then knew that Elisha, Jr. was indeed in the brokerage (not banking) business with Jennie's father.

But that was about all we knew for certain. No mention is made in "Jennie" of Elisha, Jr. or Mary Boswell Riggs or the firm of Jerome, Riggs & Company. The popular best-seller does disclose that Leonard Jerome and his wife, Clara, and their three daughters went to Paris in 1858, at which time Elisha, Jr. and Mary Boswell were living there. And one can speculate it was highly possible they met in the American colony.

Jennie was four in 1858 and Mary Boswell Riggs was 29. The Jerome's fourth daughter was born in Paris, but Leonard wrote to his brother that Paris was not as agreeable to him as New York, and he brought them all back to New York in 1859.[1]

243

In 1863, when the partnership was formed, Jennie was nine, and it is very likely that the two families visited together and Mary Boswell, then thirty-four, probably got to know the little girl. If this was the genesis of her being "a close friend of Lady Randolph Churchill, the mother of Prime Minister Churchill," despite the disparity in their ages, we will never really know. Jennie's marriage to Randolph took place in 1874.

But in any case, the unpredictable Elisha, Jr. had bounced back into the banking limelight as the partner of one of the richest and best known, albeit brash and speculative, financiers in Wall Street. And he probably discussed his new connection with characteristic pomposity when visiting his hard-working, conservative half-brother during the Christmas season of 1863.

On May 4, 1864, the Army of the Potomac under Grant finally crossed the Rapidan, marking the beginning of the bloody Battle of the Wilderness. At the same time, General William Tecumseh Sherman began the drive against Georgia that would end with the fall of Atlanta four months later.

But many dark and discouraging day lay ahead and it was too early for the President to have had any news on these crucial campaigns. For the moment he was concerned about needing a new pair of glasses. So the President walked four blocks from the White House to the small shop at 244 (later 1227) Pennsylvania Avene where Isaac Heilprin conducted his optical business.

Lincoln was a regular customer and a warm friendship had developed between the two men. Heilprin was a small, spare-bearded man who spoke seven languages and had come to America as the secretary of the great Hungarian liberator, Louis Kossuth. He had drifted into the optical business in Philadelphia as a partner of M.I. Franklin, who operated under the style Franklin & Co. He had later moved to Washington to open a branch under the same name, which he later acquired as his own.

After testing the President's eyes (Lincoln was mildly farsighted), Heilprin quickly selected the proper lenses from stock imported from France, fitted them in metal frames, and handed them to the President. Lincoln wrote his personal check for two dollars fifty cents payable to Franklin & Co.

CHAPTER 24

Our informant on these matters was Isaac Heilprin's grandson, William A. Heilprin, a cheerful, rugged octogenarian who was still operating the business at another address in the 1960's and maintaining the firm's account with Riggs National Bank. Mr. Heilprin was a frequent visitor in the bank's lobby and delighted to recount his grandfather's story, especially one particular aspect of it — the check was never cashed.

"Grandfather told me all about it before he died," he said, "but first let me explain that my grandfather was a very warm and sympathetic person, and a great family man with a lovely wife and children. Now you might think that he just kept the check because he realized it would have great historical value someday. But he reminded me that two and a half dollars was a lot more money than it is today. Grandfather said he felt sorry for Mr. Lincoln, realizing what terrible burdens he had to bear, and feeling particularly bad about the fact that Mrs. Lincoln was awfully hard on the President and very extravagant. Grandfather said he didn't cash the check because he wanted to help Mr. Lincoln out."

And so the concept of Lincoln as a poor man, which had genuine substance while he was young, followed him into the White House. It is true that Lincoln's balance at Riggs & Co. amounted to only $78.85 on the day he wrote the $2.50 check to Franklin & Company. Furthermore, the bank's records show he cashed an $800 check the next day, overdrawing his account by $721.14, and by June sixth he had run his overdrafts to $2,141.44.

The President could hardly be faulted for making errors in his bookkeeping and being preoccupied with military matters. The summer of 1864 was called "the blackest of the War." But basically the overdraft resulted from the fact that the President simply neglected to deposit his Presidential check for April of 1864, which he would have received about the time he bought his glasses. Apparently he mislaid this check — he had a habit of stuffing papers into the cluttered pigeonholes of his high-backed rosewood desk. In any event, that particular warrant didn't reach the bank until the following November.

None of his checks bounced, of course, because Riggs & Co., as a private bank was permitted to be more lenient in those days, and a Presidential account would be expected to have special treatment anyway. He did deposit his May check on June seventh, cutting his overdrafts to $118.80, and by July ninth, when his June check reached the bank, he was solidly back in the black with a balance of $1,883.53.

Franklin & Company is still in business today at 1700 K Street, northwest, and the $2.50 Lincoln check was last reported to be in the possession of one of Mr. William A. Heilprin's heirs.

As far as can be determined, about twenty Lincoln checks are still in existence. Among them is a second check to Tad for "one gold dollar;" another to "Self for Robert" represents a portion of Robert Todd Lincoln's expenses at Harvard; one to his secretary reading "John Hay for ex." was probably written for White House expenses, and a February 16, 1865 check to "R. T. Lincoln — 100 dollars," was drawn when Lincoln's eldest son was being outfitted at his expense, to serve, very briefly, as a captain on General Grant's staff.

None of the checks known to be in existence is payable to Mrs. Lincoln. She once remarked: "Money! He never gives me any money; he leaves his pocketbook where I can take what I want."

A source of disappointment is the fact that none of these surviving checks is among the very few that were drawn by Lincoln on a small, obscure second account maintained by him at Riggs & Co. which was forgotten after the war and buried in the bank's records for nearly a century. This account was entitled A. Lincoln — Hospital Fund.

Post World War II research discloses that this account was opened on August 20, 1862, after some unknown donor had sent Mrs. Lincoln $1,000 for the benefit of the hospitals in and around Washington. A telegram sent by Lincoln at about the same time (and later listed by his secretaries, Nicolay and Hay, in their first biography of Lincoln) is addressed to Hiram Barney, Collector of the Port of New York and a Friend of Lincoln's:

> Mrs. L. has $1,000 for the benefit of the hospitals, and she will be obliged, and send the pay if you will be so good as to select and send her two hundred dollars worth of good lemmons [sic] and one hundred dollars worth of good oranges.
>
> A. Lincoln.

This appears to account for the first of the two deposits of $1,000 shown in the hospital fund account, and apparently identifies the first check drawn, dated August twenty-first, in the sum of $295.75 — "good lemmons and . . . oranges."

The fact that the President handled the funds in a separate account rather than Mrs. Lincoln is not surprising. While Riggs & Co.'s ledgers of that period show quite a number of accounts for women, there is no record that Mary Lincoln ever had one. Further, she was still affected by the death of Willie, and by another more recent tragic matter reported, ironically, on August twenty-first — the day the first check was written on the hospital fund. A brief dispatch in the *Illinois State Journal*, the Lincoln's hometown newspaper, contained the following: "A brother of Mrs. Abraham Lincoln, Captain Alexander H. Todd, who was in the rebel army, was killed in the late fight at Baton Rouge."

An undated letter from Mrs. Lincoln to the President, believed to have been written on November 3, 1862, sheds some light on the second $1,000 deposit. This letter refers to "the $1,000 fund deposited with you by Gen. Corcoran." Col. Michael Corcoran, commanding the 69th New York (Irish) Regiment, was captured in the first Battle of Bull Run, spent nearly a year in Confederate prisons, and had just been released in a prisoner exchange. He was promoted to brigadier general and hailed as a popular hero in demonstrations in New York and Washington. It seems probable that the $1,000 was collected at one or both of the demonstrations in his honor, and sent to Mrs. Lincoln for the hospitals.

Corcoran dutifully rejoined the Union Army and was killed in action in late 1863.

On December 20, 1862, when thousands of wounded from the disastrous Battle of Fredericksburg were still streaming into Washington, a $650 withdrawal was debited to Lincoln's regular account, but later the entry was reversed and charged to the Hospital Fund account. Either the bank's bookkeeper made an error or Lincoln forgot to add "Hospital Fund" when he signed the check.

Mrs. Lincoln was buying provisions for donations to the hospitals of Washington. Public notice advised them to send representatives to the Executive Mansion to get "their ample quota of Christmas provisions intended for them by Mrs. Lincoln."

And they came in "a long train of ambulances and wagons". Douglas Hospital, for example, received nine turkeys, twenty chickens, a bushel of apples, fifteen pounds of butter and a peck of cranberries. The Lincolns visited many of the wounded, and at the Thirteenth Street Baptist Church Hospital, Mrs. Lincoln and Mrs. Caleb Smith, wife of the Secretary of the Interior, gave a dinner for the wounded soldiers.

The President wrote a total of eleven checks on the Hospital Fund account, all but one of them prior to Christmas, 1862. All activity in the account came to an end on January 9, 1863, when the remaining balance was $201.80. Apparently no further contributions were received and under the mounting pressures of his office the President apparently forgot all about that small balance.

With the advent of autumn, 1864, the news of the war was better. The key city of Atlanta was in Union hands and General Philip Sheridan, appointed by Grant, Commander of the Army of the Shenandoah, had won three victories in a month and completely devastated the valley which had become the "granary of Richmond".

At sea the dread Confederate raider *Alabama* was caught off Cherbourg, France, by the Union sloop-of-war, *Kearsage*, and sunk. The American merchant marine, badly damaged earlier by the debacle of the Collins Line, was almost completely destroyed by the small group of powerful Confederate raiders that were mostly built, armed and based in England and had never made port in the Confederacy. The *Alabama* alone had captured 68 prizes before being herself sent to the bottom. The Federal Navy was concentrated upon the blockade of the Southern ports and was not able to take the offensive until late in the war. But the destruction of the *Alabama* was hailed throughout the Union.

These great victories on land and sea assured Lincoln and the Union party of victory, and brought Lincoln his reelection in November, 1864, with the overwhelming defeat of the Democratic candidate, General McClellan.

Never had "Honest Abe's" star seemed brighter.

CHAPTER 24

Chapter Notes

[1] The following is from *Jennie, the Life of Lady Randolph Churchill — The Romantic Years 1854-1895*, Ralph G. Martin, 19. "The Jeromes moved to Paris in 1858, settling in a posh apartment on the Champs Elyses. Leonard Jerome noted briefly in a letter to his brother, 'We have been to the Grand Ball at the Tuileries and were presented to the Emperor and the Empress. It was universally conceded that Clara was the handsomest woman there. I never saw her look so well.'

P. 20, "Clara Jerome . . collected French aristocrats in small dinner parties and attended a series of salons that were 'delightful' and 'intimate' . . . Their fourth child was another daughter . . . . In 1859 Jerome brought them all back to New York."

Chapter 25

On January 10, 1865, the President was reportedly more relaxed and cheerful than at any time since he took office, as a result of his reelection and the favorable news from the battlefronts. On that date he wrote a brief but important letter in behalf of the Washington Gas Light Company. The company had been having increasing difficulty in obtaining transportation for the coal needed to make gas, while the demand in the teeming capital city had peaked sharply.

George Riggs had relinquished the presidency of the company after serving for eight years, but he and his associates still had a natural interest in the intervention of President Lincoln, since the company was fast becoming one of Riggs & Co.'s premier clients.

Lincoln wrote one of his humble, almost humorous little letters that so well reveals his deft and restrained handling of the enormous powers of his office. The letter was addressed to John Work Garrett, president of the Baltimore and Ohio Railroad.[1]

>Executive Mansion,
>Washington, Jan. 10, 1865

My Dear Sir:
   It is said we shall all be in the dark here, unless you can bring coal to make gas. I suppose you would do this without any interference if you could, and I only write you to say, it is very important to us; and not to say you must stop supplying the army to make room to carry coal. Do all you can for us in both matters.

>Yours truly,
>A. Lincoln.

   Down the river at Mt. Vernon, Miss Tracy mailed out notices dated January 27, 1865, containing the startling news that the first annual meeting of the Association since the War began would be held in Washington February 22, at the home of the treasurer. This was another small sign of guarded optimism.
   George Riggs had apparently intended to present to each member an elegant set of jewelry, consisting of a cameo brooch and matching earrings, with each piece containing a miniature of the Houdon bust of George Washington. Since only five sets were actually ordered, it seems apparent that not more than five vice regents risked coming to Washington via the country's overloaded and uncertain wartime transportation facilities. The likelihood is that only three of the ladies accepted and were present, and one set was intended for Mrs. Riggs and the other was presented to the faithful secretary, Sarah Tracy.
   But at least a meeting took place and the condition of Mt. Vernon was reported and some vague and hopeful plans laid for the future.
   With the advent of spring the good news that had seemed to be building up and for which all the nation hungered, finally arrived. On the morning of Monday, April 10, 1865, the loud blasts of cannon fire from units in and around the city signaled the surrender of General Lee at Appomattox, and the sharp reverberations shattered windows in the neighborhood of Riggs & Co. The startled community sprang awake to one of its most joyous days.

CHAPTER 25

The President arrived back in Washington late that evening from a cruise by steamer to survey the abandoned cities of Richmond and Petersburg. The next night a happy, relieved throng gathered in the circular drive of the White House and spilled out into President's Square to hear the President reading from an upper story window a long and somewhat rambling speech on the vital but controversial subject of reconstruction. The crowd remained restrained and polite but it was obvious they wanted to hear more about the glory and gratification of victory than the problems that lay ahead. At the very close of his speech the President said, "It may be my duty to make some new announcement to the people of the South." But he never did. This was the great wartime leader's last speech.

From what we can learn, the last two bank checks Lincoln signed in the White House were not on Riggs & Co. The first was drawn on April 13, Thursday of that fateful week, on the First National Bank of Washington, the Jay Cooke & Co. subsidiary, which would fail in the panic of 1873.

After the resignation of Secretary of the Treasury, Salmon P. Chase, in the summer of 1864, Assistant Secretary George Harrington had taken over the handling of the President's personal finances, and in some manner one of his salary warrants was deposited to the wrong bank — the First National. Lincoln's two checks on this accidentally (or otherwise) established account (Jay Cooke & Co. were probably gloating over the account of the reelected President) were for $800 each. The one on April 13, 1865, was payable to "Self" and is marked check number 2.

The second check signed by the President before his death was written in Philadelphia the same day, April 13, on the Western Bank, payable to A. Lincoln in the amount of $500 by one Eli K. Price. Presumably this check reached the President the morning of the 14th as it bears his endorsement.

The Lincoln National Life Foundation of Fort Wayne, Indiana, says of this check, "Eli Kirk Price was a Philadelphia lawyer, admitted to the Bar in 1822. He was known as the outstanding real estate lawyer in the city and was active in practice for sixty years. He was prominent in philosophical and historical circles but had little to do with politics. It is not known what the payment of $500 to Abaham Lincoln represented but it opens an interesting field of inquiry."

Apparently the President cashed $800 on the First National Bank of Washington on the day before his assassination and the $500 check on Philadelphia that fateful morning. To our knowledge, no records exist as to why the President wished to have this substantial amount of cash or what became of the funds.

Good Friday, April 14, had dawned as another delightful spring day and the city, still luxuriating in the news of victory, received the further glad tidings that the Stars and Stripes again floated over the battered walls of Fort Sumter.

Lincoln's son Robert Todd, had arrived with General Grant, and the General was invited to attend the regular Cabinet meeting.

Following that meeting, the President and Mrs. Lincoln took their customary afternoon drive through the streets and roads of the Nation's Capital, now so gayly adorned with flowering dogwoods and redbuds, with the limpid Potomac glistening in the distance between its tree-lined banks.

At about the same time the community learned from the afternoon edition of the *Washington Star* that the President and Mrs. Lincoln and the hero of Appomattox would be present that evening at Ford's Theatre for the performance of "Our American Cousin." The small article under "City Items" which announced that fact read as follows:

> *Ford's Theatre — 'Honor to our Soldiers,' a new patriotic song and chorus has been written by Mr. H. B. Phillips, and will be sung this evening by the Entire Company to do honor to Lieutenant General Grant and President Lincoln and his Lady,*
> *who will visit the Theatre in compliment to Miss Laura Keene, whose benefit and last performance is announced in the bills today. The music of the above song is composed by Prof. W. Withers, Jr.*

This public announcement that the President and Mrs. Lincoln would be present with General Grant in their customary box at the theatre was the first step in the spectacle of a nation and a government, having just won a bitter and prolonged civil war, now about to drop its guard and leave unprotected its greatest asset and source of strength — the wartime leader who had inspired and directed that triumph.

And so the script called for General and Mrs. Grant to apologetically ask to be excused from attending the performance, because they were anxious to visit their son in New Jersey. Robert Todd was simply "too tired"; and the Secretary of War and Mrs. Stanton had other excuses, and in the end, it was reported "Mrs. Lincoln had asked twelve people."

The President and his Lady thus found themselves in the outrageous position of having the festive military and the relaxed Cabinet turning their backs on the Commander-in-Chief's invitation for the celebration of victory.

It appears that Lincoln did not much want to go to the theatre that evening in any case. He had recently had a dream of his own death which he reported to the Cabinet. The ordering of the box had been Mary Lincoln's doing — it was to be at long last their (and especially her) night of triumph. But now without the military retinue that General Grant and/or the Secretary of War would probably have inspired or directed to be present, the occasion had lost some of its lustre and much of its relative security.

The President eventually bowed to the wishes of his wife, who was probably in a fit of temper at the reception of what were principally her invitations. The only other persons in the Presidential party were Major Henry Reed Rathbone and his fiancee, Clara Harris — the stepson and daughter of the New York senator. And it is doubtful that Major Rathbone had the slightest notion he had been invited to protect the President.

The song "Honor to our Soldiers" was probably never sung, since it was apparently to have been rendered by the entire company at the close of the performance. And when John Wilkes Booth fired his derringer in the second scene of the third act, Miss Laura Keene's final appearance became a horror, for her and the cast and the audience, and very soon, for the city and the nation.

And perhaps the new patriotic song was never rendered — having been stricken like Ford's Theatre with the curse and plague of the President's assassination.

Around the corner from Riggs & Co. on that murderous night an accomplice of Booth had attempted and nearly succeeded in killing Secretary of State, Seward, whose home occupied the site later covered by the Belasco Theatre and presently by the huge redbrick U.S. Court of Claims.

Seward had suffered a painful accident a few days before when his horse bolted and he jumped from his carriage, sustaining a broken collar-bone, a fractured jaw and a concussion. George Riggs was probably among those who had called at his home after the accident to express his concern for the injured Secretary, who, in addition to being an important client, had become a warm personal friend.

On the night of Lincoln's assassination, a burly stranger had rung the doorbell and told the colored porter he had brought medicine for the injured man, then pushed him aside and rushed up the stairway. Seward's son, Frederick, attempted to stop the stranger at the top of the stairs but the assassin, the half-witted but ferocious Lewis Paine, broke a misfiring pistol over his head and slashed the male nurse who emerged from the sickroom. Bounding across the bed he slashed repeatedly at the Secretary who had rolled onto the floor, and then turned and dashed down the stairs. By a stroke of good fortune the braces around Seward's neck for the broken collarbone deflected the bowie knife and saved his life.

The porter had dashed into the street yelling murder as the assassin remounted his horse. Paine rode so slowly the porter, still yelling, was able to follow him to Eye Street where he lost sight of him.

A crowd soon gathered around the mansion and soldiers and citizens pushed inside. By the time Secretary of the Navy, Gideon Welles, had rushed over from his house across the Square (the former home of John Slidell, next door to the Corcoran mansion) Secretary of War Stanton had arrived from his home on K Street and also, undoubtedly, George Riggs had hurried from his Eye Street home behind Welles' residence.

An Army surgeon summoned by Stanton was attending the injured in Seward's house when word arrived that the President was dying.

The confusion that followed was so chaotic that Stanton at first refused to credit the news, believing it to be a hoax, but a man who was hurrying past the house and had been at Ford's

CHAPTER 25

Theatre, confirmed the rumor the President had been shot. Quartermaster General Meigs who had just arrived from his home around the corner on H Street, called for an escort of soldiers, and finally the little convoy containing the Army surgeon and the Secretaries of War and Navy set out for the frightful scene in 10th Street.

A somber dawn slowly replaced the gaslit night of horror, and rain pelted the patient, loyal crowds waiting tearfully, but almost hopelessly, for word of the stricken President. At seven-thirty, bells tolled and flags were raised or lowered to half staff, as the struggle began in the small lodging house on 10th Street to maneuver the long coffin down the narrow stairs. A bareheaded Army escort followed Lincoln's coffin to the White House.

Shortly thereafter on that fateful Saturday morning, the Union had a new President. "Andy" Johnson of Tennessee, who, like Lincoln, was a pioneer's son and self-educated, was sworn in as the Nation's seventeenth President in his tightly guarded rooms at Kirkwood House at 12th Street and Pennsylvania Avenue. His "A. Johnson" on state papers, letters and checks, bears a striking similarity to the "A. Lincoln" of his predecessor.[2] And to his everlasting credit, he sought desperately to carry out the policies of Lincoln.

The nation and the capital mourned as never before. On Tuesday, weeping crowds had slowly filtered through the East Room to view the President who lay in state in his catafalque just as he had dreamed. A long line remained when the doors were closed in the evening.

At sunrise on Wednesday, the capital was awakened by a barrage of cannon fire and very soon crowds were seeking vantage points along the avenue and on roofs and in trees from which to view the funeral procession. President's Square and the Treasury collonade were packed.

Riggs & Co., like all businesses, was closed and heavily draped in black. We can be sure that at an early hour the large Hadfield-designed, three-tiered ornamental windows on the first floor and the double-step, railed stoop before the doorway were crowded with members of the Riggs family and the bank's staff, and other distinguished clients and friends. Probably the upstairs floor with its three smaller windows, vacated by the Army Pathological Association the year before, was similarly crowded.

At noon Dr. Gurley preached the funeral service in the East Room, and then the dirges of the bands, accompanied by the tolling of bells and the booming of the minute guns announced the beginning of the procession. And probably on this occasion the unique location of 32 President's Square, opposite the old State Department and across from the White House, was appreciated more than ever before as a vantage point for viewing processions of state, and, in this instance, the most solemn funeral march the capital had ever witnessed.

For one more day the martyred President lay in state under the great dome of the Capitol. Early on Friday morning, the funeral train pulled out of Sixth Street Station bearing the President and little Willie. It was Mrs. Lincoln's wish that the little son who had died in 1862, should accompany his father on the last journey and be buried beside him.

The twelve-day journey of the funeral train followed much of the route Lincoln had traveled to Washington as the President-elect, and during the course of the long journey eleven more funeral services were held.

The President and little Willie were laid to rest in Springfield on May 4, 1865. Four years before, when Lincoln had bid goodbye to his friends he had said, "I now leave, not knowing when or whether ever I may return."

Before the funeral train had reached Springfield, the patriotic and contrite citizens of Washington had formed an organization to raise funds as quickly as possible to erect a memorial in the capital city to the slain president. And one of the founders, banker George W. Riggs, was elected treasurer of the "Lincoln National Monument Association."

Chapter Notes

[1] This letter of President Lincoln is quoted courtesy of the Washington Gas Light Company and Mr. Edward T. Stafford, who was for many years Secretary of the Washington Gas Light Company and is the author of a history of the company, entitled *Growing with Washington — The Story of Our First Hundred Years.* Published by the Company in 1948. We are much indebted to Mr. Stafford for his many helpful comments and suggestions.

[2] The Riggs Bank possesses in its historical files an 1852 draft of Corcoran & Riggs on Bank of America, New York, payable to Hon. A. Johnson. "A. Johnson" on the back of the draft strongly resembles Lincoln's "A. Lincoln."

Chapter 26

Three weeks after the burial of Lincoln and little Willie, the emblems of mourning in the capital were finally taken down and replaced with a splendid display of the national colors.

The great Army of the Republic, two million strong, was breaking up and the hasty and widespread mustering out of men had begun. But a Grand Review lasting two days was to take place in Washington, involving three corps of the Army of the Potomac and four corps of Sherman's rugged and ragged Army.

For days these units had been gathering in camps and bivouacs and forts ringing the capital. Occasional glimpses of the soldiers and the evening twinkle of the lights and smoke of their encampments, had sent an air of excitement through the city.

On President's Square a huge portico had been erected before the White House, decorated with flags and bunting and crowned with the names of the great battles of the war. Across the square was another large reviewing stand, and smaller adjoining stands and banks of seats lined the entire three blocks from 15th to 17th streets.

We have no direct evidence of the fact, but unquestionably banker George Riggs, a man of large influence in the community, had hired or built a large stand in front of Riggs & Co. to accommodate as many as possible of the firm's clients and correspondents, who had probably been heating up the telegraph lines with anxious requests.

Tuesday, May 23, dawned clear and mild and at an early hour spectators began to throng the parade route from the Capitol to the White House. When the signal gun boomed at nine o'clock who but "Old snapping turtle," General George Meade, rode out on his plumed and garlanded horse at the head of the Army of the Potomac, and perhaps he even bestowed a few smiles on the happy crowds.

The greatest excitement was furnished by Sheriden's cavalry who thundered around the corner of the Capitol and filled the streets for an hour with the noise and clatter of hoofs and rattling sabers. Sheriden, himself, had been sent to the Rio Grande, but the brilliant performance of his troops soon dispelled that disappointment.

After the cavalary came engineer brigades with pontoons and artillery units with their cannon, and then seemingly endless rows of infantry marching sixty abreast, their bayonets glinting in the sunlight. These troops brought a thunderous ovation from the crowds. This was Washington's own army. They had protected the capital throughout the war and stopped Lee's two invasions at Antietam and Gettysburg, and finally fought through the mud and blood of Virginia to victory at Appomattox.

At the top of 15th Street the marchers swung left into President's Square. In front of Riggs & Co. the lines would slow after the turn and straighten, chins would go out and shoulders back as the proud moment approached for each soldier.

The emotional crowds in the stands must have alternately cheered and wept, touched by the youth of the troops and their general officers and the recollection of all those shadowy figures who would not parade here or elsewhere but had perished under those same regimental colors now so triumphantly held aloft.

CHAPTER 26

One hundred and fifty thousand men would parade during the two days — a figure hauntingly close to the total Union battle deaths of the war.

General Meade had taken his place on the reviewing stand with Grant and received a handshake from President Johnson. He was joined one by one, by the other regimental corps commanders. It was late afternoon when the last line had passed and the applause had finally subsided.

Following the parade George Riggs had probably initiated the practice of wining and dining the bank's guests and for that purpose used his own mansion and garden. A concurrent family reunion must have taken place, with Lawrason and Elisha, Jr. having come down from New York with their wives and children and also the Senator Brights, just returned from Europe. Other members of the family would be present from Montgomery County and Baltimore.

All of them, family and guests alike, must have been fascinated at the sight of the "Emperor's Bowl" in George Riggs' library. His granddaughters later confirmed the story that sometime after Lincoln's funeral Mrs. Lincoln had sent a message to Mr. Riggs saying she would like to offer for sale the Japaneses bowl Admiral Perry had brought back as a gift from the Emperor to President Fillmore. Mr. Riggs had sent word he felt the bowl belonged in the White House as the property of the state and should not be sold. When Mrs. Lincoln replied that if he didn't buy it she would sent it to auction, he hastily sent the purchase price and his carriage with his faithful messenger, Harrison, to haul it gingerly back to the mansion.

The granddaughters confirmed, too, that to accomodate its enormous size and weight (it measured 38 inches in diameter and 22 in height and was over an inch thick) he had summoned his good friend, Joseph Gawler, the cabinetmaker, who built the combination stand and cabinet on which it was displayed.[1]

The decorations on the wedgewood-like blue and white porcelain bowl — especially the flying cranes, the hairy tortoise and the plum blossoms — were said, ironically enough, to symbolize long life. But long life or not, legend also states the Emperor used the bowl as an aquarium for his fighting fish.'

Most of the guests probably bade their hosts an early good night in consequence of the next morning's resumption of parade activities. But George Riggs and a few close friends and family members may have sat for a long while contemplating the bowl and reflecting on the vagaries of fame and fortune and the fateful events which had preceded its transfer into his home.

The sun shone brightly for the second day of the Grand Review. Blue skies and gentle breezes greeted the eager crowds, made more enthusiastic by plain curiosity to see this strange army of the West.

But the figure who would dominate the day as he had the campaigns in the West and the deep South was the Commander of the Military division of the Mississippi, composed of the Armies of Tennessee, of the Cumberland and of the Ohio — the already almost legendary, Major-General William Tecumseh Sherman.

Sherman was no stranger to Washington but he had been away for a long time. An orphan, he had been adopted by Thomas Ewing, an Ohio politician who became a U.S. senator and the first Secretary of the new Department of the Interior. Sherman graduated from West Point near the top of his class and entered the Army as a second lieutenant. On his first leave, at age twenty-three, he became engaged to the daughter of the Ewing family, Ellen, but with the outbreak of the Mexican War the engagement lengthened to seven years. When he came east with dispatches in 1850, the marriage finally became possible. Thomas Ewing was then renting the Blair House as Secretary of the Interior and the marriage, which took place in the drawing room on May 1, 1850, attracted a distinguished company, including President Zachary Taylor, and the great statesmen Daniel Webster, Henry Clay and Thomas Hart Benton.

Now this one-time orphan had fought his way to the highest rungs of the Union Army and was about to lead a victory parade which would end up passing the Blair House.

When the signal gun boomed and he rode out on Pennsylvania Avenue, most of the spectators saw him for the first time — a tall, wiry soldier with deeply lined face and scraggly red beard. Almost immediately he was serenaded by the catchy new tune "Marching Through Georgia," which brought a magnificent smile to his face and wild acclaim from the onlookers.

CHAPTER 26

Sherman had been worried about the comparison of his army with Eastern troops, but he was quickly set at ease. It was true his men wore loose blouses and slouch hats instead of jackets and caps, but they had a deep rhythm to their rolling stride which had carried them through swamps and over mountains. They bore the look of frontiersmen more than of soldiers. And the crowd loved them and their strange wagon trains and pack mules and corps of fierce-looking scavangers, by which they had become a mobile army and lived off the land.

The spectators in the Riggs stand were aware for the second day of the strategic excellence of their location. It was widely recorded that, as Sherman passed the Treasury and topped the rise on 15th Street, he had turned in his saddle for a long look back at the troops he had led from the Mississippi to the Atlantic. Then, satisfied, a proud, taut figure, he had reigned his horse into President's Square to a tumultuous welcome.

And then perhaps — just perhaps — the smiling general may have tossed a salute to the bank where he had opened an account just prior to his marriage, before he turned to greet the crowd across the street at the State Department. And if he did, George Riggs and family and partners and staff must have been on their feet and cheering until the General was out of sight in the direction of the Reviewing Stand.

Some weeks after the dramatic and unforgettable events of April and May of 1865, the Metropolitan Club finally got around to putting its house in order. And, as with many such organizations, finances became an immediate preoccupation.

The first tremor came on June 22, 1865, when the board examined a financial statement prepared by Treasurer, George Riggs, and discovered it was in debt to that genial banker for $1,449.42. Other unpaid bills amounted to an additional $600.

In commenting on the subject, the Club's historian has stated: "Such a state of affairs was not an unfamiliar practice of the time, whereby the treasurer ran the finances 'out of his left pocket . . . .'" As mentioned earlier, the Club paid its bills by a check countersigned by the President and one governor, drawn on the treasurer. It could happen that the latter did not have sufficient Club funds to meet such a check, and in his loyal desire to maintain the Club's good name and credit, he would cover the needs from his own personal funds . . . . An accumulated indebtedness was the result.

"The Club then resorted to the classic formula for its solution — borrowing. The treasurer was authorized to issue $2,000 of 6 percent notes to run for three years [script it was then called].

"It is not difficult to image," continues the candid historian, "by whom most of the script was taken up — by Riggs himself, or Riggs & Co.".[3]

With many post war "comings and goings," the Club found it necessary to initiate a membership drive and, among those soon elected to membership was the preeminent military figure of the day, General Ulysses S. Grant. He was then holding the rank of General-in-Chief, Armies of the United States, and his authority extended throughout the North and West and the conquered South. His membership augured well for the young Club's future in the suddenly burgeoning Nation's Capital.

Back in Europe, banker George Peabody wrote Mr. Corcoran from Ireland, as follows:

Ireland,
August 5, 1865

My Dear Corcoran:
Since I saw you in England I have not heard a
word from you or from Mr. Morgan [his partner
and successor] relative to your intentions whether
to remain in Paris a while longer, or return to Wash-
ington during the present year. Please give me your
views and intentions.

I cannot remain in London a week without risk
of gout . . . . With the exception of ten days in
London, I have been here since 1st of May, very hard
at work fishing for salmon six or ten hours a day,
and living on a plain diet, which has kept me free of
gout and in excellent health. I feel assured that
nothing but this hard exercise in the open air will do
so, and I have leased a fine fishery on the Shannon
(for five years) to commence 1st April, 1867, and to
end 1st April, 1872, and hope we may both live to
meet there even to the last date. . . .It is my intention

to go to the United States for a year and work hard to place "my house in order" there, and then return to pass the time that may be alloted me in quiet, and, in a measure, retired from the world [Peabody was then seventy].

In the next paragraph he suddenly asks of Corcoran, "Has Elisha Riggs come out?" Evidently he had heard that the firm of Jerome, Riggs & Co. had been dissolved and Elisha, Jr. and family had left New York and were returning to Paris. This was not a surprising development, considering the opposite temperaments and life styles of the two men; the bigger surprise was that the partnership had lasted three years.

Following the return of the Riggs family to Paris, John Beverly Riggs states that, "This time he established himself and built a large hotel on Avenue Kleber, which was considered the finest residence owned by any American at the time . . . .He was a founder of the American Jockey Club and one of the oldest members of the Union Club." And once more we soon find ourselves confronted by the tantalizing question of Mary Boswell Riggs, "being a close friend of Lady Randolph Churchill."

The author of *Jennie* tells us that two years later, in 1867, Clara informed Leonard Jerome she was leaving him and moving with her daughters to Paris. He could visit his children whenever he wished, she said. She could no longer tolerate Leonard's "affairs" with other widely known women.

Thereafter, we learn that Clara and her daughters (Jennie was thirteen) moved into an elegant apartment in the Rue Malesherbs, in one of the most fashionable sections of Paris. And perhaps at this time the Riggs and Jerome families did indeed become closer, with the need of the latter for friendship and assistance from other fellow-Americans already established in the French capital.

Unfortunately we have no further information to help us. And while it seems entirely likely that the two families became warm friends and neighbors, we leave the subject for the last time in the fascinating realm of speculation.

Chapter Notes

[1] Joseph Gawler had apparently done a considerable amount of work for George Riggs. The Riggs Bank historical files contains a copy of a check from Mr. Riggs payable to Joseph Gawler in the amount of twenty dollars "for repair of furniture," along with Gawler's receipt for same "for repairing and varnishing furniture." Both are dated April 18th, 1851.

[2] The Emperor's Bowl passed into the hands of George Riggs's descendents and subsequently to the descendents of James Buchanan. It is now permanently on display at Buchanan's home, Wheatland, in Pennsylvania.

[3] The excellent *History of the Metropolitan Club* was written by the late Carl Charlick and published by the Club in 1965.

Chapter 27

Six months after Lincoln's funeral train pulled away from Washington, William W. Corcoran left England to return home. This fact is revealed in the following letter of George Peabody:

> Brighton, Feb. 17, 1866
>
> My Dear Corcoran:
> I received your letter on the eve of your departure from Liverpool, 23rd October, while near Limerick, and as I was but three hours from Queenstown, I tried to find out how long the JAVA would stop there, with a view to see you and the ladies (?) and bid you farewell for a short time, but I could get no information, and gave up the trip, but felt annoyed the next day to hear you were detained at that port from 8 A.M. to 3 P.M....
> My health is very good, and it is nearly a year since I have had an attack of gout, and I hope it has taken leave of me. Tomorrow, if I live, I shall be 71, an age that you and I, fifty years ago, used to consider very old, but my feelings and disposition,

*I am glad to say, do not keep pace with my years, and
I hope to pass my year's visit in the United States
in the same health and spirits. I have secured
passage in the Scotia on her first voyage to New
York; not yet settled when she will leave, but
(probably) ... 7th or 21st of April....*

*I had a kind note from Louly....and was glad to
hear all were well, particularly W. W. Corcoran and
George Peabody (evidently Louly's second son was
named for Mr. Peabody). Very kind regards to Geo.
W. Riggs and all his family.*

*Yours very truly,
George Peabody.*

At about the time of Mr. Peabody's letter, in early 1866, W. W. Corcoran, always something of a soft touch for a worthy cause, began a new and significant shift in the direction of his benevolences — toward the supine and ruined South. The many touching acknowledgments he received reveal how his contributions were greeted by the recipients as small rays of hope amid the wreckage of their homeland.

A few examples will show the nature of these extraordinary gifts and the urgency of their need:

Richmond, Va.

*Your very liberal contribution of one thousand
dollars was handed over to me by Mr. W. H.
McFarland of this city. This sisters are very thankful
and will often obtain for you the prayers of the
orphans, and give their own.*

*Very truly, in X T,
J. McGill,
Bishop of Richmond.*

Petersburg, Va.

*I write to acknowledge the receipt of one thousand
dollars ($1,000) sent by you through Mrs. Judge
Perkins to the Petersburg Female Orphan Asylum.*

*I am sure you know the difficulties we have
struggled through to procure necessary food, fuel,*

CHAPTER 27

and in cases of sickness, even a little medicine for the children,

> Gratefully and
> respectfully,
> Margaret F. Joyner,
> Prest. P.F.O. Asylum.

> Norfolk and Petersburg
> and Southern Railroads,
> President's Office,
> Petersburg, Va.

I was directed by General Mahone to send you the enclosed annual pass, as a slight evidence of his respect, and a token of our appreciation of your kindly interest and generosity in behalf of our distressed people.

> Very truly and
> respectfully,
> Frank Huger.

> Pendleton, Anderson
> District, South Carolina.

I hasten to acknowledge your noble gift. As soon as we can get the draft cashed, (our community is so small, and now so poor that we have to seek someone needing it) we will begin our labor of love; in the meantime, we are preparing our lists, etc.

Be good enough to remember me to Mrs. Riggs and say ... that I have received her letter and will answer it shortly.

> Anna C. Clemson.

> Winchester, Va.

I wrote you some time since acknowledging the donation sent by Mrs. Lee. In the name of our brave dead do I thank you for your aid and encouragement.

We have resumed our work of exhuming and reintering ...

> Respectfully,
> Mrs. Phillip Williams.

New Orleans,

Your handsome donation of one thousand dollars has been received, and I hasten to convey our sincere and heartfelt thanks for your generous aid and assistance....

Enclosed I send you a certificate which makes you a life member of the Southern Hospital Association.

Most sincerely,
Mrs. James Hewitt.

Pendleton, S.C.

Your letter of the 20th inst. gives me hopes that the good old State of South Carolina will still live ... We can do nothing within ourselves, and must depend entirely upon our friends without....

Thos. G. Clemson.

Fredericksburg, Va.

Mrs. Fitzgerald has handed me a contribution from you for the repairs of our desolated church.

The people manifest a just and virtuous spirit of independence so far as their own private wants are concerned, but do not feel justified in leaving the house of God a ruin.

Gratefully,
Thomas A. Gilmer.

Woodville,
Rappahannock Cty. Va.

I have just been to my old house in Culpepper, where your kind contribution has just been expended in a kitchen and stable — the first movement towards reconstruction since the desolation of this place. It inspires in me the hope I may again have a home.

The dilapidated dwelling still stands, the only relic amid the ruins, every other building, every paling, fence, etc., etc., gone.

Philip Staughton.

CHAPTER 27

> Williamsburg, Va.
>
> Be pleased to accept my acknowledgment of your letter of 18th inst. and enclosed check for $1,000 to be applied to rebuilding William and Mary College.
>
> > With the highest esteem and respect.
> > Benj. S. Ewell,
> > Prest., William and Mary College

W. W. Corcoran, rich and powerful though he was, must have been touched and rewarded by these humble acknowledgments. And as a faithful correspondent and perhaps the oldest friend of George Peabody, he must have expressed himself strongly on this subject, with the full knowledge that the latter was coming to the United States via the *Scotia* in April, 1866, for the announced purpose to "place his house in order" and distribute some portion of his even greater wealth in his native land.

And perhaps the subject thus planted, would bear fruit beyond his expectations.

Meanwhile, at Riggs & Co., George Riggs had received a letter dated, Verona, Wisconsin, March 26, 1866, from his longtime friend and former partner, Samuel Taylor.

Taylor's financial problems had considerably lessened, inasmuch as the products of his mill were in strong demand during the war and brought good prices. It appears, too, from information furnished by our helpful and attractive informant, Mrs. George Heitz (great granddaughter of Samuel Riggs) that he had opened a country store nearby which was prospering. Consequently he was requesting only that Riggs & Co. refinance and consolidate his debts into one manageable mortgage on the mill.

George Riggs, pleased to learn of the improved circumstances of his old friend, readily agreed to arrange a mortgage "at the New York rate of 8 or 9%," but wrote, "If you think this too high an interest rate, let me know, but we can even get 10% [in New York]." Rates were probably inflated, like prices, by the war. In the interim, he agreed to open a temporary credit; "You can draw on my New York house, 56 Wall Street, up to eight hundred dollars ($800.00)" he wrote. "On your drafts interest will be at 7% until we arrange the mortgage."

Samuel Taylor was proving again that high born English gentlemen can indeed adapt to the wilderness. After the "great fire" had burned out Riggs, Taylor & Co. in New York, he went West and settled in Verona, Wisconsin. He also purchased a considerable amount of land near the village of Madison. He soon met and married Sarah Elizabeth Robson, daughter of George Robson of Leeds, England, who had earlier removed to America with his family. Sarah's mother, Elizabeth Cook Robson, was the niece of Captain James Cook who discovered Australia, New Zeland, Tahiti, Hawai, etc.

At the time of his marriage in August, 1846, Samuel Taylor was forty-four and Sarah Robson eighteen. He is said to have written in family letters that the best thing he ever did in his life was to marry Sarah. And the marriage was a happy one.

It is not surprising that family lore states that this contented son of Manchester, England, rode to the hounds in his proper red jacket and dressed for dinner every night in his wilderness paradise.

George Riggs closed his letter regarding the mortgage on a personal note when he said:

> I don't know that it will please you to see my face again, but Mrs. Taylor, with women's curiousity, may be wondering what I look like. I send you a photograph which is thought to be the best I ever had taken.
> The hair on my head isn't gray — (Lawrason's is quite 'silvered o'er') but you can see the snow on my whiskers.

This was probably the photograph made by Henry Ulke, the Washington pioneer photographer, whose studio was at 278 Pennsylvania Avenue (north side, between 11th and 12th streets). Ulke's home was at 500 15th Street, northwest, in the block below the Avenue, and on the east side of the street, now covered by the Commerce Department.

By some inexplicable stroke of fortune the bank possesses a copy of this century-old photograph of George Riggs which bears his autograph on the back of it along with the printed

CHAPTER 27

name and address of Henry Ulke. An ancient photograph of Ulke's home is also contained in the bank's files, taken circa 1870, perhaps by Ulke himself (who else) before the house and neighboring structures were torn down to make room for what was later Poli's Theatre. Oldtimers will recall that this widely-known theatre with its marquee on Pennsylvania Avenue, stood there until about 1930, when the whole block was leveled for the site of the Commerce Building.

Ulke also did the fine photograph which he finished in either oil or water colors which hangs in the office area of the Metropolitan Club, and is believed to be the best likeness extant of George Riggs.

Only six weeks had elapsed when George Riggs wrote Samuel Taylor again and apologized for not having answered his intervening letters because of a family tragedy:

> Since I wrote you, my cousin Remus Riggs who had lived with me as one of my own family for ten years died at my house. He had been delicate for a long time dying with consumption. He was a great favorite of all — and his loss we feel very much.

This must have been another great blow to George Riggs's hopes of leaving another Riggs at the top of the bank. By all accounts, Remus, twenty when he had come from Brookeville to live with the family, and thirty when he died, had been like another son to him.

He was the third son of Remus Riggs — the youngest of the twelve children of old Samuel and Amelia Dorsey Riggs. He was, therefor, a nephew of Elisha, George Riggs's late father, and his own younger cousin. And he had probably been named for him — Remus George Riggs. John Beverly Riggs, who is also descended from the first Remus, says of him:

> My grandfather's brother, Remus G., was a very handsome man and a great favorite with all the Washington cousins. I have his album of photographs of family and friends. He was a close friend of Thomas Hyde and of others who were young bank clerks with him. I have always heard it said in the family that GWR recognized much ability and potential in him.
>
> He was engaged to be married to a Miss Moore of New York. I do not know her first name but she gave the font in our parish church at Olney, Md., in his memory.

Remus Riggs was buried in the family burying grounds at Pleasant Hill, not very far from old Samuel and Amelia Dorsey Riggs, and probably George Riggs and his family all went up to the old homestead for the funeral.

But most important of all, George Riggs was pushed into an immediate resolve to replace him in the bank.

In the footnote of his letter to Samuel Taylor telling him of the death of Remus Riggs, George Riggs writes, "You have probably seen [in the press] the arrival of our old friend Peabody. We suppose he will pay us a visit in a few weeks." Samuel Taylor had worked for George Peabody when he first came to the United States.

George Peabody had indeed arrived on the *Scotia's* inaugural voyage celebrating the new Liverpool-to-New York service, but it would be some months before he visited the capital.

On June 30, 1866, one month and eleven days after the death of his cousin, Remus, George Riggs hired another bright young man as a clerk in Riggs & Co. Charles Carroll Glover was nineteen and the grandson of a Washington family, but his path to the bank had been somewhat circuitous.

His grandfather of the same name, Charles Carroll Glover, was the son of Joshua Glover who had come from London circa 1740 and settled in Carroll County near Eldersberg, Maryland, on Piney Run. Joshua's son, Charles Carroll, was born in 1780, and at sixteen was sent to Frederick to study law under the supervision of Judge Roger Nelson, who had served with distinction in the Revolution and represented the State of Maryland in Congress for several terms. At nineteen, Charles came to Georgetown and later moved to Washington where he became a member of the Bar and built a home on 10th Street above Pennsylvania Avenue.

Charles Carroll Glover married Jane Cocking on August 19, 1813.[1] She was the daughter of William Cocking, a native of Nottingham, England, who had settled in Washington about 1805.[2]

Charles and Jane Cocking had three children, two daughters and a son. From the general tenor of family accounts it would appear that the son was the third child.

CHAPTER 27

The first daughter, Matilda, became the wife of Robert Harper Williamson, and lived to be eighty-seven. The second daughter, Mary Jane, wife of Abraham Ferree Shriver, lived to be ninety-four. Based on the known date of her death, she was born in 1824.

The son was named Richard Leonidas, and if our surmise is correct that he was the third child, he was born, of course, after 1824. Of him, family chronicles state: "The only son of Charles and Jane Glover was Richard Leonidas, who married Caroline Piercy of North Carolina." A later press release covering other matters of family importance amplifies this by explaining, "Richard Leonidas Glover was with the U.S. Land Office as a young man and was sent on a boundary mission to settle the boundary dispute between North Carolina and Georgia." Still a third account states that, "Richard Leonidas Glover, with his wife, formerly Miss Caroline Piercy, the daughter of William A. Piercy, in 1845 moved to a farm on Valley River about 20 miles from Asheville, North Carolina, and were living there when their son, Charles Carroll Glover, named for his grandfather, was born on November 24, 1846."

And here, for lovers of romance, which takes in most, if not all, of us, was apparently a touching romance. Young Glover had met and fallen in love with Caroline Piercy on his mission for the Land Office to the North Carolina-Georgia border, and probably much to the distress of his family (travel and communication then being so difficult and uncertain), he had resolved to marry her.

We would like to know more about the principals of this drama but the facts are few. Richard Leonidas died four years after the birth of his first son, and not long after the birth of a second son, named for Caroline's father and for him, William Leonidas Glover. Four years later, in 1854, young Charles Carroll Glover, at the age of eight, came to Washington in a stage coach to live with his father's kin.

He resided for a time with his widowed grandmother, Mrs. Jane Glover, at 421 10th Street, west, and attended Rittenhouse Academy, taught by Otis C. Wright, one of the most prominent teachers in the city. Subsequently, he lived with his grandmother's sister and her husband, Mary Jane and Abraham Ferree Shriver, at 516 (later 457) 9th Street, west.

Mr. Shriver was a bookkeeper at Riggs & Co., and it is assumed he played a part in helping young Charles enter the bank.

At age sixteen this industrious young man went to work in Frank Taylor's bookstore and he remained there three years. Pennsylvania Avenue, at the time Frank Taylor had his store and when young Glover was his clerk, was the main street for business in any form, for pedestrians, for fashionable promenades and for the city's principal hotels. The National Hotel on the north side of the Avenue at 6th Street, was a favorite of the Southern gentry, and Taylor's bookstore adjoined it on the east. The store was a gathering place for the literary and politically prominent, and young Glover benefitted immensely from serving and mingling with these famous personalities.

The story was often told that Frank Taylor, a customer of Riggs & Co. always had a word of praise for his young assistant and urged his friend, George Riggs, to take him into the bank. And, therefore, after the death of Remus Riggs, and with the further influence of his great-uncle, a faithful employee, Charles Carroll Glover became a clerk at 32 President's Square in Washington's largest and best-known bank.

Fate held many exciting prospects in store for this tall, intelligent and likeable son of the romantic but short-lived marriage of Richard Leonidas and Caroline Piercy Glover.

Chapter Notes

[1] Charles Carroll Glover, the first, was a sergeant major of the 22nd regiment, 1st Brigade of the Militia of the District of Columbia, which saw service at the Battle of Bladensburg. He died after a brief illness on March 26, 1827. His widow received for many years a pension of eight dollars per month for his services in the War of 1812. (Paper of Charles C. Glover, Jr., read before the Columbia Historical Society on Nov. 19, 1929).

[2] After his arrival in Washington, in 1805, William Cocking invested heavily in large tracts of land in what was later the downtown section of the city.

He died as a result of a widely reported accident on August 25, 1820. While he was reviewing the progress of work on the Capitol building, in which he was much interested, the scaffolding collapsed beneath him and he fell to the ground, a distance of forty feet or more, and died almost immediately.

Chapter 28

In November, 1866, Ann Pamela Cunningham, Regent of the Mount Vernon Ladies Association, having finally made her way to the capital from her home in South Carolina, sent out notices for a meeting of the Council — the first time, because of the intervention of the war, she would meet the members in Grand Council.

The notice read as follows:

> Madame:
> Whereas the VIth article of the Constitution of the Association states that the Grand Council shall be held at the call of the Regent, whenever the exigencies of the association may in her discretion require the convocation.
> Now, therefore, deeming it a duty imposed upon me by the constitution, I hereby notify you that a Grand Council will be held in Washington City on the nineteenth of November, 1866, at the house of George W. Riggs, Esqr., Treasurer M.V.L.A., 280 I

> street, at which time you are particularly requested to be present.
>
> > Ann Pamela Cunningham,
> > Regent, M.V.L.A.
>
> Sarah C. Tracy, Secty.
> M.V.L.A.
> Hour of Meeting 10 A.M.

And therefore, after a long lapse, the affairs of the Association were returning to something of a regular basis. The meeting was probably held in the Riggs mansion for the greater comfort and convenience of all the members, and perhaps later in the day a trip to Mt. Vernon was scheduled. The official record discloses that "a small but faithful band of vice regents" were in attendance.

Through good fortune and some discreet lobbying in a more relaxed Congress, an indemnity bill soon passed awarding the Association $7,000 for losses sustained during the war by the interruption of boat schedules. Miss Cunningham took up residence at the shrine and was soon reporting "visitors are coming." And so the great hazard to the dream of preserving Mt. Vernon had been survived and the on-the-site principals in the struggle to keep it intact, could breathe easier.

Miss Tracy, having valiantly discharged her responsibilities as secretary, soon retired and went home to Troy. Col. Herbert, in turn, resigned in favor of another caretaker, and returned full time to his banking firm of Burke & Herbert & Co. in Alexandria — one of the oldest correspondents of Riggs & Co.

But after a few years, these two veterans of the war at Mt. Vernon, having been partners in so many trying experiences, apparently decided to handle their future problems on a mutual basis. Whereupon, in true storybook fashion, Sarah Tracy and Upton Herbert were married, and settled down to raise a family in his home at Alexandria.

George Riggs, having surmounted the unpredictable tribulations of the war as treasurer of the Association, was soon to be the recipient of an even greater honor and responsibility which would further enhance his stature as one of the leading bankers of the nation.

CHAPTER 28

George Peabody had arrived in New York on the *Scotia* (the last and finest of Cunard's paddlewheel steamers) on May 1, 1866. After resting in a hotel for a few days (the old gentleman was in frail health and exhausted from the trip) he went on to Georgetown, Massachusetts to visit his sister and other members of his family and old friends.

While there, he made a number of endowments to hometown projects and even decided to erect a memorial church in memory of his mother who was born in Georgetown.

He also selected Robert C. Winthrop, an outstanding native of Massachusetts, to handle his American philanthropies. Winthrop was descended from the renowned Governor John Winthrop, and had studied law in Daniel Webster's office and later served in Congress. He was Speaker of the thirtieth Congress, 1847-49, but his conservative views on slavery and related matters antagonized radicals in both the North and the South and he was defeated for relection. After serving out the unexpired term in the Senate left by the resignation of Webster, he withdrew from politics, but continued to be an outstanding and highly respected public figure.

To escape the heat of the New England summer and to avoid some of the tiresome appearances planned for him, Peabody took a number of his relatives and friends on a vacation to Canada. There, after visiting Montreal and elsewhere, he managed to escape to a fishing lodge for several days of fishing and sleeping in the open air under a tent — perhaps his real motive for the excursion.

Upon his return, he soon became engaged in the more serious aspects of "putting his house in order." He made a gift to Harvard of $150,000 for a science museum, having negotiated the details through Winthrop, and gave a like amount, $150,000, to Yale for a museum and a chair of natural history. Thereafter, he turned his attention to his Peabody Institute of Baltimore. He had endowed the Institute before the war and the building it was to occupy, though completed, had never been dedicated and opened because the trustees were split into two camps — thirteen for the Union and ten for the Confederacy, and could agree upon nothing. Now he proposed to double his endowment from $500,000 to $1,000,000 and to be present for the dedication ceremony which, hopefully, with his conciliatory presence, might prove amicable.

The first step was arranged in Philadelphia where he met with some of the trustees in late October. Then, in a special railway car provided by his friend, John Work Garrett, the president of the Baltimore and Ohio Railroad, he and the other trustees started for Baltimore. (John Work Garrett was the addressee of Lincoln's letter asking for coal for Washington to make gas.) The train picked up other trustees enroute and presumably they were a united group when they arrived in Baltimore.

The dedication ceremony was held in a large meeting hall of the new institute where, after a thundeeous ovation, Peabody arose, and calmly and forcibly gave his views on the war:

> I have been accused of anti-Union sentiment. Let me say this: my father fought in the American Revolution and I have loved my country since childhood. Born and educated in the North [he had four years of schooling], I have lived twenty years in the South. In a long residence abroad, I dealt with Americans from every section. I loved our country as a whole with no preference for East, West, North or South.
>
> When war came I saw no hope for America except in a Union victory. But I could not, in the passion of war, turn my back on my Southern friends. I believed extremists of both sides guilty of fomenting the conflict. Now I am convinced more than ever of the necessity for mutual forbearance and conciliation, of Christian chairty and forgiveness, of united effort to bind up the wounds of our nation . . .

Here was almost an echo of Lincoln, from this self-educated and self-made prince of finance.

The reaction to his speech was overwhelmingly favorable and the next evening he was present at a huge reception organized by Baltimoreans in his honor. The old banker "had turned it all around" and come away in triumph. And yet, as he had explained to Winthrop, he had saved the best for last.

The master benefactor, carried along by his enthusiasm, was now envisioning a mammoth charitable project for the destitute South. And for that purpose he proposed to hold the ceremonies at the heart of the nation — in the city which had

CHAPTER 28

witnessed Lincoln's funeral procession and the Grand Review — he would make this public announcement in Washington, D.C., and involve as trustees some of the best-known figures of the war. He would capture the imagination and attention of the American public as he had previously captured that of the British public with his colossal housing project for the industrious poor of London.

George Peabody had reached his last and greatest charitable decision. And cheerfully relaxed, he bade Winthrop to work out the details, and set off for Zanesville, Ohio, to visit a favorite niece, and still other relatives and friends.

There is considerable evidence that Mr. Peabody had originally intended to establish a large fund in New York for the poor working classes, similar to his project in London. But during his travels in the United States, having previously been prompted by Corcoran, he became very much moved by reports of the poverty and misery in the South. A particularly despairing letter from William Aiken, former governor of South Carolina, had been forwarded to him by Corcoran, as well as other communications humbly confessing the need for "help from without."

Peabody had learned that most of the schools in the South had been closed during the war and many had been destroyed. A whole generation of young people had now missed four years of whatever education might have been available and now faced a worse situation, with Statehouses too dispirited and impoverished to open, staff, or rebuild the schools. The plight of the younger generation cried out for help, but the radicals in Congress were set mainly upon vengeance and punishment.

And so did this fearless philanthropist, with his wealth and power base abroad, completely independent of American politics and politicians, discover his finest crusade.

To Robert C. Winthrop, who had expressed astonishment at the magnitude of his plan for the education fund for the South, he had said: "I prayed . . . day by day that I might be enabled before I died, to show my gratitude by doing some great good to my fellow men." In the educational vacuum of the stricken South he had discovered the vehicle that was to be closest to his heart.[1]

In January of 1867 Winthrop and Peabody were in Baltimore where they sent out letters to a proposed board of sixteen trustees and received their acceptances. A meeting was scheduled with them for February 8, 1867 at Willard's Hotel where Peabody would read his founding letter. The list of trustees was as follows: Robert Charles Winthrop, Massachusetts; Hamilton Fish, New York; Bishop Charles Pettit McIlvaine, Ohio; General Ulysses Simpson Grant, United States Army; Admiral David Glasgow Farragut, United States Navy; William Cabell Rives, Virginia; John Henry Clifford, former Governor of Massachusetts; William Aiken, former Governor of South Carolina; William Maxwell Evarts, New York; William Alexander Graham, former Governor of North Carolina; Charles McAlester, Pennsylvania; George Washington Riggs, Washington, D.C.; Samuel Wetmore, New York; Edward B. Bradford, Louisiana; George M. Eaton, Maryland and George Peabody Russell, Massachusetts.

The meeting was an emotional one. Not quite two years had passed since Appomattox and for the first time statesmen from the North and South were meeting together for a peaceful purpose. There was a solemn blessing from Bishop McIlvaine while the assembled trustees knelt in prayer. Then Peabody rose and read his letter establishing the fund:

> With my advancing years, my attachment to my native land has but become more devoted; my hope and faith in its successful and glorious future have grown brighter and stronger — and now looking forward beyond my stay on earth, as may be permitted to one who has passed the limit of three score and ten years, I see our country, united and prosperous, emerging from the clouds which still surround her, taking a higher rank among the nations and becoming richer and more powerful than ever before.
>
> I give to you gentlemen, the sum of one million of dollars .. for ... education ... of the Southern and Southwestern States of our Union.
>
> > I am, Gentlemen,
> > With great Respect,
> > Your humble Servant,
> > George Peabody.

CHAPTER 28

That moment, according to President Bruce Ryburn Payne, in a Founders Day address on February 18, 1916, at George Peabody College for Teachers in Nashville, Tennessee, "was the first guarantee of a reunited country."[2]

Before the trustees adjourned, they planned a second meeting for March 19, in New York. George Peabody had already intimated to Winthrop that if all went well, he planned to donate to the fund a second million dollars which would make it one of his greatest charities.

George Riggs, as the only banker in the group, must have felt deeply grateful to his father's old partner for this signal honor, which was also an endorsement of his banking house as the probable future depository of much, if not all, of the London transfers to the credit of the Fund. The excitement and publicity created throughout the nation, and especially in the shattered South, was enormous. George Peabody was surprised and gratified on the day following the meeting, when President Andrew Johnson and his Secretary, Colonel William G. Moore, called upon him at his rooms in Willard's Hotel.

Early in March, both Houses of Congress passed resolutions thanking him for his gift and authorizing a gold medal struck in his honor. In that connection, W. W. Corcoran had received a letter from Congressman John Pruyn of New York, a member of the medal committee, which stated:

> There is no restriction in the appropriation, and the highest taste and art should be consulted in its execution.
>
> I have said this to the President [whose responsibility it was to have the medal struck] . . . but, unfortunately, such things are often overlooked. . .
> I am sure that, as a friend of Mr. Peabody, you will take some interest in this matter and give it such attention as may be in your power. Let the medal, in design and execution, be what it ought to be under such circumstances.
>
> J. N. L. Pruyn.

At about the same time the portrait of Queen Victoria painted especially for Mr. Peabody arrived from London, and was presented to him by the British Ambassador, Sir

287

Frederick Bruce. This double-barreled salute to the old gentleman filled the newspapers and raised his image to a new pinnacle on both sides of the Atlantic.

It is known that George Riggs attended the trustees meeting in New York on March 19, which was followed three days later by a large banquet given by Mr. Peabody in honor of General Grant and the trustees of the Education Fund. And he probably took advantage of his presence in New York to visit the branch of Riggs & Co. at 56 Wall Street and to review matters generally with his partner, John Elliott. Their discussion might have touched upon some of the distinguished clients doing their banking there, as shown by the letters which have come down to us from the New York files.

This would have included Dr. John Price Durbin, Chaplain of the U.S. Senate, who had requested them in 1862 to sell some bonds "on Friday, or Thursday, if it is a clear day," thus recalling that the old Curb Exchange (now the American Exchange) at nearby 44 Broad Street, was actually operated on the sidewalk until the early part of this century.

The great Mormon leader, Brigham Young, maintained an account at the Wall Street office and in a letter dated "Great Salt Lake City, Aug. 9, 1864", asked the bank to negotiate a draft on his agents in Liverpool, England, and to place the funds to his credit. This letter which must have traveled part of the distance from Utah Territory by stagecoach, was written by a scribe of the Church and merely signed by Brigham Young.

One of the earliest letters in the New York files is signed by Sam Houston, in his flamboyant, sprawling signature, four and a half inches long and three inches high. The bank has long harbored the fond, but thus far futile hope, that one day a check signed by Houston might be found and reveal how the giant Texan accommodated his enormous scrawl to the restrictive area of a check.

Franklin Pierce, from his retirement home at Concord, New Hampshire, opened an 1862 letter with the polite query, "May I presume to ask of you suggestion and advice touching the matter of the Northern Indiana Railroad Company...."

Important clients were, therefore, not restricted to the Washington office. The key locations at 56 Wall Street and 32

CHAPTER 28

President's Square gave the bank enormous influence in the money markets at home and abroad. And George Riggs's connection with Peabody and the Southern Education fund added additional lustre to the firm's name and reputation.

The files of the Washington office of March, 1867, also reveal another important facet of American history. A prized item is the check of Secretary of State, William H. Seward drawn on Riggs & Co. on Sunday, March 31, 1867, for twenty-five dollars and payable to "Vestry, St. Johns Church." Well might the Secretary have worshipped in quiet contentment on that Sunday morning, for, the day before, Congress had approved the treaty with Russia for the purchase of Alaska. This was one of the greatest acts of Seward's term as Secretary of State in President Johnson's administration.

And when, the next year, Congress would finally get around to appropriating the purchase price of $7,200,000, the banking house of Riggs & Co. would again be featured prominently in the news of that development.

Chapter Notes

[1] Payne, Bruce R. "George Peabody, an address delivered on Founder's Day, February 18, 1916." (Nashville, Tenn., George Peabody College for Teachers, 1940).

[2] Winthrop, Robert Charles. Eulogy Pronounced at the Funeral of George Peabody, at Peabody, Massachusetts, 1870. (Boston, John Wilson & Son., 1870, p. 11.)

Chapter 29

During the summer of 1867, George Riggs was much involved in plans for the first marriage in his family — that of Cecelia, twenty-three-years-old, his third daughter.

Her fiance was a young diplomat who had been appointed attache at the British Legation in Washington a year earlier. Henry Howard was a descendant of the proud, ancient English family whose forebears had included the powerful Dukes of Norfolk, as well as two unfortunate Queens of England, Ann Boleyn and Katharine Howard, both beheaded on orders of their infamous husband, Henry VIII.[1]

When young Howard arrived at his post in Washington, he found that one of the few large mansions open to the diplomatic corps was that of banker Riggs. He soon found his way there and met and fell in love with Cecelia. It was at the grand New Year's reception of January 1, 1867, that "Cecelia gave him some hope," as he hastily wrote in a note to his family.[2]

As a youth Henry had visited the Howard family seat, Corby Castle, at Wetheral, on the River Eden in Norfolk, which, like all such ancient establishments, had its own private chapel.

He must have passed some time with Cecelia visiting Mr. Riggs' country seat, Green Hill, in Prince Georges County, which, with its enormous rich acreage and tenantry, plus the old mill on Sligo Creek, reminded him of the English countryside.

The Howards were a strong Catholic family and so, of course, were the Riggs — at least Janet Madeleine Cecelia and her children; George Riggs had not yet embraced the faith. At some point, the suggestion arose to build at Green Hill a modest "Chapel of Saint Cecelia" — named for the Patron Saint of Cecelia and her mother, as well as of Mrs. Cecelia Dowdall Shedden, the late grandmother — as a private sanctuary where the young couple might take their marriage vows. This aroused much excitement and appobation in the family.

George Riggs, facing a veritable family phalanx on the subject, must have gone along with fatherly tact and good humor with their enthusiasm for the project, and plans were quickly made to erect such a chapel at Green Hill.

Not surprisingly, Henry Howard, having received a thorough English education, emerged as the architect, according to neatly-drawn specifications signed by him which have come down to us in George Riggs's private papers.

Very soon, on a site adjoining the formal gardens at Green Hill, a beautiful little Gothic chapel of fieldstone began to take shape — matching the specifications of thirty-five feet in "great height," eighteen feet "in breadth," with a "thickness of walls" of two feet, and the "height of the walls" ten feet. A triangular stained-glass window above the doorway appears in an old photo to display a madonna or the patron saint, and above it rises a slender spire and open bell tower surmounted by a cross.

Three stained-glass windows adorned each of the side walls and two others flanked the alter. A dim interior view seems to show about seven hand-carved pews on either side of the aisle. A much later colored photo reveals that the ceiling and crossbeams were beautifully decorated in gold, silver and blue patterns, suggesting the heavens, which, in combination with the richly wrought windows, must have created a jewel-like appearance at the time of its consecration by Father Lynch, of the mother church, Saint Aloysius.

CHAPTER 29

The wedding was scheduled for October 2, 1867, but a sudden emergency must have caused some trepidation among the principals. This is revealed by another brief letter from George Riggs to his lawyer, James Mandeville Carlisle dated September, 19, 1867:

> Dear Carlisle:
> This morning early a telegram came to the British Legation announcing the death of Sir Frederick Bruce at Boston at two o'clock this A.M.
> Mr. Howard has gone on. [Evidently Cecelia's fiance had gone to Boston.] Mr. Ford, Secretary of Legation, is here alone and seems doubtful of what should be done with regard to Sir Frederick's papers.
> It occurs to me that it would be proper and kind of you to go to the Legation and as legal adviser tell Mr. Ford what he ought to do.
>
> Yours very truly,
> George W. Riggs.

George Riggs, as a nervous father-of-the-bride, was apparently asking Carlisle to go to the Legation as *his* counsel to offer legal advice to Mr. Ford (who was subsequently, after an appropriate period of mourning, named minister). Sir Frederick Bruce had evidently gone to Boston to embark on a Cunard Line vessel for England. Things must have straightened themselves out in due course, for we find a notice under "Marriages" in the Thursday, October 3, *Daily National Intelligencer* announcing that:

> The daughter of George W. Riggs, Esq., Miss Cecelia Riggs, was united in marriage yesterday to Henry Howard, Esq., attache of the British Legation. On account of the recent death of Sir Frederick Bruce, the British Minister, the wedding was entirely private, and the service was performed by Rev. Father Lynch, at St. Cecelia's chapel, which is on the grounds of Mr. Riggs, adjoining his country seat. There were present members of the family of the bride and a few members of the diplomatic corps.

The *Star* of the same date added the information that "the bride's trousseau embraced a superb collection of diamonds and silk imported from England."

The family's own account indicates that Miss Fannie Whelan was the bridesmaid and Albert Bacon, Cecelia's favorite cousin, acted as best man. Miss Whelan's connection with the family is not given, but the 1867 city directory lists one William Whelan as principal of William Whelan & Co., gas fitters. This was a new and promising business located at 333 E Street, north, not far from the Washington Gas Light Company where George Riggs had been president for eight years, and might indicate a close business and personal relationship between the two families.

Albert Bacon, the favorite cousin of Cecelia and best man, was the only member of the family we have discovered who had served with the Union forces during the war. He was appointed an associate paymaster, U.S.N., and ordered to report aboard the USS *Galatia* at the New York Navy Yard on November 1, 1863. That vessel subsequently joined Farragut's fleet.[3]

Young Bacon was the son of Alice Ann Riggs, a daughter of old Romulus and Mercy Ann (Lawrason) Riggs, of Philadelphia. She had married Dr. James Ware Bacon and Albert was their third son born January 5, 1841. It was Mrs. Romulus Riggs (Aunt Molly) who had raised George W., Jr. and Lawrason after the death of their mother, Alice (Lawrason) Riggs — Elisha's first wife — and any descendant of hers was a welcome guest in George Riggs' home. Albert Bacon had been detached from sea duty in July, 1865, and had apparently been residing at the Eye Street mansion while stationed in Washington.

Witnesses were listed as James Carlisle, Francis Clare Ford, Secretary of the British Legation, and Louis Molina, Minister for Nicarague and Honduras. The young couple left for a honeymoon at the fashionable new resort area of Niagara Falls.

Most certainly George Riggs had planned to have Mr. Corcoran present at this happy affair, but fate had once again intervened to smite that star-crossed old family friend. Early in September he had been summoned to Cannes, France, by the sudden illness of Louly. Bulletins filtering back were vague at first, but indicated on November 2, "she was still sick", and on December 6 "she was dead," at the age of twenty-nine. For the second time W. W. Corcoran had been deprived of a "young Louise". Condolences came in an immense shower of sympathy. We shall mention only three.

The first was from James Carlisle, George Riggs' lawyer, who had recently lost his own daughter:

> My Dear Friend;
> You know what in God's providence I have suffered and you know, therefore, I can feel for you as only a father can feel who has laid his precious child in the grave; but, from that same desolate experience, I know too well how vain are all words of merely human consolation. Still, I cannot help hoping . . . your heart will recognize the mercy of Heaven in prolonging your daughter's life . . . until she has left you — to cheer and bless the years yet in store for you — those beautiful children whose likenesses we looked at together, and who, I trust . . . will be spared long after you and I are mouldering in the dust . . .
>
> Faithfully, your friend,
> J. M. Carlisle.

And from George Peabody:

> London, Dec. 14, 1867
>
> My Dear Corcoran
> I duly received your note of the 4th, announcing the death of your angelic daughter on that day. Although anticipated . . . no power but that of God can assuage the grief and affliction of a father at the loss of such a child, and an only child, in which, for more than a quarter of a century, a large portion of your happiness has been centered. Be assumed, my dear friend, that I sincerely sympathize and condole with you in this severe dispensation of Providence.
>
> Very truly yours,
> George Peabody.

And finally, from Lexington, Va.:

> My Dear Mr. Corcoran:
> I sympathize most deeply in the great sorrow that has fallen upon you and your house. . . .

> *I know how hard it is for you ... to relinquish her who has been your pleasure, your comfort, and your link with the future ... I remember with particular pleasure, her last visit to us at Arlington, and the recollection will always bring me happiness.*
>
> *I hope that you will visit the mountains of Virginia this summer, and it would give me great pleasure if you will come and see us at Lexington.*
>
>
>
> *Most truly yours,*
> *R. E. Lee.*
>
>

On February 4, 1868, an official letter went out from the Treasury Department as follows:

> Sir:
>
> *The Department is advised that W. W. Corcoran, Esq., of this City, will arrive at your port within a few days, by the steamer St. Laurent, bringing with him the remains of his daughter, who recently died in France.*
>
> *The object of this letter is to call your particular attention to that fact, and I will thank you to extend to him, on arrival, every facility in your power which the peculiar circumstances of the case may seem to require.*
>
>
>
> *I am, very respectfully,*
> *H. McCulloch,*
> *Secretary of the*
> *Treasury.*
>
>
>
> to H. A. Smythe, Esq.,
> Collector, New York.

On February 17, 1868, the funeral of Louise Morris Eustis took place at her father's mansion where, less than nine years before, she had been married. Huge throngs of officials and private citizens gathered to pay a last sad tribute, and the funeral cortege was one of the largest ever seen in Washington.

Among the pall-bearers were James Mandeville Carlisle and George W. Riggs. "We brought nothing into the world and it is certain we can carry nothing out. The Lord giveth, and the Lord hath taken away . . . ."

A few weeks later, it was April 15, 1868, the third anniversary of Lincoln's death.

The Lincoln National Monument Association, of which George Riggs was treasurer, had set out in grandiose fashion to erect in the capital city a fitting memorial to the slain President. But almost immediately it was discovered that kindred organizations had sprung up in most of the northern and western states and in many of the larger cities, and even in some smaller ones, and the fact was quickly recognized that no national subscription would be possible.

With one significant exception, the contributions would come from the citizens of Washington, from visitors, and from members of the armed forces stationed in and around the capital. The touching exception was an unsolicited contribution from John T. Ford, the former owner of Ford's Theatre, who had almost been thrown in jail as a conspirator during the wave of panic and suspicion that followed the assassination. His Baltimore playhouse had generously put on a "benefit" for the fund which produced eighteen hundred dollars.

The Evening Star, on the date of the dedication, stated bluntly that, "The money raised . . . although carefully husbanded . . . and invested by the Treasurer, Mr. Riggs, in government registered bonds . . . was inadequate to erect a monument on any thing like the scale originally proposed." It was soon decided that the funds were only sufficient to raise a memorial in the shape of a shaft and statue, which, though modest, would be creditable to the city. And so it came about that this shaft and statue were about to be unveiled in front of City Hall on a gloomy, rainy April afternoon.

The sculptor, Lot Flannery, was in the gravestone business with his brother, Martin, under the style, "Flannery Brothers, Marble Manufacturers, No. 496 Massachusetts Ave., north, between 4th and 6th streets." To be sure, Lot Flannery had endeavored to improve himself and had studied art abroad and in New Orleans and St. Louis. As one authority has stated, "He may not have been an artistic genius, but he was more than an ordinary artisan." His principal claim to fame at the time was the Arsenal monument which had been erected in Congressional Cemetery over the mass grave of twenty-one women who were killed by an explosion at the Washington Arsenal at the foot of 4½ Street, southwest, on June 18, 1864, as a result of the accidental ignition of rocket shells. This was the greatest civil catastrophe of the war in Washington, and members of the funeral procession, seated in 150 carriages, included President Lincoln and Secretary of War, Stanton.

Flannery's statue consisted of a weeping Neoclassical female figure of "Grief" standing atop a twenty foot high shaft, on the base of which was a low relief panel showing the disaster at the Arsenal. It was not surprising that his memorial to Lincoln was a similar composition.

Still, Lot Flannery had won his commission fairly against whatever competition had existed by furnishing a plaster model of the design which has been unanimously selected by the committee. The main difference in the two compositions was the fact that the Lincoln memorial was twice as high as that of the Arsenal disaster — forty feet compared to twenty. This would prove to be a somewhat startling height at which to view the likeness of the Civil War President, standing in approximately life size, his left hand resting on the Roman emblem of Union, his head erect and inclining forward, and his right hand partially open as if addressing an audience. Work crews had labored through the early morning drizzle to set the statue on its lofty pedestal, and it had remained shrouded during the ceremonies.

The ceremonies themselves were rendered more somber by a number of unpleasant circumstances. All departments of the government had been suspended and the municipal offices and schools closed in order to allow the populace to pay homage to the deceased President. But a rabid Senate was in process of attempting to impeach the President, and both houses of Congress had declined the Mayor's invitation, crisply, politely, but without regrets. There seemed to exist a fear that, inasmuch as President Johnson was to unveil the memorial to his predecessor, the presence of members of Congress might somehow weaken their case for his impeachment.

Furthermore, although a reviewing stand accomodating four hundred persons had been erected beside the memorial, General Grant, who was present, insisted on remaining on the sidewalk below the stand. The feud between the soon-to-be-President and the President in office was well-known to sophisticated members of the audience, but was much regretted by those in charge of this first memorial service since his death for honoring "Honest Abe."

CHAPTER 29

When the speeches had been delivered and the ceremonies were drawing to a close, Mayor Wallach, making the best of a bad situation, advanced to the front of the platform with the President, where, according to the *Star*, he said, "My friends, it is hardly necessary for me to inform you what is now to take place, or who the distinguished person is who will perform the ceremony; the anxiety depicted upon your upturned countenances plainly tells that you are awaiting the unveiling of the statue."

The President then pulled the cord, whereupon the covering of the statue fell, and vociferous cheers were given by the crowd.

Mr. Lot Flannery, the sculptor, was introduced and cheered.

The Marine Band then performed a prayer by Lonizetti, after which the Rev. Dr. Gillette pronounced the benediction and the crowd dispersed.

In his carriage returning to office, George Riggs probably felt as many did, that the afternoon had been very largely a failure, particularly because of the conduct of prominent personages from whom more respect for the occasion might reasonably have been expected. If schools could be closed and the children brought to the ceremonies, why could not elected officials set a more inspiring example by their own presence at the ceremonies. And Grant's conduct, especially, had seemed unstatesmanlike.

As for the memorial itself, George Riggs, perhaps influenced by Mr. Corcoran, was a better than average connoisseur and collector of works of art; he was also a sound thinker. He had not attempted to dominate the thirty or more members of the committee, but he had never been happy with Flannery's design, even though it was probably the best that could be found in the community for the limited funds available.

The likeness of the President itself, was sufficiently good to have invoked from one of the speakers the comment that it was a plain and simple likeness of "that unasssuming man we loved." It still might prove adequate if brought down to a more sensible level on an appropriate base.

Perhaps as he looked back again at the tall shaft in the mists, the thought might have crossed his mind, "On a pedestal above the crowd — the last place Abraham Lincoln would ever have envisioned his likeness being placed."[4]

But George Riggs had other and more depressing matters on his mind on that gloomy afternoon. Only a few weeks before, he had traveled to New York with his beloved wife, Janet, and left her and daughter, Alice, aboard a Cunard liner bound for Liverpool.

This was her first trip abroad, but it was not a pleasure trip. She was desperately seeking relief from the dread Bright's disease, which had been identified a few years before and named for Dr. Richard Bright of London.

Nothing else would have induced her, after the horror of the Collins Line disasters which she had deeply mourned, to undertake her first ocean crossing. And even though Dr. Bright had died in December, 1858, he had left a clinic which was attracting desperate patients from Britain and abroad, hoping for some miracle cure from his research staffers.

And so she had bravely and tearfully bade goodbye to her husband and set out upon the long voyage which on all other happier occasions she had smilingly declined.

Back home she had given up all social activities and even resigned from her beloved post as vice regent of the Mount Vernon Ladies Association.

George Riggs was now fifty-four, Janet, fifty-two. They had been married for almost twenty-eight years — a very long time according to the statistics of their own day.

Chapter Notes

[1]Burke's *Peerage*, founded by John Burke in 1826, and published annually ever since says of the Howard family, "The Ducal and illustrious Howards stand next to the Blood Royal at the head of the Peerage of England."

[2]*The Ancestry and Decendance of Sir Henry Francis Howard, (1809-1898)*, by Franz von Recum, (Hampton Bays, New York, 1972), p. 71.

[3]Riggs, *The Riggs Family of Maryland*, (1939), p. 377.

[4]As a result of the changes in street levels around old City Hall, the foundation on which the Lincoln monument stood became very insecure, and it was finally taken down in 1920. In that year, the Library Committee of the U.S. House of Representatives reported a resolution that had for its purpose "to disponse with the tall column and stand the statue on an appropriate pedestel on or near the original site, within easy range of the vision of the passers-by." On April 14, 1923, it was rededicated on a site in front of the old City Hall where it still stands today.

Chapter 30

Six weeks after the dedication of the Lincoln monument, George Riggs received a letter from Mrs. Samuel Taylor, advising him of the death of her husband.

He acknowledged that letter on June 10, 1868:

My dear Madam:

Your letter of last month conveying the sad and unexpected intelligence of your great loss, reached me on the eve of my departure for New York to meet my wife on her return from Europe where she had been in pursuit of her health.

I sincerely sympathize with you in your deep affliction and trust you will receive consolation from on high, trusting in the mercy of God, that your husband has gone to a better world.

Years ago I was intimately acquainted with Mr. Taylor in business . . . and I learned then to esteem him highly . . . and ever since I have had for him a high regard.

Mr. Taylor wrote me some time ago about selling the mill and confining himself to his other business . . . but as he never communicated to me the information of a sale, I presume you still hold it.

> *I hope your children are capable of conducting the business . . . and that you may find it profitable.*
> *With best wishes for your comfort and happiness,*
> *I am, my dear Madam,*
>
> Yours very truly,
> Geo. W. Riggs.

Sarah Robson had married Samuel Taylor when he was forty-four and she was eighteen. Now, she was forty, and, according to Mrs. George Heitz, our genial Taylor family historian, was left with eight children — one an infant.

"She did a good job with them," relates Mrs. Heitz. "Two were boys . . . but Samuel, Jr. died as a young man when he was working in the lumber camps of the Robsons [Sarah's family]. The other boy, George Washington Riggs Taylor, went into banking . . . but he hated all business as he was a creative person . . . Some of his historical and fictional books on Indians are said to be in the Minnesota libraries."

"Of the six girls," she continued, "the only ones with living descendants were the two Taylor sisters who married the Kendall brothers."

"One set," she pointed out proudly, "was my grandmother and grandfather . . . Sarah Elizabeth Taylor met my grandfather, Dr. Allen Orvis Kendall, on the campus of Wisconsin University . . . . She was in the first class to admit women."[1]

"The other Kendall brother [who married a Taylor girl] was a lumberman, and their son, Harry T. Kendall, became the first president and later chairman of the board of the Weyerhouser Lumber Sales Company . . . . His son, Harry, Jr. is now president [1966]."

And so the story of Samuel Taylor and his young bride who bravely carved out a home from the forest primeval, had a happy ending.

At about the time George Riggs met his wife in New York after her European trip, he and his firm were deeply involved in a crucial service to the U.S. Government.

Fifteen months before, on March 30, 1867, the Treaty with Russia had been signed, under which His Majesty, the Emperor of all the Russias, agreed to cede to the United States the territory of Alaska for the consideration of seven million two hundred thousand dollars in gold.

CHAPTER 30

Payment was to be made "within ten months after the exchange of ratifications [of the treaty]." The exchange took place at Washington on June 20, 1867 — thus the payment was to be made within ten months from that date — or by April 20, 1868.

George Riggs's letter acknowledging the death of Samuel Taylor was dated June 10, 1868 — nearly two months after the payment was to have been made. Since it had not been made, the treaty was technically in default.

What had happened, of course, in this bleak period of our history, was that the feud between President Andrew Johnson and Congress had become so bitter that on March 5, 1868, the Senate organized itself into a court to hear the impeachment case against him. All other business came to a standstill. And the Congress had refused even to recess long enough to attend the dedication of the Lincoln monument on the third anniversary of the martyred President's death.

In vain did Secretary of State, Seward, and Secretary of the Treasury, Hugh McCulloch, plead with Congress to live up to their treaty obligation and interrupt the proceedings long enough to appropriate the funds for Alaska. Their exhortations fell on deaf and defiant ears. The patient, dignified Secretary of State William H. Seward, who had become a close friend of George Riggs, began to dispair of the nation's sanity.

That "little whiffet of a man," former Secretary of the Treasury during the Mexican War, Robert J. Walker, had been retained by the courtly Russian Minister as a lobbyist in a desperate attempt to push the appropriation through Congress. As a Special Representative of the Treasury Department in London during the Civil War, Walker had been highly successful in raising funds for the Union cause by selling the country's notes to the good burghers of the low countries, Switzerland and Germany. He had constantly proclaimed the strength and inviolability of the nation's promise to pay." Now, in looking around at the scene in Congress, he said, "the country is in far greater danger than it ever was during the war."[2]

Secretary of the Treasury, Hugh McCulloch, was, if possible, even more upset by the intransigence of Congress than Secretary Seward. McCulloch was a career banker who had been appointed Comptroller of the Currency to launch the National Banking Act of 1863. He had served with distinction and was subsequently appointed Secretary of the Treasury by Lincoln in March of 1865, shortly before the Presidents assassination.

The government's wartime issues of promissory notes amounted to a colossal $450,000,000, and while Congress had called for their redemption at $4,000,000 per month in 1866, even that modest schedule was revoked in early 1868 when it became obvious it could not be met. Now Secretary McCulloch was faced with finding $7,200,000 "in gold," as stipulated by the Alaska treaty.

True, Congress had not yet appropriated the money, but McCulloch, very conscious of the nation's recently established credit standing abroad, assumed he would be called upon to make the payment before the deadline of April 20, 1868.

Under those circumstances, he had looked across President's Square as had his predecessors, and called in George Riggs as a consultant. The latter had readily consented to form a syndicate of banks in an attempt to raise sufficient gold currency to meet the purchase price. The Treasury itself could be of little assistance; its gold reserves were at a low point. It was going to be necessary to pursuade the nation's bankers to part with an uncomfortably large portion of their own gold reserves.

George Riggs argued that the banks of the North and the West that had prospered during the War, should make the necessary sacrifice of gold as a loan to the Treasury Department to meet the terms of the Treaty.

Now, having been outstandingly successful in the endeavor, he was "sitting on" $7,200,000 in gold on deposit in his name in the Treasury awaiting action by the cantankerous radicals in Congress. It is hardly surprising that his letter to the widow Taylor had sounded somewhat hasty and preoccupied.

Meanwhile, another threat to the nation's credit arose when it was disclosed that Baring Brothers & Co., of London, had advanced the Russians $2,000,000 in the fall of the preceding year on the seemingly sound assumption the funds would be forthcoming as provided by the treaty. And so did the situation involve indirectly George Peabody and W. W. Corcoran and Walker, and everybody else who had labored so tirelessly to establish the nation's credit in the first place, and to sustain it during the war.

A vote on impeachment was finally taken in the Senate on May 16, 1868, which failed by one vote of reaching the necessary two-thirds, thirty five to nineteen. A second vote was taken ten days later on May 26, and showed the same result. Impeachment had failed. Congress was now free to turn its attention to Alaska.

But instead, the hotheads on Capitol Hill were employing every conceivable tactic to delay action on the appropriation, rather than give credit for the acquisition to the hated President and his Secretary of State. They seemed to ignore entirely the fact that Seward had served as Secretary of State under Lincoln throughout the War and played a brilliant role in the handling of our foreign affairs.

Not only was the purchase referred to constantly as "Seward's Folly," but the hostile lawmakers were gleefully spending their time and energy in finding new derisive slogans for the territory. "Walrussia" and "Icebergia" were two of the favorites. This epochal purchase for two cents an acre of the vast territory where gold would be discovered on Klondike Creek in 1896, and oil on the North Slope in the next century, was in dire peril as a result of the blind vindictiveness of some members of Congress.

The fiery little expansionist, Walker, old and sick, had worked hard for the appropriation. He now wrote Seward on July 2, 1868:

> "I have done all I can here for Alaska   now I go to New York [to the Democratic convention]. The Tribune will come out for Alaska. I think & I wish the democracy [the Democratic Party] to put it on their banner.... Now, excuse me for saying that in a matter so vital, of such transcendent importance to the country, should not you & the President exert yourself with every Democratic member by fair argument to support the appropriation.... Immortal as will be the vetos of the President, sublime as was his conduct during the impeachment — yet, the

> *great act of his administration, will be the acquisition of Alaska. The theatre of our greatest triumph is to be the Pacific where we will soon have no formidable European rivals — The consequences are ultimately, the political and commercial control of the world."*[3]

This letter may have been written at Seward's suggestion for he sent it at once to the President — July 2, 1868. Walker was also very close to George Riggs who had been national treasurer of the Democratic party during the 1860 campaign. Unquestionably Walker urged him to appear at the convention in New York to seek votes for the appropriation. And Riggs probably contacted every banker in the stalled syndicate to call upon his own congressmen to support the bill.

No record has been found of the behind-the-scenes activity on this subject at the Democratic convention, but the results were soon apparent. Two weeks after the adjournment of the convention, on July 27, 1868, the Congress passed the "appropriation to carry into effect the treaty with Russia of March 30, 1867." Alaska was saved, along with the nation's integrity and its credit.

One observer has stated that the transaction (paying for Alaska) created a "sensation in the gold room of the Treasury Department." The representatives of Russia, of the bank syndicate, and of the Treasury itself, were engaged in making a final count of the unpredecented horde of gold coins, much of it in small denominations. And we can be certain George Riggs had some of his key employees present throughout the proceedings, including young Charles Glover, who was fast rising in the firm.

The final count was completed on Saturday, August 1, 1868, at which time de Stoeckl signed a special receipt which read as follows:

> *"The undersigned, Envoy Extraordinary and Minister Plenipotentiary of his Majesty the Emperor of all the Russias, do hereby acknowledge to have received, at the Treasury Department in Washington, $7,200,000 in coin, being the full sum due from the United States to Russia in consideration of the cession by the latter to the former of certain*

territory described in the Treaty entered into by the Emperor of all the Russias and the President of the United States on the 30th day of March, 1867.
Washington, Aug. 1, 1868

Stoeckl

The whole amount was to be shipped on Baron de Stoeckl's order to Messrs. Duncan, Sherman & Co. of New York, the correspondents of Messrs. Baring Brothers & Co. They were to deduct the $2,000,000 plus costs of the loan due their clients, and ship the balance of $5,000,000 odd, to Russia via London, on a properly insured Cunard Line vessel. The payment to the New York brokers was to be handled there by the U.S. Sub-Treasury.

Baron de Stoeckl had also received a Treasury Warrant Draft for $7,200,000 payable "at sight," which authorized the transaction. He and Secretary McCulloch and other Treasury officials, and probably Secretary Seward, hurried to the mansion of George Riggs on Eye Street, where, on the big desk in the library, de Stoeckl endorsed the back of the draft, "Pay to George W. Riggs or order," and signed his name "Edward de Stoeckl" as the instrument was drawn.

George Riggs finally held the valid Treasury draft for repayment of the banks. They also eventually received an agreed-upon fee for their participations.

And probably at this point corks were popping and glasses were held aloft in repeated toasts to all parties in the historic transaction.

The rest is more or less legend. Oldtimers in the bank always maintained that the gold was loaded on a New York bound train preceded by a second engine pushing a flat car. This was a protection from a possible charge of dynamite placed on the tracks. A third engine and cars followed, carrying a heavily armed contingent of federal troops. The publicity and passions aroused by the purchase and the accompanying long debate and delays, were said to have rendered it virtually impossible for the Treasury agents to mask the time and route of the payment.

Three weeks later another great event occurred in George Riggs's life when his first granddaughter was born at Green

Hill on August 22, 1868. On the following day, Sunday, August 23, Father Lynch came out to baptize the baby and to hold a service in the sparkling little chapel of Saint Cecelia, where he had married Cecelia and Henry Howard the preceding October 2nd.

The baby's nurse gently carried the infant from the big house past the rose garden to the chapel, where the adoring family had gathered, including the proud grandmother, Janet, now much afflicted by her illness.

This child would grow up to be Baroness Marie Ernestine Howard von Recum, the mother of Franz von Recum, and the eldest surviving granddaughter of George W. Riggs we were privileged to interview in 1949 at the Gramercy Park Hotel in New York.

The day after the christening, down at 32 President's Square the beaming grandfather was probably indulging his penchant for passing out expensive cigars in celebration of his new link to posterity.

While happily receiving congratulations and good wishes from a host of customers and friends, the faint hope must have formed in his mind that perhaps his own "Riggs Bank," having witnessed and participated in so many dramatic events, might itself enjoy a "posterity" and somehow survive the hazards of the future to continue serving, even a century hence, his beloved namesake city and the Capital of the Nation.

And if such a thought did occur to George Riggs it could only be characterized as an extravagant but noble dream.

Chapter Notes

[1] Letter from Mrs. George Heitz of February 16, 1966
[2] Robert John Walker, *A Politician from Jackson to Lincoln*, P. 214. James P. Shenton, Columbia University Press 1961.
[3] *Ibid*, p. 213.

Index

A

Acadia, ship, 102
Adriatic, steamship, 154, 177, 180
Age of the Superliner, 111
Agg, John, 98, 150-151, 181
Aiken, William, 285-286
Alabama, warship, 248
Allen, George, 170, 174-175
Allen, Mrs. George (Grace Brown), 170, 174
Anderson, Col. Robert, 214
Anderson, Robert (of John), 44
Andrews, Richard Snowden, 181
Annapolis and Georgetown Mail Ship, 30, 40
Appleton, William, 223-225
Army-Navy Club, 115
Artic, steamship, 105, 155, 169-175, 177, 180, 189, 192
Artists of the Nineteenth Century, 121
Ashburton, Lord Alexander, 131, 191, 237
Atlantic, Steamer, 105, 170

B

Baalham, second mate *Artic*, 173-174
Bache, Mary, *see* Walker, Mrs. Robert
Bacon, Albert, 294
Bacon, Dr. James Ware, 294
Bacon, Mrs. James Ware (Alice Ann Riggs), 227, 294, 300
Baltic, steamer, 130, 192
Baltimore Museum of Art, 28
Bancroft, George, 89
Bank of Columbia, 14, 47
Bank of the District of Columbia, 11
Bank of the Metropolis, 22
Baring, Thomas, 87
Baring Brothers & Company, 84, 87, 89, 90, 107, 194, 306, 309
Barney, Hiram, 246
Barnum, P. T., 111, 118
Barry, Joseph, 81
Bates, Joshua, 87, 107, 111, 194
Bates, Mrs. Joshua, 194
Beale, Edward Fitzgerald, 147-149, 159
Beall, George, 46, 51
Beall, Col. Ninian, 46
Beall, Thomas, 51
Beall House, Georgetown, 46
Belasco Theatre, 256
Belmont, August, 69, 89, 91
Belt, Col. Joseph, 33
Bentley, Caleb, 33

INDEX

Benton, Jesse, see Fremont, Mrs. James C.,
Benton, Thomas Hart, 75, 147-148, 159, 264
Benton-Beale Expedition, 145-146, 149, 157-159
Black, Jeremiah, 75
Blair, Francis, Jr., 215
Blair, Francis Preston, 149, 215, 220
Blair, Montgomery, 215, 220, 224
Boleyn, Ann, 291
Bolton, Mr. (1850's), 96, 129
Booth, John Wilkes, 255
Bordley's Choice, 24
Boswell, Mary Keene, see Riggs, Mrs. Elisha, Jr.
Boucicault, Dion, 206-207, 210
Bradford, Edward B., 286
Brandywine, warship, 195
Braynard, Frank O., 111
Breckenridge, John C., 221
Bright, Sen. Jesse D., 196-198, 201, 228, 239, 263
Bright, Mrs. Jesse D., 228
Bright, Mary Turpin, see Riggs, Mrs. Lawrason
Bright, Dr. Richard, 300
Britannia, ship, 102
Brooke, Deborah, see Thomas, Mrs. Richard
Brookeville, Md., 25, 33, 34, 38, 43, 66, 138, 275
Brown, Alexander Crosby, 162, 170, 175-176
Brown, Bill, 170
Brown, Grace, see Allen, Mrs. George
Brown, James, 102, 153-154, 169-170, 175
Brown, Millie, 170, 174
Brown, Stewart, 102, 153
Browning, Elizabeth Barrett, 119
Bruce, Sir Frederick, 288, 293
Buchanan, James, 75, 106-107, 155, 179, 199, 208, 209, 211-212, 220, 268
Bull, Ole, 206
Bulwer, Sir Henry, 131
Burche, John Covington, 133
Burche, Mrs. John Covington (Eleanor Jones Karrick), 133
Burgdorf, Lewis, 199
Burke, John, 301
Burnside, Gen. Ambrose, 235

Butler, Gen. Benjamin F., 215
Byron, Lord, 79

C

Caledonia, ship, 102
Canada, steamer, 169
Carlisle, James M. 239, 293-296
Carson, Kit, 147-148, 158
Casey, James P., 160-161
Caton, Mr. (Annapolis Innkeeper 1802), 30
Cedars, Georgetown estate, 49
Charlick, Carl, 268
Chase, Salmon P., 214, 253
Chesapeake and Ohio Canal Co., 37, 39
Chillum Castle Manor, 178, 239
Churchill, Lady Randolph (Jennie Jerome), 243-244, 267
Churchill, Sir Winston, 243-244
City Hall, Washington, 74
Clagett, Darius, 39, 40, 49
Clagett & Riggs, merchants, 39, 41
Clarke, John G., 146, 167
Clarke, Mathew St. Clair, 131-132
Clarke-Ashburton House, 125, 130-133, 138, 166
Clay, Henry, 75, 104, 105, 111, 133, 264
Clayton-Bulwer treaty, 131
Clemson, Anna C. 271
Clemson, Thomas G., 272
Clifford, John Henry, 286
Cloak, F. Theodore, 210
Cockburn, Adm. George, 22
Cockenderfer, Thomas, 30
Cocking, Jane, see Glover, Mrs. Charles Carroll
Cocking, William, 276, 279
Codlentz, E. D., 162
Coleman, Sarah H., 132
Collins, Edward Knight, 100-103, 106, 126-127, 154, 169-170
Collins, Mrs. Edward Knight, 171
Collins, Henry, 171
Collins, Capt. Israel Gross, 101
Collins, Mrs. Israel G. (Mary Ann Knight), 101
Collins, Joseph, 101
Collins, Mary Ann, 171
Collins Steamship Line, 100, 103, 107, 110, 114, 123, 125, 127, 128, 130, 144, 153-154, 169, 172, 177, 180, 192, 194, 248, 300

313

Colman, Edna M., 133
Columbia, ship, 102
Comegys, Mrs. (Vice Regnet, Mt. Vernon), 218
Congress, frigate, 147
Constitution, frigate, 15, 19
Cook, Henry, 30
Cook, Capt. James, 274
Cooper, Jane Agnes, 146, 150
Coote, Sir Charles, 119
Cora, Mr. (accused murdered), 160-161
Corcoran, Charles Morris, 17
Corcoran, Eliza, 13
Corcoran, Harriet Louise, 17
Corcoran, James, 13
Corcoran, Mrs. James (Harriet Reynolds), 17, 88
Corcoran, Louise Morris see Eustis, Mrs. George
Corcoran, Martha Ellen, 13
Corcoran, Col. Michael, 247
Corcoran, Sarah, 13
Corcoran, Thomas, Sr., 12, 13, 30, 31
Corcoran, Mrs. Thomas, Sr. (Hannah Lemmon), 12, 13
Corcoran, Thomas, Jr., 13, 17
Corcoran, William C., 167-168
Corcoran, William Wilson,
  early employment, 11; birth, early life, 12-13; death, 12; military service, 14; marriage, 15-16; partnership with Riggs, 59; manages first large loan, 64-65; banking career, 75-76, 83-90, 106-109; pays off old debts, 77-79; purchases H St. mansion, 103-104; purchases Greek Slave, 116-119; retirement, 154-158; sells interest in bank, 189; concern for daughter's health and European trip (1855), 189-194; death of father-in-law, 195; marriage of daughter, 202; builds art gallery, 213; residence aboard during Civil War, 213, 229; involvement in Trent Affair, 223-225; benevolence of 270-273; death of daughter, 294; 19, 45, 58, 73, 93, 102, 105, 110-111, 120, 123-124, 126, 129-132, 140, 148, 159-160, 163-164, 168, 179, 198, 201, 202, 205, 228-231, 239, 266-267, 269-270, 285, 287, 299, 307
Corcoran, Mrs. William Wilson (Louise Amory Morris), 15-19, 190

Corcoran family, 33, 42
Corcoran Gallery of Art, 22, 71, 119
Corcoran and Riggs, 63, 64, 66-68, 73-75, 83-87, 89-91, 99, 103, 106, 108, 109, 140-141, 143, 148, 150, 157, 159, 163, 259; see also Riggs & Co. and Riggs National Bank
Corn Rigs, 67, 68, 97, 104, 105, 109, 113, 131, 150, 166, 228
Cosway, Maria, 73-74
Coward, Adm. K.K., 187
Cox, Col. John, 48, 49
Cox, Mrs. John (Jane Threlkeld), 49
Cox, Sally, 49
Cox's Row, Georgetown Row Houses, 15, 48, 59
Crane, Sylvia E., 121
Cruttenden, Joel, 58
Cruttenden, Mrs. Joel (Mary), 59
Cruttenden, Sophia Theresa see Riggs, Mrs. Lawrason
Cumberland, frigate, 195
Cunard, Samuel, 102
Cunard Line, 102, 106, 107, 283, 293, 300
Cunningham, Ann Pamela, 182-185, 203-205, 208, 215-217, 281-282
Cunningham, Mrs. Robert, 183

D

Dahlgren, John A., 241
Dallas, Alexander J., 75
Dallas, George Miflin, 75
Darius Clagett and Co., 49
Davies, H.E., 190, 193
Davis, Jefferson, 147, 211, 214, 228
Davis, Thomas, 24
Davis family 25
Day, Jeremiah, 54
de Astaburuaga, Don Francisco, 126, 133
Decatur, Stephen, 15
Decatur, Mrs. Stephen (Susan), 14-15
Decatur House (Lafayette Square), 132
Degges, William H., 67, 69
Demidov, Prince Anatol, 119
de Montholon, Marquis, 213
de Stoeckl, Baron Edward, 182, 308-309
de Stoeckl, Eliza, 182
Dick, Thomas, 46
Dick, Mrs. Thomas (Margaret Peter), 46
Digges estate, 239
Dorsey, Amelia, see Riggs, Mrs. Samuel
Dorsey, Capt. Philemon, 24, 39

Dorsey, Mrs. Philemon (Catharine Ridgely), 24
Dorsey, William H., 27
Dorsey family 25
Douglas, Stephen A., 220
Dowdall, Mathilda Cecelia, see Shedden, Mrs. Thomas William
"Dramatic Line" 102
Durbin, Dr. John Price, 288

E

E. Riggs & Son, 58
Eaton, George M., 286
Ebbitt House, 50
Ecker, Mrs. Grace Dunlop, 46, 52
Edouart, August, 69-70
Edward VII, 208
Elliott, John, 137, 168-169, 205, 207, 288
Eustis, George, 202, 223-224, 231
Eustis, Mrs. George (Louise Morris Corcoran — "Louly") birth 17; marriage 202; death 294-295; 88, 189-191, 193-197, 223, 225, 228-231
Eustis, George, Jr. 202
Evarts, William Maxwell, 286
Everett, Edward, 185, 190-191, 195-198, 205
Everett, Mrs. Edward, 196
Ewell, Benjamin S., 273
Ewing, Ellen, see Sherman, Mrs. William Tecumseh
Ewing, Thomas, 264

F

Farmers and Mechanics Bank, 26, 37, 38, 44, 178
Farquahar, Roger, 242
Farragut, Adm. David Glascow, 286
Farragut Square 115
Federal Republican, 39
Federal Republican and Commercial Gazette, 42
Federalist, 28, 29, 40
Fillmore, Millard, 103, 106-107, 190-194, 209, 239, 263
First National Bank of Washington, 253-254
Fish, Hamilton, 286
Flannery, Tad, 297-300
Flannery, Martin, 297
Ford, Frances Clare, 294
Ford, John T., 201, 297
Ford's Theatre, 254-256, 297

Forestall, E. J., 89
Forrest, Richard, 50
Forward, Walter, 64, 65, 75, 85
Franklin, Benjamin, 73-74
Franklin, M.I., 244
Franklin & Co., 244-246
Freeman, Mr. & Mrs. William Grisby, 132
Freeman House, 237
Fremont, James C., 158-160
Fremont, Mrs. James C. (Jesse Benton), 159
Fremont Expedition of 1846, 158

G

Gaither, George R., 53
Gaither, Henrietta, 53
Gaither family, 25
Galatia, warship, 294
Gales, Mrs. Joseph, 132
Gardner, Julia, see Tyler, Mrs. John
Garrett, John Work, 251, 284
Garrick, ship, 102
Gawler, Joseph, 263, 268
Geberding, C.O., 160
George Peabody and Company, 43, 144
George Peabody, A Bography, 162
Georgetown College, 13, 50
Georgetown Packet, 139
Gerolt, Baron, 238
Gibson, Mr. (art teacher, 1823), 47
Gillette, Rev. Abraham, 299
Gilmer, Thomas A., 272
Globe, 160, 220
Glover, Charles Carroll (son of Joshua), 276, 279
Glover, Mrs. Charles Carroll (Jane Cocking), 276-277
Glover, Charles Carroll (son of Richard), 276-278, 308
Glover, Charles Carroll, Jr., 279
Glover, Joshua, 276
Glover, Mary Jane, see Shriver, Mrs. Abraham
Glover, Matilda, see Williamson, Mrs. Robert
Glover, Richard Leonidas, 277-278
Glover, Mrs. Richard Leonidas (Caroline Piercy), 277-278
Glover, William Leonidas, 277
Goster, Bill, 46
Goster, Henry, 46
Graham, Mrs. Katharine, 178

Graham, William Alexander, 286
Grandfather's Legacy (W. W. Corcoran's autobiography), 12, 14, 21, 87, 117
Grant, John, 117-118
Grant, Gen. Ulysses S., 236, 244, 246, 248, 254-255, 263, 266, 286, 288, 298-299
Grant, Mrs. Ulysses, S., 255
Gratz, Benjamin, 104
Gratz, Rebecca, 104
Great Eastern, steamship, 180
Greek Slave, statue, 116-120, 156
Green, Dr. (1861), 223
Green Hill, 237, 239-240, 292, 309-310
Griffith family, 25
Growing with Washington, Story of the first 100 Years, 259
Guerriere, frigate, 15, 19
Gurley, Dr. Phineas D., 231, 236, 258

H

Hadfield, George, 73, 74, 163, 232, 257
Haggarty, Ogden, 155
Hamilton, Alexander, 203
Hamilton, Miss (1859), 203, 217
Harewood (Corcoran's estate), 213
Harriet Lane, cutter, 208
Harriman, Averell, 51
Harrington, George, 253
Harris, Clara, 255
Harrison, William Henry, 63, 64, 111
Harrison, Mr. (servant), 263
Hay, John, 227, 246
Heilprin, Isaac, 244-245
Heilprin, William A., 245-246
Heitz, Mrs. George, 57, 273, 304, 311
Henry, Joseph, 191, 192, 231
Henry, Mrs. Kate Kearney, 50
Henry VIII, 291
Herbert, Upton, 203-204, 208, 217, 282
Hewitt, Mrs. James, 272
Hill, Rev. Stephen P., 201
History of American Sculpture, 121
Hodge, Dr. Hugh I., 183
Holland, Sir Henry, 191
Holland, Isaac, 174
Holland, Stewart, 174-175
Hooker, Gen. Joseph, 235
Hostick, King, 233
Houston, Sam, 288
Howard, Henry, 220, 291-293, 310
Howard, Mrs. Henry (Cecelia Riggs), 97, 220, 291-294, 310

Howard, Sir Henry Francis, 301
Howard, Lady Jessie, 182
Howard, Katharine, 291
Howard family, 301
Huger, Frank, 271
Hull, Capt. Isaac, 15
Humboldt, Baron, 193, 239
Hyde, Anthony, 45, 168
Hyde, George A., 45, 50
Hyde, Thomas, 167-168, 275
Hyde family 46

I

Independent American, 38
Ingersoll, Mr. (1852), 136

J

Jackson, Andrew, 11, 14, 37, 38, 149, 220
Jackson Square, 119, 131, 218, 236, see also Lafayette Square and President's Square
James, Charles H., 167
Jay Cooke & Co., 253
Jefferson, Thomas, 12, 73-74
Jerome, Jennie, see Churchill, Mrs. Randolph
Jerome, Leonard W. (Clara) 243, 249, 267
Jerome, Mrs. Leonard W. (Clara) 243, 249, 267
Jerome, Riggs & Company, 242-243, 267
Johnson, Andrew, 257, 259, 263, 287, 289, 298, 305
Johnson, Christie, 185
Johnson, Edwin F. 148-149
Johnson, Sen. and Mrs. Reverdy, 197
Johnson, William, 226
Johnston, W. P., 55
Joyner, Margaret F., 271

K

Karrick, Eleanor Jones, see Burche, Mrs. John
Karrick, Joseph, 133
Karrick, Mary Ann, see Riggs, Mrs. Elisha
Karrick, Rebecca Ord, 133
Kearny, Stephan, 147
Kearsage, sloop, 248
Keene, Laura, 254-255
Kellog, Mr., 118
Kendall, Dr. Allen Orvis, 304
Kendall, Harry T., 304
Kennedy, John F., 51

INDEX

Kennedy, Mrs. John F. 51
Key Francis Scott, 108
Kieckhoefer, A.T., 95, 96, 167-168, 205
King, James of William, 157-161
Kirkwood House, 258
Knight, Mary Ann, see Collins, Mrs. Israel
Kossuth, Louis, 244

L

Lafayette, Marquis de, 31, 49, 195
Lafayette Square, 103, 108, 166, 195, 220, see also Jackson Square and President's Square
Lane Harriet, 208
Lawrason, Alice, see Riggs, Mrs. Elisha
Lawrason, James, 31
Lawrason, Mrs. James (Alice Levering), 31
Lawrason, Mercy Ann, see Riggs, Mrs. Romulus
Lee, Gen. Robert E., 229, 235, 252, 262, 296
Lee, Thomas Sim, 40, 41, 44
Lomman, Hannah, see Corcoran, Mrs. Thomas, Sr.
L'Enfant Plan, 167
Levering, Alice, see Lawrason, Mrs. James
Life of Lady Randolph Churchill, 249
Lincoln, Abraham, 207-209, 212-215, 218-221, 224, 226-229, 233, 235-238, 240, 244-248, 251-260, 263, 269, 284-285, 297-298, 300, 306-307
Lincoln, Mrs. Abraham, 217, 226, 245-248, 252, 254, 255, 258, 263
Lincoln, Edward, 225
Lincoln, Robert Todd, 225, 246, 254-255
Lincoln, Tad, 225-227, 233, 246
Lincoln, William Wallace, 225-227, 236, 247, 258, 261
Lincoln National Monument Association, 258, 297
Lind, Jenny, 107, 111
Lizst, Franz, 206
Longfellow, Henry Wadsworth, 206
Luce, Capt. James C., 171-175
Lyons, Lord, 225, 229
Lynch, Father, 297-298, 310

M

McAlester, Charles, 286
McClellan, Gen. George B., 219, 227, 235, 248
McCulloch, Hugh, 295, 305-306, 309
McFarland, W.H., 270
McGill, Bishop, J., 270
McIlvaine, Bishop Charles Pettit, 286
McLaughlin, Charles, 30, 40
McMakin, Miss — — — (1861), 219
McMullen, J.B., 54
McMullen, Mary, 54
Madison, James, 13, 32, 33, 34, 38, 75, 111
Madison, Mrs. James, 32, 34
Marini, Mrs. Glynn, 55
Martin, Ralph C., 249
Mason, Betsey C., 84
Mason, J.Y., 193
Mason, James M., 223
Meade, Gen. George, 235, 262-263
Meigs, Montgomery C., 150-151, 229, 257
Merrimac, ironclad, 226
Metropolitan Club, D.C., 238, 265, 268, 275
Metropolitan Railroad, 150
Militia of Anne Arundel County, 32
Mills, Clark, 218, 220-221
Moale, Capt. Samuel, 32
Molina, Louis, 294
Monitor, ironclad, 226
Monroe, James, 34, 38, 44, 166
Montgomery County Militia, 32
Moore, Col. William G. 287
Morgan, J. Pierpont, 144
Morgan, Junius S., 144
Morris, Commodore Charles, 15-17, 195-196
Morris, Mrs. Charles, 195
Mount Vernon, Va., 183-184, 204, 208, 215-219, 227, 241-242, 252, 282
Mount Vernon Ladies Association, 184-185, 190, 203, 207, 210, 221, 241, 281-282, 300

N

Nash, Sylvia, 35
National Hotel, 94-95, 133, 278
National Intelligencer, 17, 53, 169, 170, 182, 213, 293
National Theatre, 107
Nelson, Judge Roger, 276
New National Hall, 107
Newbold, George, 65
Nicholson, Mrs. (widow-1803), 13

317

Nicolay, John George, 246
Norris, Margaret, see Riggs, Mrs. Samuel, Jr.
Norris, Rebecca Smith, see Riggs, Mrs. George Washington
Noyes, Pauline Riggs, 70

O

Old Ironsides (Constitution), 15, 19
Old Stone House, Georgetown, 27, 28
Ould, Paulina (Gaither), 133
Ould, Robert, 133
Ould, Mrs. Robert (Henrietta), 133
Ouseley, Lord W. G., 229-230
Owings, Capt. Thomas, 32

P

Pacific, steamship, 105, 130, 180, 194
Paine, Lewis, 256
Parker, Franklin, 162
Patriotic Bank, 131
Payne, Bruce Ryburn, 287, 290
Payne, John Howard, 108
Peabody, George
    hired by Elisha Riggs, 41; early life mentioned, 42; established as London banker, 43; return to U.S. and benevolence of, 283-286; portrait of Queen Victoria presented to, 287-288
    57, 58, 69, 87, 91, 96, 116, 117, 138, 143, 144, 150, 154-156, 159, 160, 189, 190, 192, 230-231, 266-267, 269-270, 273, 276, 289, 290, 295, 307
Peabody, John, 42
Peabody Institute of Baltimore, 283
Perry, Commodore Matthew C., 173, 263
Peter, Margaret, see Dick, Mrs. Thomas
Peter Rober, 12
Peter, Mrs. Robert, 46
Philadelphia, frigate, 15
Phillips, H.B., 254
Pickins, Gov. Francis W., 211
Pierce, Franklin, 140, 209, 288
Piercy, Caroline, see Glover, Mrs. Richard Leonidas
Piercy, William A., 277
Pierson, G. W., 55
Pigman, Capt. Nathaniel, 32
Pleasant Hill, plantation, 25, 33, 66, 138, 276, 292
Poli's Theatre, 275

Polk, James K., 74-75, 76, 83, 111, 158, 209
Potrait of Old Georgetown, 46, 52
Potomac Company, 39, 40
Powell, Lucien, 103
Power, Tyrone, 206
Powers, Hiram, 116, 118-119
President's Square, 11, 22, 73, 74, 149, 167, 176, 179, 186, 196-197, 213-215, 220, 228, 232, 253, 257-258, 261-262, 264, 278, 289, 306, 310 *see also* Jackson Square *and* Lafayette Square
Price, Eli K., 253
Proctor, John Clagett, 16, 67, 69
Pruyn, John, 287

Q

Queen Mary, ocean liner, 180

R

R & E Riggs and Co., 54
Railroad to the Pacific, 149, 159
Rathbone, Maj. Henry Reed, 255
Reintzel, Dr. Henry, 46
Rich Neck, plantation, 24
Richards, Paul, 19
Richardson, Mr. (Federal Marshall), 160
Ridgeley, W.D., 38
Ridgeley & Riggs (mercantile company), 39
Riggs, Alice Ann, see Bacon, Mrs. James Ware
Riggs, Cecelia, see Howard, Mrs. Henry
Riggs, Col. E. Francis (grandson of Elisha), 32, 70
Riggs, Elisha
    settles in Georgetown, 23-34; invests in Georgetown real estate and early business career, 28-31; marriage, 31; military service in War of 1812, 32; banking career, 38-45; remarriage, 42; association with Collins Line, 114, 154, 177, 180, death, 151;
    33-35, 49, 54, 56-58, 64, 69-70, 75, 84-85, 91, 100, 102-103, 115, 137-138, 143-144, 168, 239, 275
Riggs, Mrs. Elisha (Alice Lawrason), 31, 32, 41
Riggs, Mrs. Elisha (Mary Ann Karrick), 42, 54, 93, 133, 135
Riggs, Elisha, Jr.
    birth, 43; enters Corcoran & Riggs,

INDEX

86; letters to father, 91-96, 114-116, 123-124, 127-130, 135-136, 140; marriage 104; Benton-Beale Expedition, 145-149; 102, 125-126, 132-133, 137, 154-155, 157-160, 166-168, 178-179, 181, 182, 197, 198, 220, 242-243, 244, 263, 267

Riggs, Mrs. Elisha, Jr. (Mary Keene Boswell), 104, 115-116, 132, 179, 181, 198, 242-244, 267

Riggs, Elisha Francis (son of George Washington Riggs, Jr.) 139, 181

Riggs, Francis Blair (son of Elisha, Jr.), 147

Riggs, George Smith (son of George Washington, Jr.), 32

Riggs, George Shedden (son of George Washington, Jr.), 105, 181

Riggs, George Washington, Sr., 23, 24, 27, 28, 32, 35, 40, 138

Riggs, Mrs. George Washington, Sr. (Eliza Robertson), 28

Riggs, Mrs. George Washington, Sr. (Rebecca Smith Norris), 138

Riggs, George Washington, Jr.
birth, 32; attends Yale, 47, 54-56; romance, 50-51, 58; marriage, 59; partnership with Corcoran, 59; purchases Corn Rigs, 66-69; disagreement with Corcoran, 84-85; withdraws from bank, 86; returns to bank, 163, 167; treasurer of Mount Vernon Ladies Assn., 185-186; president of Washington Gas Light Co., 199, 251; association with Mount Vernon Ladies Assn., 203-208, 215-217, 227, 241-242, 252, 281-282; treasurer Metropolitan Club, 238, 266; connection with bank for reviewing Army of the Republic, (1865), 262-265; treasurer Lincoln National Memorial Assn, 297, 299; involvement with purchase of Alaska, 308-310; 41, 45, 48, 57-58, 70, 91, 93, 96, 98-100, 104-105, 109-110, 113, 115, 124-126, 128-132, 137-138, 141, 143-145, 150, 153, 155, 164, 166, 100-109, 177-182, 180, 107 108, 201, 211-212, 220, 232, 237, 239-240, 256, 258, 268, 273-276, 278, 289, 291-294, 296, 300, 303-306

Riggs, Mrs. George Washington, Jr. (Janet Shedden), 48, 50, 51, 58, 59, 96, 97, 98, 105, 113, 126, 138-139, 150, 153, 163, 178, 181, 186, 198, 207-208, 211, 220, 228, 242, 300, 310

Riggs, George Washington (son of Lawrason), 100

Riggs, Illinois (daughter of Romulus), 54

Riggs, Jane (daughter of George Washington, Jr.) 54, 152

Riggs, Jane Agnes, 153

Riggs, Janet Madeleine (daughter of George Washington, Jr.) 211, 292

Riggs, John, 24

Riggs, Mrs. John (Mary Davis), 24

Riggs, John Beverly, 24, 145, 147, 148, 152, 166, 242, 267, 275

Riggs, Joseph Karrick, 94, 125-126, 133, 140, 143

Riggs, Mrs. Joseph Karrick (Rosalie Van Zndt), 144

Riggs, Karrick, 70

Riggs, Kate (daughter of George Washington, Jr.), 227

Riggs, Lawrason
birth 41; settles in St. Louis, 58-59; first marriage 58-59; second marriage 97-99, closes St. Louis business and settles in New York City 198, third marriage 201 45, 47, 48, 54, 56, 57, 92, 94, 100, 110, 114, 124, 128-129, 131, 136-137, 139, 143, 145, 150, 199, 263, 274, 294

Riggs, Mrs. Lawrason (Sophia Cruttenden), 58, 59, 100

Riggs, Mrs. Lawrason (Frances Clapp), 97, 99

Riggs, Mrs. Lawrason (Mary Turpin Bright), 152, 197-198, 201

Riggs, Mary Alice (daughter of Elisha Sr.), 97, 126, 130

Riggs, Mary Griffith (daughter of George Washington, Jr.), 97, 104

Riggs, Remus, 275

Riggs, Remus George, 275-276, 278

Riggs, Richard C. (great grandson of Lawrason), 152

Riggs, Romulus, 23, 24, 31, 33, 37, 41, 42, 45, 46, 49, 51, 53, 54, 143, 178, 294

Riggs, Mrs. Romulus (Mercy Ann Lawrason), 31, 41, 294

319

Riggs, Samuel, 24, 30, 32, 34, 35, 53, 137, 273, 275-276
Riggs, Mrs. Samuel (Amelia Dorsey), 24, 34, 39, 137, 276
Riggs, Samuel, Jr., 138-139, 141, 143, 154
Riggs, Mrs. Samuel Jr. (Margaret Norris, 138, 141
Riggs, Samuel James (son of Romulus), 32
Riggs, Thomas, 94, 137, 138, 153
Riggs, Thomas, 94, 137, 138, 153
Riggs, Mrs. Thomas (Mary Hammond), 138
Riggs, Thomas Lawrason (son of George Washington, Jr.) 186, 212
Riggs, Wiliam (son of Elisha, Sr.) 94
Riggs, William Henry (son of Elisha, Jr.), 97, 145-146
Riggs, William Corcoran (son of Elisha, Jr.), 179
Riggs family, 25, 257
Riggs Family of Maryland, 24, 35, 44, 56, 61, 142, 145, 167, 187, 301
Riggs Bank, 209, 310 see also Corcoran & Riggs and Riggs National Bank
Riggs & Company, 157, 163, 167-168, 175, 176, 179, 199, 205, 207, 213, 214, 220-221, 227-228, 232, 236, 243, 245-247, 251-253, 255, 257, 262, 266, 273, 276, 278, 282, 288, 289
Riggs Hills, plantation, 24
Riggs Mansion, I St., 54, 152, 206
Riggs National Bank, 21, 26, 44, 56, 65, 67, 108, 168, 218, 220, 226, 233, 236, 239, 245 see also Corcoran & Riggs, Riggs & Co. and Riggs Bank
Riggs, Peabody & Co., 42, 43, 138
Riggs, Taylor & Co., 56, 274
Rives, William Cabell, 286
Robb, James, 118-119
Robertson, Eliza, see Riggs, Mrs. George Washington
Robson, Elizabeth Cook, 274
Robson, George, 274
Robson, Sarah Elizabeth, see Taylor, Mrs. Samuel
Rockhill, T.C., 79
Roscius, ship, 102
Rothschilds, 69, 89, 202
Russell, George Peabody, 286
Riggs, Peabody & Co., 42, 43, 138
Riggs, Taylor & Co., 56, 274

S

Sang, Philip D., 220
San Jacinto, warship, 223
Schafhirt, Frederick, 232
Scolia, steamship, 273, 276, 283
Scott, Gen. Winfield, 111, 120, 125, 140, 148, 215, 217, 219
Searle, Ann, 47
Searles & Smith, school, 46
Second Bank of the United States, 11, 14, 21, 22, 73-74
Selden, Dudley, 117-118
"Sessford Annals" 182, 187, 213
Seward, Frederick, 256
Seward, William H., 224, 256, 289, 305-309
Shakespeare, ship, 102
Shedden, Catharine Ann Teresa, 48
Shedden, Jane Agnes, 48
Shedden, Janet Madeleine see Riggs, Mrs. George Washington, Jr.
Shedden, Thomas William, 48
Shedden, Mrs. Thomas William (Matilda Cecilia) 47-50, 59, 97, 178, 292
Shenton, James P., 81, 311
Sheridan, Gen. Philip, 248, 262
Sherman, Gen. William Tecumseh, 244, 261, 264-265
Sherman, Mrs. William Tecumseh (Ellen Ewing), 264
Shriver, Abraham Ferree, 277-278
Shriver, Mrs. Abraham Ferree (Mary Jane Glover) 277-278
Siddons, ship, 102
Simmons, Robert Hilton, 121
Simms, Joe, 139
Sinclair, Catharine, 156
Skirving, John, 67
Slidell, Sen. John, 213, 223, 228, 256
Slidell, Mrs. John, 197
Smith, Mrs. Caleb, 248
Smith, Clement, 38
Smith, Gamaliel, 78
Smith, Gurdon B., 88
Smith, Mrs. Isabella, 47
Smith, McCall & Co., 77
Smithsonian Institution, 115, 191-192, 231
Smyth, Jeannette, 71
Smythe, H.A., 295
Soldier's Home, 150, 213, 228
Stafford, Edward T., 259

INDEX

Stanton, Edwin M., 226, 255-256, 298
Stanton, Mrs. Edwin M., 255
Stephens, Alexander H., 211
Stephenson, Robert Louis, 195
Stockton, Commodore Richard, 130, 132
Stuart, William, 207
Suter, Mrs. John, 22
Suter's Tavern, Georgetown, 22
Sutter's Mill, 83

T

Taft, Lorado, 121
Tarbell, Ida M., 236-237
Taylor, Charles Franklin, 57
Taylor, Frank, 278
Taylor, George Washington Riggs, 304
Taylor, Samuel, 56, 57, 98, 109, 124, 137-138, 144, 273-276, 303-305
Taylor, Mrs. Samuel (Sarah Robson), 137, 145, 274, 303-304, 306
Taylor, Samuel, Jr., 304
Taylor, Zachary, 103, 106-107, 111, 209 264
Taylor, of Messrs Ward & Taylor, 38
Ten Eyck, L., 164-165
Thomas, Richard, 33
Thomas, Mrs. Richard (Deborah Brooke), 33
Thomas Collyer, steamer, 217
Threlkeld, Jane *see* Cox, Mrs. John
Todd, Capt. Alexander H., 247
Townsend, Col. E. D., 219
Tracy, Sarah, 215-218, 221, 227, 241-242, 252, 282
Trent, packet, 223
Truman, Harry S, 17
Tyler, John, 63, 64, 67, 68, 111, 191, 209
Tyler, Mrs. John (Julia Gardner), 68
Tyler, Mrs. John (Letitia Christian), 68

U

Ulke, Henry, 274-275
Union Bank, 30, 39
Union Hotel or Tavern, Georgetown, 15, 39, 40, 41
United States Mail Steamship Company, 103

V

Vail, Emilie L., 196-197
Van Buren, Martin, 63
Van Zndt, Rosalie *see* Riggs, Mrs. Joseph Karrick

Vesta, ship, 172-173
Victoria, Queen, 116, 233, 287
Von Recum, Franz, 47, 48, 58, 61, 69, 70, 93, 143, 153, 166, 220, 301, 310
Von Recum, Baroness Marie Ernestine (Howard), 182, 220, 237-238, 310

W

W. W. Corcoran & Co., 13
Walker, Robet John, 71, 74-76, 86, 108-109, 305, 307-308, 311
Walker, Mrs. Robert John (Mary Bache) 74-75
Wallace, Dr. William, 226
Wallach, Richard, 299
Ward, Lord, 118
Ward, Messrs, 38, 94, 95
Washington, Betty, 59
Washington, George, 24, 32, 39, 40, 44, 59, 168, 183, 203, 205, 216, 252
Washington, George C., 37, 178
Washington, John Augustine, 184-185, 204, 207
Washington, Lawrence, 60
Washington Acqueduct, 150
Washington Gas Light Co., 199, 212, 251, 259, 294
Washington & Georgetown Railroad, 227
Waters, Mrs. Clara (Erskin) Clement, 121
Waters family, 25
Webster, Daniel, 64, 68, 86, 91, 103, 105, 108, 111, 131, 132, 191, 264, 283
Webster-Ashburton treaty, 131
Welles, Gideon, 256
Wetmore, Samuel, 286
Wetmore, William Shepard, 126, 130, 154
Whelan, Fannie, 294
Whelan, William, 294
White Silence, 121
Whitney, William, 78
Whitney, Mrs. William (Julia), 78
Wickliffe, Charles A., 68, 91
Wilkes, Capt. Charles, 223-24
Wilkes, Capt. Charles, 223-224
Willard Hotel, 50, 66, 206
Williams, Mathilde D., 19
Williams, Mrs. Philip, 271
Williams, S., 227
Williamson, Robet Harper, 277
Williamson, Mrs. Robert Harper (Matilda Glover), 277

321

Wilson, Elizabeth, 12
Wilson, H., 243
Wilson, H. 243
WIlson, Mr. & Mrs. William, 12
Winder, Gen. William, 32
Winthrop, Gov. John, 283
Winthrop, Robert C., 76, 283-287, 290

Wolper, David A., 233
Women and Children Last, 162, 170, 176
Wright, Otis C., 277

Y

Yardley, Miss (governess), 189, 194, 196
Young, Brigham, 288